Army and Nation

Army and Nation

THE MILITARY AND INDIAN DEMOCRACY

SINCE INDEPENDENCE

STEVEN I. WILKINSON

Harvard University Press

Cambridge, Massachusetts
London, England
2015

Library of Congress Cataloging-in-Publication Data

Wilkinson, Steven I., 1965–
  Army and nation : the military and Indian democracy since independence /
Steven I. Wilkinson.
    pages cm
    Includes bibliographical references and index.
    ISBN 978-0-674-72880-6 (hardcover : alk. paper)
    1. India. Army—History.   2. Civil-military relations—India—History.
3. India—Politics and government—1947-.   4. India—Military policy—
History.   I. Title.
    UA840.W55 2014
    322'.50954—dc23   2014016505

To Donald L. Horowitz

Contents

Introduction

ARMY AND NATION

ON SEPTEMBER 12, 1946, shortly after taking office as minister for external affairs in India's pre-independence cabinet, Jawaharlal Nehru sent a long letter to the Commander in Chief and Defence Secretary to press for large-scale reforms to the Indian Army. To the colonial officials who read Nehru's letter this seemed a dangerous and even reckless proposal, given the bloody and almost uncontrollable communal riots in Calcutta the month before, during which six thousand people were slaughtered. The last thing India needed, from their perspective, was to destroy the one force standing between the country and mass disorder. But Nehru argued, on the contrary, that reform of the military was absolutely necessary to safeguard India's new democracy. The most urgent thing to do, he said, was to "transform the whole background of the Indian Army," which meant changing the composition of the "martial class" regiments, drawn heavily from the Punjab and a handful of other provinces, so that they reflected the broader Indian nation and its aspirations.[1] Only if there were more Indian officers at the higher ranks, where not one of the four Lieutenant Generals or twenty Major Generals was Indian, and more representation from provinces and communities that had previously been excluded from the army, would India and its new freedoms be truly secure.[2]

In pressing for these changes, Nehru was reflecting more than three decades of nationalist opposition to India's "divide and rule" army. By the mid-1930s nationalist Indians were openly arguing in the central legislature that the dominance of Punjab in the army was a real threat, and that "Democracy can never function in this country satisfactorily unless the basis of recruitment for the army is radically changed."[3] The Indian Army had been designed by the British, like most imperial armies, to be loyal to the colonial regime and not to the people. These armies were effective because they recruited disproportionately from a few communities and were kept apart from society, so that they lacked what John Stuart Mill termed "fellow feeling" with those they might be ordered to fire upon (Enloe 1980; Gutteridge 1962, 1969; Horowitz 1980, 1985; Mill 1861). In the European colonial empires, this practice often led to local armies populated disproportionately by minorities: a largely Punjabi and Pashtun army in India, northerner-dominated armies in colonial Togo, Ghana, and Nigeria, a Sunni-dominated army in Iraq, an army of Karens, Chins, and Kachins rather than the Burmese majority in colonial Burma, and to the recruitment of Ambonese and Minahassans rather than the majority Javanese in Dutch-controlled Indonesia.[4]

In country after country, such ethnically imbalanced armies proved fatal to democracy soon after independence. New democracies were overthrown as minority-controlled militaries sought to preserve their power against new democratic majorities, and as ethnic majorities used force to try to displace minority groups from power (Enloe 1980; Gutteridge 1962, 1969; Harkness 2013; Horowitz 1980, 1985). Where the ethnic imbalance between a group's representation in the army and its representation in the population, government, or the economy was very high, the chances of violence and civil war increased sharply (Horowitz 1985, 458). Where, as in postcolonial states such as Australia, Canada, Botswana, and Malawi, the imbalance between the population and army was low the chances for stable democracy increased (Chandra and Wilkinson 2008). One recent statistical study of all African states after independence, for instance, finds that there were much higher numbers of coup attempts in those countries where there was a "mismatch" between the proportion of the ethnic group in the army and that in control of politics. This was especially true where there was no external guarantor of security, such as a French or British military base that could allow foreign powers to step in and protect the local regime (Harkness 2013).

The Question

This book asks why India, which inherited a deeply imbalanced colonial army, a "mercenary army" as nationalists sometimes derisively called it before independence, has been able to largely solve the problem of "army and nation" posed by Nehru in September 1946. Like its neighbor Pakistan, and like many other states in Africa and Asia, India inherited an ethnically unrepresentative, cohesive, and politically conservative military that was seen by nationalists as a major threat to democracy. New data I have collected for this book (see Chapters 2 and 3) show that immediately after independence in 1947 around three quarters of India's officers and men were from a small number of provinces and "martial classes," with only 10 percent of India's overall population. Half of all India's most senior officers came from one single province, Punjab, with only 5 percent of the new state's population.

This kind of narrowly recruited and cohesive army is dangerous, according to scholars such as Morris Janowitz, because "armies with high internal cohesion will have greater capacity to intervene in domestic politics" (1977, 144; see also Horowitz 1985, 532–559; Janowitz 1964). After independence, in country after country, narrowly based and cohesive armies overthrew democratically elected governments drawn from a much wider swathe of the population, which seemed to threaten their power, in a pattern that was repeated from Sierra Leone to Syria (Horowitz 1985, 472–496, 527–528). In some former colonial states, such as in Francophone West Africa and South East Asia (Singapore and Bhutan), leaders tried to overcome such domestic imbalances by relying on the continued presence of troops from the former colonial power, at least until the local military could be rebalanced (Bedlington 1980). But India's new leaders were clear from the beginning that they did not want to rely on an external power for security. Yet despite these challenges India has succeeded in keeping the army out of politics and preserving its democracy, unlike its neighbor Pakistan, which has had three long periods of direct military rule and a lot of indirect army control and interference besides. This book seeks to explore the reasons why? How and why has India successfully managed its military when Pakistan has failed, despite similar institutional inheritances at independence in 1947?

Explanations for the Divergence

The answer to this question might initially seem obvious. First, experts on Indian defense often point out that India inherited a professional British-style military in which politics was kept out of the mess, generals were kept out of politics and the public eye, and the lines of civil-military authority were clear. In his reply to Nehru's September 1946 letter, for instance, the Commander in Chief, Field Marshal Sir Claude Auchinleck, reassured him that "The Armed Forces of India understand very well, I think, that they exist solely to carry out the policy of the Government which is in power, and that officers, whether British or Indian, and men must not allow their political views, if they have any, to influence them in any way in the execution of their duty. . . . This fact has been impressed continuously on all ranks of the Navy, Army and Air Force."[5] The autobiographies of India's post-war generals and lieutenant generals all talk about their commitment to civilian rule and political oversight and minimize any possibility of a coup ever being possible (Cariappa 1964, 34; Khanduri 2000, 60–61). General J. N. Chaudhuri, Chief of Army Staff from 1962–1966, wrote in his autobiography that "I can say now with the utmost confidence that to the best of my knowledge, no officer in the Indian Army, however senior, has ever thought of a military coup at any time" (Chaudhuri 1978, 178–79). India, according to this view, is an instance of the kind of military Samuel Huntington describes in his classic book *The Soldier and the State*: a professional army under objective civilian control (Huntington 1957). This view does capture an important truth. The colonial Indian Army was indeed strict about its professional norms, and it insisted that officers not get involved in politics—by which of course the Raj meant nationalist politics—or talk to the press. When General K. M. Cariappa took over as the army's first Indian commander in chief in January 1949 he immediately sent out orders and made several public statements warning against entanglement in politics —"Politics in the Army is a poison. Keep off it," he told his officers—and emphasizing the importance of civilian supremacy.[6]

Such professional traditions are important. But they are also clearly not able on their own to explain the democratic divergence that we observe between India and Pakistan. For one thing, the most senior Indian officers and Pakistani officers had all trained at Sandhurst and served together before 1947, and one internal army analysis of their political views in 1946 identified little difference between them (S. K. Sinha 1992, 79–80). So why did this common professional experience lead ex-Indian Army officers to participate in a coup in Pakistan in 1958, but not in India? More generally, why did similar British professional military training and professionalization not prevent coups in Nigeria, Sierra Leone, and many other former British colonies?

Second, as Samuel Finer pointed out, professionalism might at times actually increase the chances of intervention (Finer 1962, 20–25).[7] General Cariappa, General Chaudhuri, and other senior Indian officers recruited to the armed forces between 1919–1934 were professional, but they were also politically conservative, mistrustful of politicians. Many of them, after independence, expressed their deep concern at rising levels of corruption, political conflict, and social discontent. The first Indian Commander in Chief, General Cariappa, argued on several occasions after his retirement in 1953 for a suspension of civil liberties, the imposition of emergency President's Rule on the states, the disbanding of political parties, suspension of parliament until "law and order" had been restored, and the replacement of universal suffrage with a franchise that was restricted to literates.[8] When he stood for election in 1971, he was backed up at a press conference by a retired lieutenant general, a rear admiral, four brigadiers, three colonels and lieutenant colonels, and an air marshal, which suggests that his views cannot be completely dismissed as unrepresentative of India's senior officers.[9] It is not hard to imagine that these Indian professionals, had the external and domestic crises faced by India seemed greater, might have considered intervention in the same way as their Pakistani former Batchmates.[10]

A second explanation for India's ability to overcome the challenges of a deeply imbalanced colonial military inheritance focuses on the supposedly rapid ethnic rebalancing of the army before and immediately after independence. The *Official History of the Indian Armed Forces in World War II (Second World War)* and several other authors, for instance, have argued that World War II, by forcing recruitment from many new communities to staff the more than two-million-strong Indian Army, effectively "exploded the myth of the martial classes" (Deshpande 1996, 183–184; Prasad 1956, 84–85; Venkateshwaran 1967, 187–189). According to this official view, the job of diversifying the army was then quickly tackled in the first few years of independence through a succession of new orders and policies that quickly opened the army to all. Defence Minister Sardar Baldev Singh announced in 1948 and 1949 that recruits would no longer be classified as belonging to "martial" or "non-martial" classes, and recruitment to the army would "henceforth be open to all Indians, specifically including Scheduled Castes, Muslims, and members of other regions and communities that had been excluded."[11] Then, shortly after General Cariappa had been appointed in January 1949, the Government of India announced that it had "decided to abolish class composition based on fixed percentages . . . [and that] recruitment to the army will now be open to all classes and no particular class of Indian nationals will be denied the opportunity of serving in the Army."[12] General Cariappa also promised that all *new* infantry and armored regiments would be open to members of all provinces, a policy that has been reiterated by Indian defense ministers and Chiefs of the Army Staff (COASs) ever since.[13] Every Defence Minister from the 1950s to A. K. Anthony (2006–2014) has emphasized that the Indian military is open to all, that it now largely reflects the diversity of the country, and that recruitment is now based on the recruitable male population of each state and union territory.[14]

The problem with this argument, however, is that it reflects political promises rather than what has actually happened. As the new data collected in this book show, India has largely *not* followed through on its 1949 promises to radically change the composition of the infantry and armored corps. Far from dismantling its colonial-style army, independent India instead doubled the number of its "martial class" units by the beginning of the 1970s, to deal with the threat from China and to a lesser extent from Pakistan. The specific wording of the army promises and orders given in 1949—which stated that *new* infantry and artillery *regiments* would be open to members of all provinces, and that all other branches of the army would be open to members of all provinces—had much less effect in broadening out the army than most politicians thought it would. This was because, as the generals knew, the Infantry and Armored corps had expanded in World War II by adding new battalions to existing class regiments, rather than through the logistically much more complex and uncertain step of adding whole new regiments, training centers, recruitment areas, and fighting traditions. Since independence, for instance, the Punjab Regiment (which recruits mainly Sikhs and Dogras) has increased from five to twenty-nine battalions while the Rajputana Rifles (mainly Jats and Rajputs) has increased from six to twenty-one battalions. Because expansion has largely happened through the existing regiments, most of India's infantry and armored corps battalions are still disproportionately recruited from the same regions and castes that provided the bulk of the army at independence in 1947, though these imbalances have lessened substantially in recent decades and are not as threatening as they were before independence.

In Figure I-1, using data from parliamentary replies in the Lok Sabha and Rajya Sabha, I display the state-level patterns in army recruitment from 1998 to 2009, showing the extent to which states were overrepresented or underrepresented relative to their RMP, the "recruitable male population" of a state (which is supposed to serve as the basis for recruitment). As we can see from the map, the main traditional recruiting states in the north—Punjab, Haryana, the Dogra region of Jammu and Kashmir, Himachal Pradesh, and Uttarakhand (Uttaranchal)—still have from two and a half to six times their proportional representation in army recruitment even today, while states such as Gujarat and Jharkhand are considerably underrepresented.

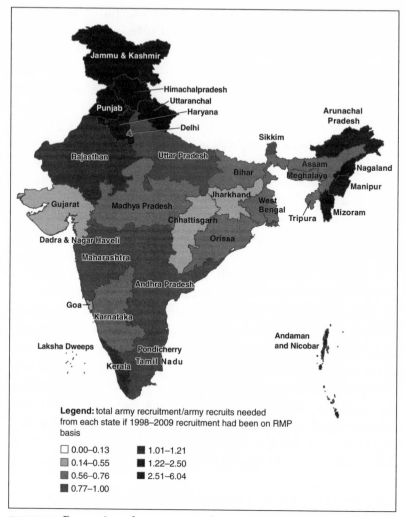

FIGURE I.1 Proportion of army recruits from each Indian state 1998–2009
relative to recruitable male population (RMP)

The Argument

So if neither professional traditions nor a restructuring of the army
in the 1940s and 1950s (that did not in fact happen) seem to explain
the variation in civil military outcomes, what does? The argument I
make here is that India's ability to control its military since independence and the larger puzzle of the India-Pakistan civil-military

divergence after 1947 is explained by three factors: (1) the far worse socioeconomic, strategic, and (especially) military inheritance that Pakistan received in 1947 compared to India; (2) the greater political institutionalization of the Congress Party compared to the Muslim League in Pakistan, and in particular its broad ethnic and regional support. This broadly representative ethnic and religious character allowed, and in some cases forced, the party to take a series of steps in the 1940s and 1950s, which crosscut and moderated cleavages in India that might otherwise have been as deeply divisive as they were to prove in Pakistan; and (3) the specific coup-proofing and balancing measures the new Indian state undertook, especially in its first decade, which reflected several decades of Congress thinking about the urgent need to control the military, and ways to achieve that goal.

1. Good and Bad Inheritances

The first factor I highlight is the fact that Pakistan really *did* have a much worse inheritance than India at independence in its trained officers and officials, state institutions, army, and the stocks of capital and goods it received as part of the division of the country. The new state also had to cope with the outflow of much of its most productive human capital, the influx of huge numbers of refugees (10 percent of the population in West Pakistan compared to 1 percent of India's population), the loss of much of the productive industry, communication hubs, and tax base of the former country, and a thousand-mile gap between the two parts of the new state, East and West Pakistan. And there were of course enormous strategic challenges, including the need to pay for a large army to defend both the Afghan border and the new borders with India. All of these aspects have been well explored by others, especially in several very good studies by Ayesha Jalal and Philip Oldenburg, as well as in an important volume edited just after independence by C. N. Vakil (Jalal 1987, 1992, 1995; Oldenburg 2010; Vakil 1950; Weiner 1989). I agree with many of the points these authors have made, especially with Jalal's points about the strategic and financial weakness of Pakistan at partition and how these pushed the state and its generals to seek a US alliance as well as preventing the new state from dealing with many important domestic issues.

Table I.1. Explaining the India-Pakistan Civil-Military Divergence

	India	Pakistan
1. Unequal military, strategic and fiscal inheritances	• Imbalanced army • Strategic depth and greater external security • Greater fiscal strength	• Very imbalanced army • No strategic depth and great external security challenges • Fiscal weakness
2. a) Party Institutionalization	• Strong, internally democratic party with broad ethnic support and legitimacy	• Weak party with narrow ethnic, geographic, and class support
2. b) Measures to reduce social cleavages in society and army	• Ban on religious claims • Caste reservations • Linguistic states	• Acceptance of religious claims • No caste reservations • No states reorganization to cross-cut existing identities and grant autonomy to main groups
3. Strategies to coup-proof and reduce army's ability to coordinate against the state	• Fixed class units at battalion level • Officer level with diversified recruitment and multiple recruitment streams • At top command level by maximizing the ethnic diversity of officers and restricting their tenures • At command and control level by replacing C-in-C structure with three separate commands with strong civilian oversight • Civilian-controlled paramilitaries act as strong indirect and direct hedge	• Fixed class units at battalion level but less diverse than in India • Less diverse officer corps with single stream entry • Overwhelmingly Punjabi and Pashtun officer corps in centralized leadership structure • No substantial civilian-controlled paramilitary hedge

Bad inheritances are not always destiny, of course. In a recent book Maya Tudor points to the experience of countries such as Israel to demonstrate that the fact that it "does not necessarily follow that a state with a large militarized population or a high proportion of military officers cannot create a stable or democratic regime" (Tudor

2013, 27–30, 291). Tudor makes a good point when she says that the number of officers and veterans in the new state, by itself, was not critical. But there was, however, one other crucial difference between the armies that Israel and Pakistan inherited at independence. That is the fact, which I highlight in this book, that the partition significantly *reduced* the degree of ethnic imbalance in the Indian military, to a much less threatening level, while it made the degree of ethnic imbalance in the Pakistani military much worse.[15] It was for just this reason, in fact, that a prescient B. R. Ambedkar in his 1941 book *Thoughts on Pakistan* had urged that Indian nationalists should not object to the idea of Pakistan, because India would, he argued, be much better off with a "safe army" in which Punjabis were no longer so dominant (Ambedkar 1941, 93).

The partition led to such a massive imbalance in Pakistan's army because the new state was formed by joining together the most over-represented recruiting regions in pre-independence India (West Punjab and NWFP) with populous East Bengal, the most under-represented recruiting region in the country. (The two other provinces that made up Pakistan, Baluchistan and Sind, each had less than 10 percent of the national population.) That left a new state in which virtually all the army came from two provinces with 35 percent of the population, while East Bengal, with 55 percent of the population, had no representation at all. In India's new army, on the other hand, there was still substantial regional overrepresentation, but as a result of the secession of the Pakistani provinces, it was actually much less than it had been in the army before independence. Punjabis were still the largest group, but now they had only 32 percent of the infantry (see Table 3.2), far from the Punjabi majority in the army that had existed prior to World War II. This provincial overrepresentation of Punjab, moreover, was also softened by several crosscutting cleavages: Hindu versus Sikh, and among the Sikhs a clear caste divide between the upper-caste Jat Sikhs who were found in many units and the lower-caste Mazhabi and Ramdasia Sikhs who had been recruited to the Sikh Light Infantry, a new unit raised in 1941 (Table 3.1). And India also retained many of the Gorkha regiments from Nepal, who acted as an additional hedge against any threat from the army; at independence these amounted to, by my estimates, around 20 percent of the Indian infantry.

Pakistan also inherited the expense of guarding the northwest frontier, which had consumed huge amounts of money before 1947, and it now had the additional cost of defending its new frontier with India. But Pakistan inherited only a small amount of the tax revenue that had paid for this military infrastructure. Ambedkar had understood what was likely to happen. In 1941 he argued that "it is the money contributed by the Provinces of Hindustan which enables the Government of India to carry out its activities in the Pakistani provinces," and he predicted that if Pakistan left, India would benefit from redirecting the revenue that supported military expenditure in the Punjab and NWFP to a variety of civilian purposes (Ambedkar 1941, 93–95). This was exactly right. The massive costs of having to keep up with India militarily in Pakistan's first years left little money for other important domestic priorities, such as social spending and education; 70 percent of the Pakistani budget in the first few years of independence went to the military (Jalal 1987, 306).

The resulting fiscal and strategic weakness of the new Pakistani state meant that Pakistani elites perceived, as Paul Staniland points out, a much greater strategic threat than those in India. This could only be addressed, they concluded, by reaching out in the early 1950s to the United States, in what was to be the beginning of a very tangled alliance (2008, 347–348; Jalal 1992; Nawaz 2008). These strategic imperatives increased the risk of foreign interference in Pakistani politics. In India however, as Stephen P. Cohen has pointed out, Nehru's policy of nonalignment, or what we might think of as the "diversification" of risk internationally, was also deeply related to the policy of "diversifying" risk in terms of India's domestic military arrangements. The fewer entanglements with foreign governments and militaries, the more the Indian Army could be kept insulated from politics at home. India, secure in its ability to take on Pakistan, could reduce links with the British and American militaries. In Pakistan, however, the generals and politicians, confronted with a much graver strategic threat, felt that they had no option but to cultivate close ties with foreign friends for military and financial support, despite the obvious risks these ties posed to domestic politics (Cohen 1988, 2010, 353; Jalal 1992; Nawaz 2008).

2. Party Institutionalization

The Congress Party had a much greater degree of what scholars have called "party institutionalization" compared to the Muslim League. Party institutionalization has been identified as important, for instance, in a wide variety of other democratizing contexts by Mainwaring and Scully, who define it as "stability in interparty competition, the existence of parties that have somewhat stable roots in society, acceptance of parties and elections as the legitimate institutions that determine who governs, and party organizations with reasonably stable rules and structures" (1995, 1).[16] By 1947, the Indian National Congress was over sixty years old and had been a substantial mass presence across India for three decades, supported by a broad social coalition that included members of all India's main religious groups. The Congress Party was also internally competitive, with a transparent and open structure and clear rules for both challenging incumbent leaders and replacing them when they left office. Congress's leaders also, crucially, had experience in government and the art of political management and compromise, going back to the party's first provincial election victories in the 1920s and especially after the party's clear victories in eight out of eleven provinces in the 1936 provincial elections. The Muslim League, by contrast, was oligarchical and had a much weaker party organization and far less experience in governing, having failed to win in any province in the 1936 elections. The League had only won the 1945–1946 elections in most of the provinces that became Pakistan (it lost in the North-West Frontier Province, or NWFP) by hastily building a party structure in 1944–1945 and then by co-opting local leaders and parties that wanted to be part of a winning national ticket (Weiner 1989; Oldenburg 2010, 36–37). So the party clearly lacked what Mainwaring and Scully think of as "stable roots in society" at the local level (1995).

These important differences in the degree of party institutionalization between the Muslim League and the Congress Party have been recognized and written about many times before (see, for example, Jalal 1992; Kothari 1964; Morris-Jones 1967; Oldenburg 2010; Tudor 2013; Weiner 1989). But what differentiates my argument here is that I link these differences in the strength of the parties to several specific outcomes that affected civil-military relations after independence: first, the determination and knowledge among Congress's senior leaders (but not the Muslim League's) that they had to fix the problem of the military soon after independence; and second, the way in which Congress's broad, ethnically and regionally diverse, and internally competitive party structure allowed it to make much better choices than the League in managing the divisive religious, ethnic, and caste conflicts that might otherwise have increased conflict in the country at large, potentially drawing the army further into politics. It was these ethnic and religious conflicts that seem, judging by contemporary and subsequent events in Pakistan (the secession of East Pakistan, insurgencies in Sind, Baluchistan, and NWFP, and the growth of religious extremism), to have been the most important ones to get right.

Congress was a party that had been conscious of the "problem of the military" for at least three decades, and had developed ideas on both the scope of the problem and some likely solutions. In a series of studies in the 1930s and 1940s, as well as in many parliamentary debates, nationalists pointed to the deep regional and caste imbalances that existed and the use of the army as a coercive force against Indians, and suggested ways to reduce the threat these posed to democracy (All-India Congress Committee 1934; Ambedkar 1941; N. Chaudhuri 1930a, 1930b, 1931a, 1931b, 1931c, 1935; Nehru to Defence Secretary 1946).[17] Twelve years before independence, for instance, as part of a series of fiftieth-anniversary policy papers outlining different aspects of the Congress program, Nirad Chaudhuri analyzed the problems in the structure of the army at length and argued that "A national army for India should be commanded and controlled by Indians, be recruited from all parts of the country and be animated by a national spirit. It should be a self-contained fighting machine able to do without the help and guidance of foreigners (N. Chaudhuri 1935, 8–9). Nehru, in his classic *The Discovery of India*, written while he was imprisoned in Agra jail in 1944, also analyzed and criticized what he termed the army's "policy of balance and counterpoise" (Nehru 1982, 329).

Nehru is sometimes accused, no doubt through the prism of the disastrous defeat by China in 1962, of being inattentive to and unin-

terested in military issues. In a recent book, for instance, Zoltan
Barany says that "Nehru had little interest in defense matters, was
indifferent to the armed forces, and had no strategic vision. He
famously said, 'India doesn't need an army, it needs a police force.
We have no enemies'" (Barany 2012, 260). This view, however, is
not correct. One of the first things Nehru did, when taking office
at the national level in September 1946, was to set to work addressing the reform of the army in his long letter to Auchinleck and the
Defence Secretary. Nehru's other letters to officers prior to independence in 1946–1947 and the steps that he took in the first years
of independence demonstrate that in fact he and his party were far
from indifferent to the armed forces. Nehru and Sardar Patel had
a very keen sense of what the domestic potential civil-military issues might be, and they acted decisively to prevent them. Many of
the most important actions they took, moreover, were in the first
few years of independence, well before events in Pakistan in the
mid-1950s made the potential threat from the military clear to
everyone else.

This pre-independence thinking about the necessary reform of
the military—something that, as I show, was not present in the Muslim League—was not just a matter of chance. It reflected the fact
that Congress was a broad regional party, with substantial representation from many of the biggest "deficit" provinces such as Madras,
Orissa, and (above all) Bengal that had been excluded from the military and were pressing for reform of the system. It also reflected the
fact that the Congress Party representatives had been in politics for
thirty years, which had allowed them to ask many difficult questions on the military, as well as to force public debates on the structure of the army. This attention also reflected the party's strong links
with academics, journalists, and intellectuals, who put forward the
working papers and policy briefs that provided much of the blue-
print for post-independence India (N. Chaudhuri 1935; Oldenburg
2010, 10).

The second factor, again linked to Congress's degree of political
institutionalization, was that the party's broad ethnic and religious
base and federal structure led it to make better decisions than Pakistan in the first years of independence on a number of religious,
linguistic, and caste issues that might have easily pulled the country

apart and drawn the military into politics. At independence the Congress Party faced a number of difficult choices. Should it abolish religious reservations in politics and the civil service, even though these were supported by many Sikh, Muslim, and Christian representatives? Should it institute Hindi as the new national language, even though this might be strongly opposed by speakers of other languages, especially in the south? Should it carve up the existing provinces to create new linguistic states, or would this just encourage secession and more conflict? And should it abolish caste in all aspects of government, or allow reservations in politics and jobs for members of the backward classes?

The wrong decisions on these questions would have made national-level conflicts in India much worse because, as Horowitz says, "To understand ethnically based military coups, civilian and military ethnic politics must be viewed in tandem" (1985, 459–460). If Congress had kept religious reservations or instituted Hindi as a national language, for instance, that would have immediately focused politics around the national cleavages of Hindu versus Muslim, Hindi-speaking versus non-Hindi-speaking Indians, and north versus south. Instead India made the right decision on these issues, banning discrimination on the basis of religion and delaying (it turns out indefinitely) the full implementation of the Hindi-only policy, which would have been deeply resisted by the non-Hindi-speaking regions. Unfortunately for Pakistan, and reflecting the much narrower geographic, religious, and organizational base of the Muslim League compared to the Congress Party, the League initially instituted Urdu as a national language, though it was spoken by less than 5 percent of the population as a first language (and by hardly any of the 55 percent of the population who spoke Bengali as a first language), and retained separate religious reservations in politics. Both of these decisions turned out very badly and led to significant ethnic and regional conflicts. Many of these decisions reflected the belief of the League before independence that a common Muslim identity would solve all problems and a consequent absence of the deep thinking about institutions and planning for independence that we see in the Congress Party (Oldenburg 2010, 10; Tudor 2013, 157). When Muhammad Ali Jinnah was interviewed in 1946–1947 by *New York*

Times correspondent George Jones about how he planned to deal with minority issues in Pakistan after independence, his response was simply "Give us Pakistan, and we will take care of that problem when we come to it" (1948, 115).

Tudor has argued that two key conflicts in Pakistan after independence, over the form of representation and the installation of an elected chief executive, were not centrally about the macro-cleavage of ethnicity, and that "the economic threat posed by Bengali control over the state, and not Bengali identity per se, was the driving rationale for authoritarian intervention in Pakistan" (2013, 33–34). I would suggest, though, that the many complaints that Jinnah received in 1947–1948 on these issues, and the language that was used, make it clear that language and ethnicity—rather than class dynamics—*were* key aspects of these conflicts.[18] Ayesha Jalal for instance has explored at length the many ethnic and provincial tensions in post-independence Pakistan, over issues of language, discrimination, the economy, and defense (Jalal 1992, 49–135). Given the long pre-1947 history of Bengali-Punjabi disputes over defense and financial issues—which I explore in Chapter 6—many aspects of state building in Pakistan's first decade were inevitably framed in group rather than class terms.

In India Congress also made two important decisions, again in contrast to the Muslim League in Pakistan, which multiplied what social scientists term "cross-cutting cleavages" in politics, identities that cut across macro-Indian identities and help to make sure that there are no permanent losers in politics. Since the 1950s, social scientists have realized that cross-cutting cleavages, the "interdependence of conflicting groups and the multiplicity of noncumulative conflicts provide one, though not, of course, the only check against basic consensual breakdown in an open society" (Coser 1956, 78–79). The first important decision was taken by Nehru in 1951, when he backed down in his opposition to passing a constitutional amendment that would allow reservations for "backward classes" (that is, castes), something that was being demanded by these castes in the state of Madras. This decision was taken, against Nehru's own preferences, because he recognized that a substantial part of the party in the south was opposed to him on the issue, and that with the first general elections on the way, not bending on it might cause problems for Congress in Madras, where backward castes were a very large share of the population. The second important decision was taken in 1952, after violent protests in the Telugu-speaking areas within Madras, when a hunger striker died in support of his goal of a separate Telugu-speaking state. As he had done on the issue of caste reservations, Nehru again conceded on the issue of language. He allowed the creation of a Telugu-speaking Andhra Pradesh state, and also announced the setting up of a new commission on states reorganization, which would eventually lead to the process by which the nine Indian states at independence have been carved up into twenty-nine states today (the most recent a February 2014 parliamentary vote to carve up Andhra itself into two states).

Both of these measures were controversial at the time, and they still have their supporters and opponents. But from the conflict-management perspective they have worked to prevent religion from becoming a "macrocleavage" in India and instead helped defuse tensions by channeling identities along the less damaging lines of caste and language. It is sometimes said that India's great inherited diversity has made conflict less likely, because no single group or cleavage can dominate the polity. But in fact this mistakes the outcome of India's good policy choices since 1947 for their cause. India and Pakistan were, in fact, actually quite similar in their initial degree of ethnic diversity, each with a substantial linguistic majority group (Hindi, Bengali), a substantial religious minority (Muslims and Sikhs in India, Hindus in Pakistan), and a whole host of smaller language groups, as well as many caste and tribal identities. India, though, diminished the power of religious cleavages by abolishing religious electorates, job reservations, and discrimination on the grounds of religion. At the same time India increased the importance of the cross-cutting cleavages of language and caste through reorganization of states and caste reservations. Pakistan, however, retained separate religious electorates, and did not implement either the caste reservations or a process of reorganization of states that might have cross-cut the strong provincial and religious identities that it, like India, inherited in 1947.

These policy decisions should not be seen as idiosyncratic, I argue, because at their heart they were the result of the Congress Party's institutionalization; in particular its strong regional structure and internal competitiveness and pluralism, combined with the need to respond to political competitors from outside the party (Kothari 1964). Nehru took two of the key measures—on caste and language— not because he wanted to, but because this party structure and the strong feeling on these issues in the south compelled him to. In the Muslim League's much more centralized structure, however, Jinnah was free to go to Dacca in March 1948 to tell the unhappy Bengalis that Urdu would be the sole official language whatever their views and that they had better like it (Zaidi 2002, 272–275).[19] The fact that Congress was a broader and more responsive party in this way, more willing to compromise, negotiate, and deal with dissent, was to be vitally important in providing India's diverse groups with the feeling that they had a stake in the regime—which, as Luttwak has pointed out, is one important factor in reducing the levels of discontent that can lead to a coup (Luttwak 1968, 87–88).

The Congress Party's ability to deal with the religious, linguistic, and caste conflicts that might have pulled India apart—as regional and linguistic conflicts did pull Pakistan apart in 1971—was vital to establishing the party's legitimacy as a governing party in the 1950s and 1960s. And this in turn was very important in limiting the involvement of the military in politics. This is because, as Stephen P. Cohen pointed out half a century ago, "the mere repetition of the slogan 'civilian control' is not enough to guarantee its existence: that the civilian leadership must demonstrate its capability to rule is no less important than that it maintain the tradition of apolitical professionalism in the military" (Cohen 1963–1964, 4).

3. Coup Proofing

The third set of factors I highlight are the specific coup-proofing strategies that the Congress Party used to balance the power of the military, especially during India's first decade. Party institutionalization and the decisions on ethnic and religious issues from 1947– 1953 were important in providing democratic stability and legitimacy, and in preventing the sort of political crisis in which the military felt obliged to intervene. But not all coups happen through such political crises and the vacuums they create, so it is also important that the political leadership took preemptive steps to prevent the military from becoming a threat. The Congress Party's institutionalization was also important, therefore, because it put the issue of what to do about the military clearly on the party's political agenda well before 1947 and made the party leaders feel it was a pressing issue at independence.

What options did the party have to prevent a coup? The radical restructuring of the army that the party leaders had envisaged in 1946–1947 was temporarily off the table after independence because of the internal conflicts caused by partition, the 1947–1948 war with Pakistan, and other strategic threats. Sardar Vallabhai Patel, for instance, told Nehru that India had to reconsider "our retrenchment plans for the army in light of . . . new threats" posed by Pakistan, Burma, and especially by communist China (quoted in Munshi 1950, 175–181).[20] The menu of options that India was left with is well covered by James T. Quinlivan, who has examined coup proofing in Saudi Arabia, Syria, and Iraq, and by Donald Horowitz's analysis of coups and coup prevention in ethnically divided societies (1985). Quinlivan argues that "in practice a regime seeking to become coup-proof tries to break down the corporate identity and corporate loyalty of the military; at the same time, it may try to increase the expertness of the military in a strictly technical sense" (1999, 152). He also highlights the important role of developing parallel militaries and praetorian guards packed with ethnic loyalists to the ruling regime, and of developing security agencies that watch everyone, including the other security agencies (1999, 135). Horowitz looks at similar mechanisms, and also identifies various methods of introducing "balance inside the army" to hedge some groups with others in the officer corps and rank and file (1985, 534–536).

The Congress Party's democratic and secular character meant that India was not about to develop new praetorian guards packed with ethnic loyalists. But Nehru did employ all of the other methods that Quinlivan describes—in a few cases by continuing systems that had first been developed by the British, but more often by innovating and through new command and control structures, careful attention to promotions, tenures, and balancing ethnic groups at the top of the military, and attention to top generals' career pathways after retirement. Nehru also changed the symbolic structure of power, something less well covered in the literature on coups, by altering the status of the army in the warrant of precedence and in public life, by limiting the wearing of uniforms in public, and by personally taking over the commander in chief's house in New Delhi as his new prime ministerial residence.

The most important measure Nehru, Deputy Prime Minister Sardar Patel, and their first Defence Secretary H. M. Patel (1947–1953) and his successor M. K. Vellodi (1953–1957) took was to minimize the army's ability to coordinate against the state. Given the external threat from Pakistan that India faced after the 1947–1948 war, as well as the shortage of money, India could not afford either to disband the "martial class" military it had inherited or to massively enlarge the army to draw in many new groups that would immediately reduce the potential threat the army posed to democracy (Horowitz 1985, 536–537). One thing India could do, and did, was to "balance inside the army" by continuing the British system of having the majority of the army's infantry battalions structured in "fixed class" units, in which each of the four companies was ethnically cohesive, but the battalion as a whole contained at least two different ethnic groups. For instance, the typical Punjab Regiment battalion contains two companies of Sikhs and two of Dogras, while a typical Jammu and Kashmir Rifles battalion contains four different groups: Dogras, Gorkhas, Sikhs, and Muslims (Palit 1972). This offered the fighting advantages of cohesiveness, but also introduced enough diversity to make it harder for individual units to easily coordinate against the state (Horowitz 1985, 536).[21] Nehru also blocked attempts to introduce new provincial or class regiments that might serve as a focal point for provincial or community conflicts, pushing back strongly in 1948 when regional leaders demanded that new regiments be created to represent their regions and communities.[22] Most of the new units the infantry and armored corps have added since independence, however, have been fixed-class units.

Under Nehru the Ministry of Defence also innovated and took a number of other measures to make the military high command less cohesive and less likely to coordinate against the political leadership. Perhaps the most important steps were two decisions, in 1947 and 1955, that downgraded the political position of the army commander in chief and intensified interservice rivalries, therefore making overall military coordination less likely. Prior to 1947 India had a weak Defence Department and a very strong commander in chief, who served in the governor-general's executive council and was also superior to the chiefs of the navy and air force. In 1947 the commander in chief was taken out of the cabinet and was made responsible to the Defence Minister, with overall expenditure decisions now to be approved by the Ministry of Defence (and increasingly also by the ministry of finance) rather than the army's own military finance department, as previously (Chari 1977, 8–10). The commander in chief was still represented in high-level committees, but the army was now directly responsible to elected politicians and Ministry of Defence bureaucrats (in particular secretaries Patel and Vellodi) in a way it had not been before. Then in 1955 the commander in chief's power within the military itself was reduced when his position was downgraded to the new position of "Chief of Army Staff," which was made equal, at least in theory, with the chiefs of the much smaller air force and navy (Chari 1977, 2012). The bureaucrats and politicians in the Defence Minister's committee could now play the three chiefs off against each other and encourage interservice rivalries as a way to prevent the possibility of successful coordination against the political leadership.

The Congress Party leadership also carried out several other steps to decrease the cohesion of the military. One of the most important was to maximize the ethnic heterogeneity of the most senior officers so that the top command was much more diverse than it would have been otherwise. This made the top military leadership less internally cohesive and hence less threatening to democracy (Janowitz 1977).

As we will see in Chapter 3, the officer corps after independence was disproportionately drawn from the "martial classes" in general, and from Punjab in particular, which accounted for almost half the senior officers (Sikhs, who came mainly from Punjab, were 26 percent of the total). So to prevent Punjabis in general and Sikhs in particular from having too much influence at the top, there seems to have been a de facto policy of ensuring that they were less successful than they would have otherwise been in getting appointed to the top corps commands, and in particular to the top job of COAS. From 1947 to 1977 all but one of the Army COASs was from outside the traditional Punjabi heartland of the Army; the men appointed came from Coorg, Mysore, Rajasthan, Bombay, Madras, and Kashmir, and even from the hugely underrepresented state of West Bengal. Only one Punjabi, though, was ever appointed to the top position, and that was a very unusual case; there were allegations that General Thapar (1961–1962) was appointed by Defence Minister Krishna Menon because of his perceived pliability, and because Menon had blocked many of the other plausible candidates in an effort to promote one of his own protégés, Lieutenant General B. M. Kaul (Thorat 1986, 176–178; S. D. Verma 1988, 122).

As well as using this "compositional strategy" of diversifying the military's upper levels, Nehru took several additional steps to decrease the group cohesion and increase the professionalism of the army (Horowitz 1985; Quinlivan 1999). One important step was to limit the tenures in office of the most senior generals, which was costly in terms of military effectiveness; as a result of the slow Indianization process before the war and the rapid promotions after the top British officers left from 1947 to 1949, the top Indian officers were still comparatively young men when they advanced to the highest commands, and they might have provided useful service for many more years. But Nehru and the Defence Ministers thought that the political dangers of extending tenures—which might increase the cohesion of the top command—exceeded the military benefits, and refused either to extend tenures or to employ retired officers in significant defense roles after retirement. A logical next step, of course, was to provide some other roles for the key officers after retirement, as Nakanishi shows was done extensively in the case of the Burmese military, where retired senior officers were moved into the ruling party, the parliament, and various council and ministerial positions (Nakanishi 2013). India did nothing on this scale, but several of the retired army chiefs were instead sent off on extended diplomatic postings that took them far away from India: General Cariappa as High Commissioner to Australia, General Chaudhuri as High Commissioner to Canada, and General Thimayya to a UN peacekeeping role in Cyprus.[23]

Another step, which diversified the military officer corps and increased its professional competence, was to increase the number of recruitment streams, training academies, and midcareer training institutes. At the junior level, officer recruitment was now opened to men from all over India, rather than preference being given to candidates from "martial" backgrounds; and the number of ways officers could join and train for the army was increased, which reduced the tight bonds among officers that intensive training at a single institution—Sandhurst, Dehra Dun, or Kakul—could create. Then once officer cadets had enrolled they were put through several different institutions instead of just one. Sardar Patel and Defence Secretary H. M. Patel decided to found a separate National Defence Academy, which was eventually to open near Pune in Maharashtra in 1954, far from the main Indian Military Academy at Dehra Dun, and over what the NDA's first director describes as protests from the top officers (Habibullah 1981, 97–98). This diversification of communities and training institutions and streams was critical to breaking the tight cohesion that might have led to dangerous results. As S. S. Khera pointed out, "The heterogeneous mixture of officers from different parts of the country is represented throughout the structure of the officer cadres, and right up to the high command. They would not hold together for long, if they participated in an attempted coup" (Khera 1968, 85).

As well as taking these measures, Nehru, especially through his Defence Minister Krishna Menon (1957–1962) and his successors, made sure that the Intelligence Bureau kept tabs on what the generals (including some retired generals) and the rest of the military were up to. Lieutenant General S. D. Verma described how in 1960–1961 he was "certain my telephone was tapped and my mail censored under orders of Menon and Kaul. When General Thimayya resigned from the post of Chief of Army Staff after a series of disagreements with Menon, I rang him up to say that we were all with him [and] that was held against me as it transpired later" (1988, 120–121). Verma goes on to describe how when he wanted to have a frank talk with his friend the COAS General Thimayya in Kashmir in 1960 the two of them were forced to take a boat out in the middle of Nagin Lake, "as we did not feel safe anywhere else" (Verma 1988, 120–121). There is also direct evidence that retired General Cariappa was under surveillance after his retirement (Khanduri 2000,

176–177). And we have many documented reports that the Intelligence Bureau has, since independence, been keeping an eye on important troop movements and military events, including closely monitoring the roads in the national capital region.[24]

Finally, Nehru and the new state paid attention to symbols as well as structures. Shortly after independence the prime minister moved into the commander in chief's impressive New Delhi mansion, which as "Teen Murti" (named after the World War I memorial statue of three soldiers outside its gates) now became his official residence. The Defence Ministry under its secretary, H. M. Patel, also changed the warrant of precedence, again over the objections of the top officers, so that at public meetings and state occasions the top generals were clearly below the senior civil servants and elected representatives of the people. And one of the first things the Indian Army did after an Indian took over as commander in chief in 1949 was to raise a new regiment, The Guards, which unlike existing regiments was to recruit from all over India, in its full diversity, and which in consequence was to be ranked senior to all of the other class and mixed regiments.

Nehru took most of these important measures in India's first decade, but after India's defeat by China in 1962, the Indian Army had to be massively expanded because of the strategic threat posed by China. This raised the question of whether the coup prevention strategies in place would be sufficient to control an army that doubled in size by the end of the decade. The Indian state initially responded by strengthening its intelligence capabilities and monitoring of the top generals and of army movements. One of Nehru's close political allies was reportedly also brought in to "coup proof" the capital, preparing contingency plans to get the leadership away from danger if trouble should arise (Maxwell 1970, 439–441).

The major new tactic to deal with the potential political threat caused by a greatly expanded army drawn mainly from the traditionally recruited groups, however, was "balancing outside the army" (de Bruin 2014; Horowitz, 1985). The size of the country's paramilitary forces, which were much more reflective of the country's overall population than the army, was increased from a relatively paltry 29,000 just before the China war (when the army strength was 458,000) to 202,000 by 1972 (when the army had grown to 850,000). By 2011 these forces had been massively increased to more than 852,000 paramilitaries, which made them greater in size than the infantry and armored corps, though not the army as a whole. These paramilitary forces lack heavy equipment and are no match for the regular army, so while they are superior in strength in the capital, where several paramilitary barracks have been built since the 1960s, they are clearly not a direct military hedge against the army in the same way that the well-equipped Saudi National Guard is an effective balancing force for the regime there against the Saudi national army (Quinlivan 1999, 142–144). More importantly the paramilitaries act as an *indirect* hedge against risk, by freeing up troops for other uses and by ensuring that the regular army is not used more than is absolutely necessary on internal security and counterinsurgency tasks that might draw the military into a more public political role.[25]

Control or Autonomy?

After discussing these many control measures it might be easy to conclude that the military is completely under the thumb of the politicians. But as several observers have pointed out, it has been easier for the military to put up with these various constraints, albeit grudgingly, because it has been given a wide degree of control over operational matters, especially at the periphery of the country where it has increasingly been used on counterinsurgency duties (Cohen and Dasgupta 2010; S. Raghavan 2010b). A tacit deal seems to have been struck, most probably during the calming tenure of Defence Minister Y. B. Chavan from 1962–1966, that as long as the military rendered unto Caesar what was Caesar's, it could have substantial autonomy in its own operations.

This arrangement has not always been good for Indian democracy, however, because of course the line between what is "operations" and what is "politics" is not always clear. For instance, in 2011 the democratically elected chief minister of Jammu and Kashmir, Omar Abdullah, publicly called for modifications to the Armed Forces Special Powers Act (AFSPA) in Kashmir, under which the Army has substantial extrajudicial powers and immunities in that highly militarized area. Abdullah was only reflecting the widespread feeling in the valley over the issue, similar to tensions over the same issue in the northeast, where the AFSPA is also in force (Baruah 1995; Haksar and Hongray 2011). The extent of militarization in these peripheral conflict zones is extensive, and one indicator of the military's influence in these areas is that over the past three decades around 40 percent of the governorships in these states have been held by retired generals.[26]

In Jammu and Kashmir, however, the army publicly criticized any such move to soften the AFSPA as one that would gravely impede its operational effectiveness, and this stance seems to have been successful in blocking political change on the issue. Another instance in which the army flexed its muscles on an "operational" issue was over government feelers to Pakistan to consider a joint demilitarization of the Siachen glacier and possibly the Line of Control. The army, which had lost many troops in both areas, publicized its opposition to demilitarizing Siachen—on operational grounds, citing the difficulty of retaking the glacier if it was demilitarized—only a few days before a Ministry of External Affairs mission to Pakistan in 2007, effectively wrecking the negotiations (Staniland 2013, 943, 952).[27]

Working out exactly how much the civil-military policies that prevented coups have hurt the army's military effectiveness is very difficult. Assumptions about the extent and effects of civilian interference often seem to depend on whether the Indian military succeeded or failed; the defeat by China in 1962 demonstrated that civilian interference had been too much, while victory against Pakistan in 1971 demonstrated that civilian oversight had been just right. Srinath Raghavan is one of the few authors to do the necessary thinking in terms of counterfactuals here. He has put forward a well-argued case that the military had no better ideas to combat the threat from China in the 1950s and early 1960s than the politicians—referring to politicians' promotion of the disastrous "forward policy" on the border—which, he argues, invalidates the traditional narrative that it was civilian interference that led to the bad results (2012). Without completely overturning the conventional wisdom that the civilians did make serious strategic mistakes, Raghavan argues that it was "the military's inability to come up with proposals to meet these intrusions [that] gave the civilians the upper hand in the formulation of strategy" (2009, 151).

Overall, though, it seems likely, given important studies by various experts on the Indian military, that the civil-military constraints that have helped prevent a coup have hurt military effectiveness and preparedness in at least three important ways: (1) the weakening of the army before the 1962 China war; (2) the problems caused for defense coordination and preparation by the unwieldy defense bureaucracy, duplication of functions among the different branches, and lack of sharing of information across branches; and (3) the gradual downgrading of pay and perks since independence, which has left the army with a huge shortage of officers that has affected the force's discipline and capabilities (Cohen and Dasgupta 2010; Menon 2009; Mukherjee 2011). The February 2000 Kargil Review Committee, for instance, pointed out that India's strategy of developing and controlling nuclear weapons outside of the army, while it may make sense from the perspective of civil-military relations, "puts the Indian Army at a disadvantage vis-à-vis its Pakistani counterpart. While the former was in the dark about India's nuclear capability, the latter as the custodian of Pakistani nuclear weaponry was fully aware of its own capability. Three former Indian Chiefs of Army Staff expressed unhappiness about this asymmetric situation" (Menon 2009, 114–115, 117).

The Structure of the Book

I begin in Chapter 1 by examining the inheritance of India's colonial military structure. As I show, the colonial Indian Army was deliberately constructed both to maximize its fighting potential and to hedge against the threat of any repeat of a mutiny like the one that had almost ended British control in 1857. Other much smaller mutinies that took place over the following decades made senior officers always aware of the issue even as memories of 1857 receded, and confidential army reports make it clear the ethnic balance of the army and the need to hedge against a mutiny was always a concern.[28] However, this "divide and rule" army structure was increasingly criticized by Indians in the 1920s and 1930s. Nationalists complained about the "martial caste" bias, the economic unfairness of recruiting from only some regions using taxes reaped from others, and the potential political threat posed by a "mercenary force" if India ever became a democracy. Already in the 1930s Congress was putting forward thoughtful and detailed policy proposals to reform the military and its composition, as well as motions in the central assemblies, which ensured that the issue was immediately on the political agenda after independence (e.g., Chaudhuri 1935).

In Chapter 2 I explore the impact of World War II, both on the army's composition and on the development of strategies to manage political criticism of its recruitment policies that the army and Ministry of Defence have continued, in some respects, to use to this day. I show that the army did not radically change the composition of its frontline combat forces during the war, and used the many new recruits from new regions to fill in the gaps in service, technical, and rear locations while it continued to rely on its traditional "martial class" units for all the important frontline roles.

The partition in 1947 led to almost all of India's Muslim officers and other ranks leaving for Pakistan. The senior officer corps that was left in each country after the mass departure of most of the British officers in 1947–1948 was politically conservative, drawn from just a few ethnic groups, and very cohesive—all the officers having trained together in the same companies at Sandhurst, then served together in the same eight "Indianized" regiments, and having forged additional bonds in subsequent training and military assignments. This ethnic and organizational cohesion, when combined with senior officers' political conservatism and distaste for politicians, posed a major challenge to both new states (Janowitz 1964, 1977). In Pakistan this challenge was made worse by the deep imbalance in the army between the representation of different provinces and their share in the army.

In Chapter 3 I look at how the new Congress Party government in India dealt with these challenges in its first decade and a half. Although Nehru and other Congress leaders originally wanted to reshape the army's rank and file to make it reflect the nation's composition, this proposal had to be dropped for two reasons. First, the outbreak of war with Pakistan in 1947–1948 and the possibility of renewed conflicts, especially coming on the heels of the massive

instability caused by partition, made the radical restructuring envisaged before independence now seem strategically unwise. Second,
it was difficult to restructure the army by creating lots of new units
drawn from more diverse regions and groups, because India's political leadership wanted the military—by far the country's largest
budget item, accounting for around 50 percent of central expenditures—to shrink rather than grow, to free up money to use for the
country's larger economic and social development.

In the absence of large-scale change in the overall composition of
forces, the government relied on several other policies to minimize
the military threat. First, new policies to control the senior defense
officers and reduce the army's institutional autonomy. Second, new
measures to deter coordination among the officer corps. The third
important thing the Congress Party did in the 1950s that helped
with civil-military issues was to provide political stability and legitimacy, which lessened the chances of the military being drawn into
politics to deal with political crises. A very important element here
was the defusing of the ethnic and regional conflicts that could have
spread to the army or created the sort of political crisis that might
have precipitated army intervention. In particular, the constitutional ban on religious discrimination and the acceptance of the
principle of linguistic states and caste reservations helped cross-cut
the damaging cleavages (Hindu versus Sikh and Muslim, north versus south, Hindi speakers versus non-Hindi speakers) that might
otherwise have arisen.

In Chapter 4 I consider the impact of the China War, the 1975–
1977 emergency, and the Sikh militancy of the late 1980s, three major challenges to the civil-military control strategies that India had
developed since independence. First, after the disastrous defeat by
China in October and November 1962, the country was forced to
more than double the size of the army in just a few years. With speed
and military efficiency as the main criteria, almost all of this expansion was in fact done by adding new "martial class" recruits to existing class regiments, something that was deliberately hidden from
sight in most official statements. This massive expansion of the
military of course caused some anxiety in civilian ranks, especially
after the death of Nehru in 1964 and the weakening of the Con-

gress Party, both internally due to faction fights and externally with increased competition from the Swatantra, Communists, and various regional parties. As General Chaudhuri (the COAS at this time) puts it in his memoirs, the civilian leadership was worried: "Would they [the generals] get ideas above their station?" (J. N. Chaudhuri 1978, 193).

Preoccupied by these worries, the political leadership decided not to fundamentally weaken the cumbersome Ministry of Defence command and control structures that Nehru, Patel, and a succession of Defence Ministers had introduced to control the army in the 1950s, and which many army officers had blamed for the country's poor preparation and military performance in 1962. The intelligence services still kept tabs on the most senior officers and kept them well away from positions of political influence.

The rise of Sikh militancy in the late 1970s and 1980s and the serious insurgencies in Jammu and Kashmir and the northeast in the 1980s and 1990s posed the most serious challenges since independence to the strategies that India had evolved to manage its military. The Sikh militancy reminded the country again of the potential dangers of regionally imbalanced recruitment, as ex-soldiers fought the government forces in Punjab and several Sikh units mutinied after the military action at the Golden Temple in Amritsar in June 1984. These events prompted a major challenge to the class recruitment model, as General Vaidya, the COAS at the time of Operation Bluestar in 1984, considered whether to switch the army over to all-India recruitment. As I show, this effort ultimately failed and the army in fact switched these mixed units back to class units in the late 1990s because of worries about their military effectiveness compared to the traditional format. The long-running insurgencies in Jammu and Kashmir and the northeast posed a different but just as serious challenge as Bluestar; how to preserve a militarily effective force that also keeps out of politics when massive portions of the army are being deployed for long periods to put down serious local insurgencies. The state has dealt with these challenges in two main ways. First, the state has increased the size of paramilitary forces even more, to more than 852,000 today, as an indirect hedge against the military. The paramilitary forces perform politically sensitive policing and internal security roles that would otherwise have to be done by the army or the ill-prepared state police forces. Second, beginning in 1990, the state has created a separate military force, the Rashtriya Rifles, specifically for domestic counterinsurgency roles. One benefit of both these forces is to insulate the regular armed forces from roles that might weaken its military effectiveness against external foes and also, potentially, draw it more into politics.

In Chapter 5 I consider the condition of the Indian Army and the country's civil-military control structures today. Because of continuing civilian concerns over having a powerful military and COAS, despite persistent criticism from senior officers and defense analysts, the country still relies on a very cumbersome command and control structure, which creates problems in intelligence gathering, defense coordination, procurement, and strategic development. Neither the Arun Singh report in 1990 nor the more recent Kargil Committee Report in 2000 have been able to change this structure and succeed in moving to a new one headed by a Chief of the Defence Staff (CDS), in part because the CDS would likely have to come from the army, as the largest force; neither the civilian leaders nor the heads of the air force and navy find this prospect attractive (Menon 2009, 114–118).

The intensification of caste, religious, and regional politics in India over the past twenty years and the distributional claims these identities create have threatened, but so far not overturned, the army's ability to recruit from its traditional communities for its single- and fixed-class units. For more than two decades, the major national parties have been forced to form large coalitions in order to form a government in New Delhi, and these coalitions have given regional and ethnic parties a powerful voice. As it did in earlier periods, the army has so far successfully resisted demands to introduce Scheduled Caste (SC), Scheduled Tribe (ST), and Other Backward Class (OBC) caste reservations (as opposed to the de facto caste reservations it already has in its class regiments), to create new caste regiments to represent OBC and SC communities, or to release systematic information about the religious, caste, and regional patterns of recruitment. The Sachar committee's 2006 attempt to highlight the issue of low Muslim recruitment in the army was beaten back on the grounds that it was an attempt to "communalize" the army.

There are indications, however, that the army's autonomy over recruitment is likely to lessen in the years ahead. First, the regional parties now play an important part in political coalitions at the center and, as I show, MPs from these parties are asking an increasing number of questions about why some states and communities are less represented than others. In response to this, and to a decreasing demand for army recruitment from some traditional regions—in part due to the long-term economic growth that the flow of army recruitment has helped to sustain—the army is already more ethnically balanced than it was in the 1960s. Second, there are still legal questions being asked about whether "martial class" recruitment is compatible with a secular state, including a major public interest petition to the Supreme Court, filed in 2012 by a doctor from Haryana, I. S. Yadav that challenges the whole basis of class recruitment in the army as unconstitutional discrimination on the basis of caste.

From the perspective of India's civil-military control issues there are also a few worrying signs. First, in 2012, the country stood back aghast as a public fight broke out between the chief of army staff, General V. K. Singh, and the country's Defence Minister, A. K. Anthony. This conflict was damaging because it was public, and because it exposed allegedly severe conflicts within the army over promotions, some of which were along religious and caste lines. The conflict was also worrying because one of the main protagonists, General Singh, was actively backed by civilian politicians from his own Rajput caste and by some quarters of the media during the crisis, and since his retirement he has entered politics as a BJP MP and Minister of State. Second, there are signs that growing caste consciousness, especially when combined with increased education and the widespread availability of the mass media and mobile phones, is hampering the army's ability to retain its traditional hierarchies and insulate itself from societal conflicts. Incidents of "fragging," the murder of officers by troops, have apparently been on the increase, with sixty-seven reported fratricides in the armed forces from 2003 to 2007, the army being worst affected.[29] And in the past four years there have been several incidents in which soldiers, bristling at the poor treatment they have received from officers, have used physical force against them or refused to carry out orders. Media reports make it clear that the growing number of "backward caste" soldiers, like their counterparts in civilian life, are increasingly unwilling to work in the undignified roles to which they have traditionally been assigned by their still largely upper-caste officers.[30]

In Chapter 6 I explore why Pakistan's experience with civil-military relations has been so much worse than India's. The first factor is the real weakness of the Pakistan Muslim League as a political party and its inability to provide political stability and legitimacy in the first decade after independence. The second factor is the extremely bad hand that Pakistan was dealt in 1947; a deeply ethnically imbalanced and overlarge military, very weak public finances (partly caused by the need to spend 65–70 percent of its central budget on the military to keep up with a much larger India), the loss of much of its human and economic capital to India, preexisting rivalries between east and west, and the thousand-mile physical distance between the country's two wings.[31] A third factor is the relative lack of thinking about the issue of civil-military control before and just after independence among the Muslim League's top leaders. This partly reflected the optimism of the secessionists that all problems would be solved by the creation of the new state, and partly reflected the fact that Muslims were an overrepresented minority in the pre-independence army. All three factors combined, unfortunately, to prevent the country from taking the sort of decisive steps taken by India in the 1940s and early 1950s to rein in the power of the military. Instead, the military was left largely autonomous, and its senior officers were gradually drawn into politics both by their own ambitions and by the chaotic void created by the lack of legitimate, strong national party alternatives. In particular the civilian leadership used the army for some purposes, such as a relatively successful imposition of martial law in Lahore in 1951, that convinced some senior officers as well as many in the country that the army might offer a solution to some of the country's problems. Once the early autonomy of the army had been established, and then strengthened during the long military rule of Ayub Khan, it could not be overturned. When, after the Pakistan Army's defeat by India in 1971 and the loss of Bangladesh, Prime Minister Zulfikar Ali Bhutto tried to redress the balance, it was too late. Bhutto tried to rein in the military's autonomy through command and control measures similar to those India adopted in the 1950s, including death penalties for treason, and to "balance outside the army" by establishing a Federal Security Force (FSF), armed with modern weapons and tanks, and responsible only to the political leadership (Nawaz 2008, 338–339; 343). The army resisted all these measures and abolished them (and the eighteen-thousand-member FSF) soon after the 1977 coup that led to Bhutto's execution. Since then, if anything, the power of the military has grown, as the Fauji Foundation—a number of military welfare and pension corporations—now controls a fair chunk of Pakistan's land and businesses directly, and operates as a state within a state; as private career opportunities stagnate, the highly compensated military seems (unlike in India) one of the best careers open to the country's ambitious middle classes as well as the children of serving officers (Siddiqa 2007).

Finally, in the Conclusion I draw some general lessons from the Indian and Pakistani experience of managing civil-military relations, which might be useful as we consider other transitions from authoritarian rule. One lesson is that the timing and sequencing of civil-military controls is very important; reforms that might have worked in the 1950s in Pakistan were too late by the mid-1970s. Another lesson is that hedging works, both within the army and in terms of what Horowitz might term "balancing from outside" with paramilitaries (Horowitz 1985). Finally, structural reforms that are often not highlighted in the comparative literature on coup proofing, such as multiplying the number of different routes into the officer corps, can end up making a big difference in terms of the effective obstacles to coordination they might pose to potential coup makers.

Note on Spelling

This book follows US conventions in spelling and capitalization except for quoted material, proper nouns (for example, "Ministry of Defence," not "Ministry of Defense"), and those military terms and ranks in which Indian convention uses capitalization (for example, "Lieutenant General," "Army," and so on) even though these might not be capitalized elsewhere.

1

Divide and Rule

Introduction

THE BRITISH RAJ, like most colonial regimes, used several divide-and-rule strategies to maintain control of India and its army. First, like empires throughout history, it preserved its power by recruiting disproportionately from some groups and not others. After the mutiny and rebellion of 1857, the British stopped recruiting troops from the Hindi-speaking heartland of north India, and instead began to recruit in very large numbers from the newly conquered areas of Punjab and the North West Frontier Province (NWFP), areas that had remained loyal and from which additional troops had been raised to help put down the rebellion.

Second, even though the British now recruited disproportionately from groups seen as loyal, they were still nervous enough, especially as they increased the number of "pure" Punjabi and Pashtun units to guard against a potential Russian threat in the late nineteenth century, to use a variety of additional strategies to prevent a mutiny. To make it more difficult for Indians to coordinate against the British, they continued to deploy most Indian soldiers in "fixed battalions" in which men from different regions and groups served in homogenous companies alongside each other. The purpose of this, quite explicitly, was to prevent the troops finding common cause against the colonial ruler. The Secretary of State for India, Sir Charles Wood, wrote in 1862 that he wanted to "have a different and rival spirit in different regiments, so that Sikh might fire into Hindoo, Goorkha into either, without any scruple in case of need" (Sarkar 1983, 16). In some regiments the rule was also enforced that men from the same regiment on guard duty had to be drawn from different subcastes, so as to make it less likely that they would unite to betray their officers (*Regimental Standing Orders*, Pathan Regiment, 1919). On the same principle, care was taken, once Indian officers began to be given King's Commissions into the Indian Army after 1919, not to post them to units of their own ethnic group (Thorat 1986, 12).

Third, the Indian Army practiced a policy of what Horowitz terms "balancing" outside the army; hedging the potential risk from Indian soldiers with British soldiers (one British unit for every two Indian units, after 1857) and with Gorkha soldiers recruited from Nepal. British and Gorkha troops were always kept within easy reach of large concentrations of Indian soldiers (Horowitz 1985; de Bruin 2013). Right up to the end of British rule, Gorkha units were also officered only by British officers, never by Indians, to prevent any possibility of coordination between Gorkha units and potential Indian mutineers (Palit 1997, 297).[1] Lord Kitchener, when he was Commander in Chief, analyzed the security risks posed by the composition of the army, and concluded that "The most loyal Native soldiers are beyond all doubt the Gurkhas. They have very little in common with the rest of our indigenous troops and are hardly likely to coalesce with them; their individual personal sympathy with the British soldier is well known, and except by the grossest folly on our part, I see no danger of alienating their friendship. So convinced am I of this that I consider we should be perfectly justified in eliminating them altogether from our calculations when estimating the relative proportions of British troops."[2]

Fourth, remembering the repressive policies and the mismanagement of troops and their home regions that had led to the 1857 mutiny and rebellion, the army used a variety of strategies to try to ensure political stability in the main recruiting regions, as well as to maintain its social and political isolation and loyalty. The Raj lavished benefits and development projects on its main recruiting regions, in addition to the money it spent directly on military wages and pensions, so these regions grew much faster than average. From 1898 to 1939, central expenditure on rail, roads, power, and irrigation in the Punjab, the recruiting heartland of the army, was twice as high per capita as in the rest of India, and economic historians think it very likely that these differences in public investment increased regional disparities in growth and income (Kumar 2005, 915). The Raj also intervened on controversial issues as diverse as Punjab agricultural policy in 1907 and the Sikh Akali movement over the control of *gurd-waras* after 1919, when these seemed to threaten the political loyalties of its main recruiting classes, such as the Sikhs, Jat Hindus, and Punjabi Muslims.

There was never any reason for the British, however, to change the centralized command structure of the army. The interests of the British colonial administration and the British-controlled army were closely aligned, and the only serious problem was the personal power struggle between General Kitchener and the Viceroy in 1905 over whether the Commander in Chief should continue to be both the head of the army and "Military Member" of the council. The army won, and this led to the Viceroy's resignation. The overwhelming bulk of the officer corps was still British, and the interests of the army and the political leadership were aligned, at least most of the time. The army was also represented politically in India through the Commander in Chief's membership of the Viceroy's council, and in London through its access to contacts at the India Office and War Department, whose officers had often served at one time or another with their counterparts in the Indian Army. Many of the official letters between Indian officers and London begin with the use of familiar nicknames—such as "Dear Pug" and "Dear Mo"—that emphasize the closeness of these formal and informal ties.[3]

A Primer on Indian Army Recruitment and Organization

Before we discuss the historical forces that shaped the Indian Army, a brief account of its basic recruitment strategy and organizational structure is in order (see also Table 1.1). In the Indian Army, "class" means the religious, regional, or caste category used to define recruitment to particular units in the infantry, armored corps, and artillery (the other branches recruit on an all-India basis). It does not mean "class" in the sense of socioeconomic status. For example, Jats, Mazhabi and Ramdasia Sikhs, Jat Sikhs, Dogras, Kaimkhani

Table 1.1. Organizational Structure of the Indian Army

Division	In the infantry a unit with, nowadays, at least three infantry brigades combined with armored, artillery, mechanized, and mountain units as required. Headed by a Major General, who is responsible to the Lieutenant General in charge of the Corps.
Brigade	An operational unit of (in the infantry) three battalions, together with transport, HQ, engineer, communications, and other support as needed. Usually attached to a division, but sometimes independent. Headed by a Brigadier.
Regiment	A hundred years ago the infantry's combat regiments were each a battalion size unit of approximately 850 men. The army's current regiments, however, vary widely in size, and in the infantry the regiment typically serves as the focal point and training organization for a large number of linked battalions; the Naga Regiment has only three battalions, while the Mahar Regiment, Jat Regiment, Kumaon Regiment, and Rajputana Rifles each have more than twenty battalions. The army's largest regiment, the Rashtriya Rifles, had more than sixty battalions as of 2014, trained not by a central Rashtriya Rifles regimental infrastructure, as in the case of other regiments, but by the regiments to which its battalions are individually linked. In the armored corps, however, regiments are still battalion sized.
Battalion	In the infantry a unit of 825–850 men, composed of four companies, additional platoons of signals, pioneers, and such personnel, and an administration company with clerks, transport, medical and the like. In the armored corps a battalion is smaller: a unit of around 650 men composed of three squadrons in addition to support units. In class units the companies in a battalion are made up of the specified class or classes, but the men in noncombat roles are drawn from many different areas and groups. As of 2012 the Indian Army had around 650 infantry battalions and armored regiments. Each battalion is headed by a colonel.
Company/ Squadron	The subunit of the battalion—in the infantry, a unit of around 120 men. In the infantry's single- and fixed-class units these companies—four to each battalion—are often composed of men of a specified regional/religious/caste group, termed a "class." In the armored corps regiments are subdivided into three squadrons, also frequently recruited on a class basis.
Platoon	Infantry companies are divided into three platoons, each under the command of a subedar, a junior commissioned officer rank, with the assistance of havildars (sergeants) and naiks (corporals). In the armored corps, regiments are divided into squadrons and troops, commanded by daffadars and lance daffadars.

Muslims, and Gorkhas are all considered "classes" for the purposes of military recruitment. What the military considers a "class" is often not really a single caste at all, but aggregates of several different groups. For instance, the class of "Dogras" includes several different castes from the hills of Jammu, Punjab, and Himachal Pradesh; "Kumaonis" includes several castes from the hill areas of Uttarakhand; "Gorkhas" includes several different castes from east and west Nepal; and "South Indian Classes" includes a variety of Hindu, Christian, and Muslim castes from South India.

The system goes back to the nineteenth century, when the British designated certain groups, such as Sikhs and Gorkhas, as "martial classes" (often termed "martial races") and recruited them disproportionately on the basis of their presumed martial abilities and traditions as well as their proven loyalty to British interests. The process of "martialization" of the Indian Army accelerated in the 1880s as the Raj became more worried about the threat from Russia, which led it to increase the number of units from "martial classes," especially from Punjab, and decrease those from supposedly less martial areas in the south and west.

The term "class unit" refers to the type of regiment or battalion. Some regiments, such as the Sikh Regiment and Sikh Light Infantry, are "single class," and therefore recruit combat troops only from members of a specified class, such as Jat Sikhs and Mazhabi and Ramdasia Sikhs. A larger number of regiments are "fixed-class" units and recruit only from specified classes according to a particular percentage. For instance, in the Punjab Regiment, out of the four companies in a typical battalion, two will be Sikh and two will be Dogra. In the Bihar Regiment, most battalions are composed of two companies of Biharis and two of "Adivasis" recruited from Bihar, Jharkhand, Chhattisgarh, and Orissa. An increasing number of infantry and armored units (now close to 30 percent of the total) are not single- or fixed-class units but are recruited on an all-India basis, in which troops of all different classes are recruited or mixed together. This is usually done on a regional (zonal) basis to ensure that the differences in language, food, and other matters are not so great that they create logistical difficulties in training and the field.

Since independence, officers are no longer formally recruited on the basis of their "class." Since many officer candidates come from

army families—often through army schools—or from traditional
recruiting areas, there may still be some overrepresentation of traditional army communities. Officers are supposed to be assigned to
units without regard to community. In practice the facts that many
officers who do well in training (and therefore have a choice of unit)
have a clear preference for serving with particular units and that the
army still is reluctant to post too many officers from a particular
group to a unit of the same community mean that there may be a
larger representation of some groups in particular units than a ran-
dom unit assignment would predict.

The "Martial Class" Army

The Indian Army that was developed after the costly British defeat
of the 1857 rebellion was designed to meet two goals, goals that the
colonial administration often saw as in tension. First, the colonial
government was determined to prevent a repeat of the 1857 mutiny
and rebellion, and to maintain Britain's hold on India. Second, the
government wanted to field the most effective possible fighting force
against any foreign powers that might threaten India and British
imperial interests (Cohen 1969, 1990a; Omissi 1994; Roy 1997; Mazumder 2003; Yong 2005).

First, and most importantly from the colonial government's perspective, after 1857 the army had to be restructured in a way that
preserved British power in India and prevented a repeat of the mutiny and rebellion. To begin with, the European proportion in the
Indian Army was sharply—and, given the roughly threefold cost
difference between European and Indian troops, expensively—
increased, from a ratio of one British soldier to six Indian soldiers
before 1857, to a new ratio of one British to every two Indian soldiers. This ratio was later relaxed to 1:2.5 when the Bombay, Bengal,
and Madras presidency armies were merged in 1894, on the grounds
that improvements in transport and communications since 1857 now
allowed the quicker and more effective deployment of (British and
Gorkha) troops to deal with any mutiny.[4] The risk from Indian
troops' potential ability to overwhelm these British forces was also
hedged in other ways; Indian-staffed artillery units were disbanded
after 1857, Indians having used artillery very effectively against the

British during the uprising, and Indian troops were also issued inferior rifles. These worries eased somewhat over time, and after 1893
Indian troops began to be issued the same rifles as British soldiers.
But the trust in Indians and belief in the capacity of the Raj to deal
with the threat of rebellion went only so far. When the Commander
in Chief, General Kitchener, proposed that a few Indian artillery
units be created to serve on the frontier, he was overruled by the
Viceroy, Lord Curzon, on the grounds that the risks of training
Indians in field artillery were still too great.[5] The first Indian artillery
regiment, the First Field Brigade, was only raised in 1935, with different classes—Madrasis, Rajputs, Punjabi Muslims, and Ranghars—in
each of the four batteries (Marston 2014, 32). We can speculate that
this composition, which provided the maximum possible diversity
among batteries, probably reflected the fact that even in 1935 the British were nervous about providing artillery to Indians, and therefore
wanted to provide as many barriers to prevent coordination against
them as possible.

In addition the British made sure to always balance concentrations
of Indian troops with nearby concentrations of British and Gorkha
units. The Nicholson committee reminded senior officers in 1913
that "care must also be taken in the internal defense arrangements
not to associate small detachments of British soldiers without artillery support with large numbers of Indian troops" (Army in India
Committee 1913). For internal security purposes, some of these
practices continued right up until the end of British rule. One retired
Indian officer who served at Indian Army headquarters in 1946–
1947 remembers a map of India that "had brown pins for Indian
units, green for Gorkha units and red for British, and the strategy
was, do not allow clusters of brown pins on their own with no reds
or greens."[6]

In addition, the regional and ethnic recruiting basis of the Bengal
Army (the largest of the three presidency armies) was rebalanced
away from the "Poorbeah" recruits from Bihar, Agra, and Oudh and
the Central Provinces, the areas from which the bulk of the military
mutineers had come and where the general rebellion had been concentrated, and instead toward increased recruitment from Punjab
and the NWFP, recently conquered areas that had remained largely

loyal to the British and from which additional troops had been recruited during the conflict (Peel Commission 1859).

The British also wanted to make it much harder for troops within each Indian regiment to coordinate against them as they had done in 1857. In its debates on the causes of the rebellion, the British administration worried that the mixed regiments that existed before 1857 had allowed Hindus, Muslims, Sikhs, and Poorbeahs to lose "to some extent their racial prejudices and became inspired with one common sentiment" (N. Chaudhuri 1930a, 47).

The solution to this problem, in the Bengal Army, was the "class company" model, in which each regiment would contain several homogenous "class companies" drawn from different groups. This seemed to offer the fighting advantages of homogeneity at the company level, with the security advantages of balancing different groups against each other at the regimental level and regiments from different communities against each other. The central idea here, again, was expressed by Sir Charles Wood, the Secretary of State for India, in a letter in May 1862: "If one regiment mutinies, I should like to have the next so alien that it would fire into it" (B. Moore 1966, 223–224).

In 1864, as a result of this policy, the Bengal Army began to change most of its regiments over to the new fixed-class company system. For example, a Punjab regiment might have two companies of Punjabi Muslims, one of Dogras, and one of Jat Sikhs. The principle of reducing risk to the British by increasing the diversity of ethnic groups was also sometimes used when carrying out specific tasks within a regiment; for instance the Fortieth Pathan Regiment, which recruited from various tribes of Pashtuns, had a standing order that "guards will always be composed of men of different classes" (*Regimental Standing Orders* 1919, 18–19).[7]

The second main goal of the British after 1857, which became of increasing concern with Russian expansion into Central Asia after the 1870s, was to build an Indian Army capable of fighting the troops of a major Western power (Mazumder 2003). Costly foreign campaigns in Burma and Afghanistan in the 1870s and 1880s, during which units suffered many reversals, convinced the senior military leadership that it urgently needed to bolster the fighting quality of its Indian Army. There were many differences of opinion among senior officers on what exactly the problems were and how to solve them. But with regard to the army's composition, the view that dominated by the mid-1880s, especially after General Roberts became Commander in Chief in 1885, a position he held for eight years, was that two big changes were needed: an increase in the proportion of "martial classes" from the north, and an increase in the proportion of class company regiments, which were thought to be superior in combat to mixed units.[8]

Roberts and other senior officers believed that the army needed to reduce the number of troops that were from "nonmartial" groups and regions that had not performed well on campaign and increase the number of recruits from "martial" areas and castes whose allegedly superior performance on campaign had shown that they were better equipped for the battles the army was likely to fight in the future, especially on the northwest frontier (Marston 2014, 10).[9] That meant fewer Madrasis and soldiers from Bombay, fewer lower-caste soldiers such as the Mahars, and more recruitment from "martial classes" from the Punjab, the NWFP, Nepal, and a few selected hill regions. This "evidence" on the poor battle performance of Madras and Bombay units was in fact rigged. Officers from Madras and Bombay, furious at the negative comments made about "their" men's fighting ability, pointed out that the "battle proven" argument was largely the product of their troops not having been deployed because of other senior officers' biases, despite their regiments' past records and proven fighting abilities (Eden Commission 1879). Sir Frederick Haines, the Commander in Chief at the time of an 1879 commission that examined the issue and a proud product of the Madras Army, argued that the claim that the Madras soldiers were not as martial as Punjabis and other martial classes was simply wrong. The Madrasis, he argued, could not be blamed for being "untested" in battle, when this lack of combat experience was simply the product of blinkered officers deciding not to deploy them on the battlefield. He pointed out that the Madras sappers, the only unit that had been deployed on the frontier, had done just as well as troops from the north, and said that "I cannot admit for one moment that anything has occurred to disclose the fact that the Madras sepoy is inferior as a fighting man. . . . In drill, training and discipline the Madras sepoy is inferior to none. . . . I have no doubt all I have said for Madras may be judged equally justly for Bombay" (Eden Commission, 1879, 1: 120).

But despite these protests, the "martial class" and pro-Punjabi lobby emerged victorious. The proportion of Madras and Bombay regiments in the army was substantially reduced, and the few lower-caste regiments in service were gradually disbanded. By 1907 forty of the fifty-two Madras battalions that had existed in 1860 had been disbanded (twenty-six battalions), turned into noncombat units (three battalions) or converted to Punjabi battalions (eleven battalions)[10] (Mason 1974, 349–350; 361). In addition all the lower-caste troops except those in Sikh units were forced out of the Bengal Army in 1883 (Willcox Committee 1945, 1: 209–210). As memories of 1857 receded and worries about Russia grew, senior officers also increased the proportion of class regiments that consisted solely of Sikhs or Hindus, which they saw as generally more cohesive and effective in battle than the fixed-class companies that had been created in response to worries about mutiny. In 1893 alone, eighteen Bengal regiments were converted from a fixed- to a single-class structure. The army proceeded cautiously with this strategy, though; fixed-class regiments were still the majority, and the army also did not create any single-class Muslim regiments, because of lingering worries over the political reliability of Muslim troops.

After the replacement of most Bombay and Madras regiments by those from the north was completed in the 1890s, the ethnic composition of the Indian Army's main frontline "class" regiments was to remain essentially the same for half a century: a heavily Punjabi and Pashtun force from Punjab and the NWFP, with significant numbers of "martial class" Gorkhas, Rajputs, Dogras, Garhwalis, Jats, and Marathas, and very little representation of anyone else. The overall caste and religious balance of the army for the next decades can be seen in Table 1.2.

Some adjustments were made to this basic formula from time to time, if one or other of these communities seemed to be at somewhat greater risk of opposing the British or was perceived as "unreliable" or hard to recruit on some other grounds. The 1913 Nicholson committee, for instance, concerned about disaffection among Jats

Table 1.2. Comparison of the Provincial and Class Composition of the Indian Army, 1914–1931

	January 1, 1914	January 1, 1931	Percentages January 1, 1914	Percentages January 1, 1931
Punjab				
Punjabi Muslims	38,055	40,618	26.5	35.3
Sikhs	32,645	22,506	22.7	19.6
Punjab and Western Uttar Pradesh				
Hindu Rajputs	14,577	6,786	10.1	5.9
Hindu Jats	9,728	9,677	6.8	8.4
Garhwalis	1,723	4,156	1.2	3.6
North West Frontier Province				
Pathans	13,456	7,440	9.4	6.5
Jammu and Kashmir				
Dogras	8,888	11,348	6.2	9.9
Madras				
Muslims	3,127	366	2.2	0.3
Hindus	6,431	3,373	4.5	2.9
Bombay				
Mahrattas	6,321	4,589	4.4	4.0
Others				
Muslim Rajputs	4,988	3,271	3.5	2.8
Deccani Muslims	3,862	906	2.7	0.8
	143,801	115,036		

Source: Derived from tables in Government of India, *Legislative Assembly Debates*, September 15, 1931, Volume 5, No. 7, 427. Totals exclude Gorkhas. Percentages add up to slightly more than 100 because of rounding.

and Sikhs, recommended that their proportion in some regiments be reduced in favor of Punjabi Muslims, Dogras, and Pathans (Army in India Committee 1913, 130). Similar shifts in composition took place after World War I, resulting in Punjabi Muslims displacing Sikhs by 1930 as the largest single group recruited from Punjab (N. Chaudhuri 1931a). But the overall balance remained about the same. Reflecting the growth in the "martial class" ideology within the army, European ideas about race current at the time, and the army's preference for "reliable" and less educated farmers over more politicized and educated urban dwellers, a series of recruiting handbooks was drawn up to highlight, in a pseudoscientific and frankly racialist manner, (1) the alleged characteristics of particular martial communities, (2) ways to sift out "true" members of the community from "impostors" from less favored castes, and (3) the best areas and times of year to obtain what were referred to as recruits of good "stock," such as after harvest and before planting (Chaudhuri 1931c, 464).[11] For instance, the handbook on the most heavily recruited single group, the Punjabi Muslims (so ubiquitous that internal army correspondence usually refers to them simply as "PMs"), emphasized that the best soldiers were those from "districts which are essentially Muhammadan, *viz.*, that portion of the Punjáb which lies between the Indus and the Jhelum rivers and the Gujrat, Shahpur, Jhang and Multan districts. In the other districts where the Hindu and the Sikh predominate, the Punjábi Mussalmán (Rájput and Jat) appears to hold an inferior position which has naturally affected his soldierly qualities. There the superiority of the Jat Sikh over the Punjabi Musalman Jat of the same stock, is most marked."[12]

The 1930s handbook for Jats, Gujars, and Ahirs, on the other hand, referred to them as "thick headed and manly . . . yeoman cultivators . . . eminently adapted to the profession of arms" (cited in Deshpande 1996, 178).

Recruits from these desired "martial classes" were enticed by military tradition, the regular pay, the status of military service, and the not insignificant land grants and pensions that one could expect on retirement, especially in the new irrigated "canal colonies" that were developed in Punjab from the late nineteenth century. These government pensions and grants came to be a very significant share of the overall economy in the most heavily recruited districts, such as Rawalpindi, Jhelum, Attock, and Amritsar in Punjab, where government expenditure greatly improved the economic status of recruits and their families (Mazumder 2003, 24–30; 175–189). In addition to these benefits, the government also lowered the land tax in the most heavily recruited districts and rewarded local religious leaders and landlords who encouraged or at times strong-armed their community members to join up. Tan Tai Yong shows that the total amount of military pay and pensions received in one tehsil in Punjab was almost three times the land tax owed to the government (2005, 78–96).

This reliance on only a few areas and communities for recruits came under severe strain in World War I, when there was a very high demand for Indian troops to fight, initially in France and then later in the Middle East, and reports from troops sent to the front early in the war began to discourage others from joining up (Gajendra Singh 2006). One strategy to deal with this, which began in 1917, was to recruit traditional communities from districts that had previously been regarded as providing poor-quality recruits. Another was to specify recruiting targets for each district, which were often met by local bigwigs through heavy-handed methods (Leigh 1922, 35–43). Although resisted by many—some recruits even mutilated themselves to avoid service—these and other methods eventually allowed the army to meet almost all its recruitment needs from the traditional classes such as Pashtuns, Punjabi Muslims, Sikhs, Jats, Garhwalis from Uttar Pradesh and Punjab, rather than from provinces such as Bengal and Bihar that the British now associated with political radicalism and opposition to British rule. Punjab alone provided 41 percent of all troops, and more than 50 percent of combatants from 1914 to 1918. To deflect political pressure from excluded groups the British did recruit one or two new units from disfavored provinces; but as we can see in Table 1.3 this did not greatly affect the combat composition of the army, because Bengalis and men from Bihar and Orissa were given mainly support roles rather than used as frontline combatants. Bengalis were 5.4 percent of all recruits but only 1 percent of combat troops. This strategy—to recruit a little more broadly to deflect political pressure and fulfill overall manpower needs, but make sure that the fighting arms were still recruited from the traditional and "tested" groups—would be used again, both in World War II and in the postindependence period.

Once the war ended in 1918, the few regiments that had been recruited from outside the favored groups, such as the Bengal detachment that had served in Mesopotamia, were quickly disbanded on the grounds that they had "not performed well." In the case of the Forty-Ninth Bengalee Regiment, which had mutinied in Mesopotamia, this was largely because it had been deployed in a campaign that had been monumentally mismanaged by the British (J. N. Chaudhuri

Table 1.3. Army Recruitment by Province, 1914–1918 (British India)

Province	Total Recruits	Percent of All Recruits	Percent of Combatant Recruits
Madras	92,340	8.4	7.5
Bombay	71,483	6.5	6.0
Bengal	59,052	5.4	1.0
United Provinces	281,143	25.6	23.9
Punjab	446,976	40.7	51.2
North West Frontier Province	45,231	4.1	4.7
Baluchistan	2,088	0.2	0.3
Burma	18,673	1.7	2.1
Bihar and Orissa	41,552	3.8	1.3
Central Provinces	15,007	1.4	0.8
Assam	15,124	1.4	0.1
Ajmer-Merwara	8,973	0.8	1.1
TOTAL	1,097,642		

Source: Calculated from data in *India's Contribution to the Great War* (Calcutta: Superintendent of Government Printing, 1923), Appendix C, 276–277. Nepal recruited 58,904 troops.

1978, 13). Despite the same sort of protests on behalf of the "cleansed" ethnic groups such as Bengalis and Mahars that had accompanied the "Punjabi-ization" of the army thirty years before, the army was homogenized once more.[13] In 1929, as we can see from Table 1.4, the broad ethnic composition of the army after World War I was still deeply imbalanced in favor of Punjab, the NWFP, and a few other "martial" areas. The province of Punjab, with 6.5 percent of India's pre-1947 population, accounted for around 54 percent of the troops. The NWFP, with 1 percent of India's population, accounted for a further 3.5 percent of the troops. Gorkhas (12 percent of the army) and Dogras from Jammu and Kashmir, Rajputs from Rajputana, Garhwalis from U.P., and Marathas from Bombay accounted for nearly all the rest. So British military control of India rested fundamentally on Punjab and the NWFP which between them had around two thirds of the Indian troops in the army, together with the Gorkhas from Nepal (not included in Table 1.4), and the British infantry, cavalry, and artillery regiments that constituted around one quarter of the Indian Army forces by 1939.

Table 1.4. The Provincial Army Imbalance, 1929

Provinces	Share in Indian Population (1921)	Share in Army (1929)	Absolute Imbalance	Share in Army Relative to Provincial Population
Punjab	6.5%	54.4%	+48%	838%
NWFP	0.7%	3.5%	+3%	502%
Baluchistan	0.0%	0.2%	+0.2%	473%
Kashmir	1.0%	4.1%	+3%	397%
Rajputana	3.1%	4.4%	+1%	144%
United Provinces	14.2%	10.4%	−4%	73%
Bombay	6.1%	4.4%	−2%	73%
Burma	4.1%	1.9%	−2%	46%
Madras	13.3%	2.5%	−11%	19%
Hyderabad	3.9%	0.4%	−3%	11%
Central India	1.9%	0.1%	−2%	7%
Mysore	1.9%	0.1%	−2%	3%
Bihar and Orissa	10.7%	0.2%	−10%	2%
Central Provinces (including Berar)	4.4%	0.1%	−4%	1%
Other Chief Commissioner's Provinces (Delhi, Ajmer-Merwara, Coorg, Andamans)	0.4%	0.0%	0%	0%
Assam	2.3%	0.0%	−2%	0%
Other Indian States and Tribal Agencies	10.2%	0.0%	−10%	0%
Bengal	14.6%	0.0%	−15%	0%
Nepal	0.0%	12.0%	+12%	—
Miscellaneous	0.0%	1.2%	+1%	—

Source: Calculated using data in *1921 Census of India: 1930 Indian Statutory Commission Report*, Volume 1 (Cmd. 3568), map at 96–97.

Set against the martial class provinces, though, were a large number of important provinces with hardly any representation at all. Madras, Bengal, and Bihar and Orissa, with a combined 39 percent of the Indian population, accounted for only 3 percent of the troops. The Central Provinces had only 1 percent of their proportional share in the army, Bihar and Orissa were little better with 2 percent, and the huge province of Bengal, with 15 percent of India's entire population, had no representation at all.

These provincial imbalances in recruitment were enormous. But even these figures understate the true scale of the imbalance of recruitment into the colonial army, because the patterns of regional and district recruitment *within* each province were also very uneven. In Bombay province there was hardly any recruitment from Sind and Gujarat, and most of the recruits came from a few Maratha districts around Pune, such as Satara. In the United Provinces (now Uttar Pradesh) there was heavy recruitment from the hill districts, moderate recruitment of Jats and "Hindustani Muslims" from western U.P., and hardly any recruitment from the rest of the province. And within each district, of course, only some castes were recruited; many others were not.

The Political Pressure for Reform

The approach of independence in India, as in other colonies, raised the issue of whether this highly imbalanced colonial military structure was suitable for a democratic state, both in terms of reflecting its democratic values and also in terms of whether such an unbalanced army posed a threat to the country's stability. Even the colonial government, albeit in a self-serving way designed to justify its own military presence, had acknowledged in 1930 that "the peaceful unity of a self-governing India would be exposed to great risks if it relied, for the purpose of maintaining and restoring internal order, solely upon Indian troops drawn from selected areas and special races, such as the Punjabi, the Pathan, the Sikh, the Mahratta, or (to go outside India) the Gurkha."[14]

Throughout the 1920s and 1930s, especially after an influential series of critical and data-rich articles by Nirad Chaudhuri on the issue in *Modern Review* in 1930–1931, nationalist Indians grew increasingly critical of the army's martial class recruitment policy (1930a, 1930b, 1931a, 1931b, 1935). In Chaudhuri's articles, in the central and provincial assemblies, in the press, and in several official Congress Party pamphlets, Indians made several arguments against the martial-class military.

The most common argument was the distributional unfairness of a system in which provinces and communities paid taxes to support an army from which they were excluded. The army was very expensive, and paying for its wages, pensions, and other costs accounted for around half of all central government expenditure. Was it fair, representatives from Bengal, Madras, Bihar, and Orissa asked, that their taxes go to support a force from which their communities were excluded? These arguments had been made in the 1910s and 1920s in the central assemblies and councils, usually by moderates, but they took on a new force in the 1930s with the general rise in nationalism combined with economic hardship and government retrenchment that made the economic and employment imbalances seem particularly hard to bear. The anger over this issue was particularly strong in Bengal, which ever since 1916 had seen massive central taxes on its primary export product, jute and jute manufactures, used to finance up to half of the central government's budget. These taxes went to support the costs of a military that recruited from Europeans, Punjabis, Pashtuns, and Gorkhas, and which deliberately excluded Bengalis. Meanwhile Bengal's own domestic tax burden and provincial fiscal deficits continued to rise.[15]

Second, Indians argued that the system of class recruitment reflected false official prejudices about which groups were good at fighting. Representatives from Madras, Bihar, Orissa, Bengal and the Central Provinces, as well as from formerly recruited communities such as the Mappilas, Mahars, and Uttar Pradesh Muslims pointed out that their regions and communities had strong martial traditions, had fought well in the past, and deserved to be recruited once more.[16] For instance, one Bengali representative in the 1930s argued against the army stereotype that shorter Bengalis and Madrasis made worse soldiers than taller men from the Punjab and NWFP, saying that "during the last Great War, the Gurkhas, although pigmies, distinguished themselves and proved their mettle in the Western Front against the surging tide of German invasion. If the Bengalees are given an opportunity, there is every reason to hope that they will turn out as efficient as any other martial race in British India."[17]

A third set of arguments was over the dangers that martial class recruitment posed for the Indian nation and any future democracy. Part of this was a simple matter of power, the fear that if the army was recruited from only one or two provinces, then these provinces would call the tune in terms of politics, and could pose a real danger to a fledgling Indian democracy. In an article in the *Manchester Guardian* in 1930, perhaps authored by Nirad Chaudhuri, the writer pointed out the disparity in recruitment, and argued that "in a self-governing India the Punjab would be sorely tempted to regard with contempt the less martial areas, and to use its overwhelming military strength to reinforce the weakest arguments when any interprovincial controversy arose. If a self-governing India is to have a purely Indian Army on which all can rely, all the provinces must make some substantial contribution to its man-power."[18]

Finally, there was also a worry that army recruitment policies were preventing the development of a broader national Indian identity that could transcend caste, region, and religion. For instance, Nirad Chaudhuri showed how the army's insistence on recruiting "authentic" members of various castes and communities and then sharpening these community identities to increase military effectiveness inevitably intensified community feeling at the expense of national sentiment. He criticized the division of the army "into small tribal, caste and religious groups, distinguished by strong local, communal and section loyalties" on the grounds that this led to the absence of "any sense of national unity and the patriotism that springs from it." "This sense of nationality," he argued, "has always been regarded as one of the most valuable moral assets of a modern citizen army" (1930a, 45). In contrast, Chaudhuri pointed out, the reification of caste in the army—which put a premium on subcaste affiliations and "authenticity" and affiliation to traditions—had made it much more rigid than Indian society as a whole. He cited the regulations from the Eleventh Sikh Regiment (which had a mixed Muslim and Sikh class composition) to demonstrate how adherence to particular religious practices was enforced and adherence to often common syncretic practices was punished. In that regiment it was required that "men will observe the customs of their faith. A Sikh found smoking tobacco, or with his beard, moustache, or the hair of his head cut, or who dyes or pulls out the hair of his head or face—and a Musalman found drinking alcoholic liquor or disobeying in part or in whole the rules laid down for observance of Ramzan will render themselves liable to punishment for disobedience of regimental Standing Orders" (Chaudhuri

1931b, 219). In India, as in Africa and other regions where these martial classes strategies were employed, this military insistence on "authenticity" sharpened group identities and reduced the extent of syncretic practices, which arguably could reduce the intensity of communal conflicts (Fox 1985; Parsons 1999).

The protests became much louder in the 1930s, as many Indians demanded independence and more nationalists were elected or appointed to the central representative bodies. Three motions, all unsuccessful, that requested a total reform of the policy of martial class recruitment, were put forward in the Council of State, one in 1935 and two in 1938. The proposer of the 1935 resolution, Pratap Narain Sapru, was the most eloquent Congress opponent of the policy during the 1930s. He argued that although many of the previous debates on the army had focused on the Indianization of the officer corps, and the slowness of that process,

> it is quite clear that it is not enough to Indianise the officer ranks only. It is also necessary to go further and make the army a truly national army. That is to say, the army must not be allowed to remain the close preserve of certain classes or provinces. It must be thrown open to all classes and all provinces. The army must not be allowed to remain a purely professional or mercenary army, but should be recruited from all classes who satisfy the tests of efficiency and character. Sir, our future self-government—and I would like the question to be approached from this point of view—must not be dependent for its functioning upon a military class recruited largely from certain areas and classes only. A system like that might very easily prove to be a menace to the civil power. . . . If you shut out certain peoples and provinces from enlistment in the army, you make it possible for certain classes and provinces to dominate other classes and other provinces. Therefore it is necessary to have a wider basis of recruitment, wider areas both territorially and racially.[19]

Sapru also pointed to the fiscal injustice of the system, which was paid for by taxes from all provinces but whose salaries, pensions, and land grants benefited only two or three. In 1938 Sapru made the point again, this time more forcefully. "If you want to confine recruitment to the North-West Frontier and the Punjab," he demanded, "then, let them pay for this army."[20]

All these efforts to broaden army recruitment before 1939 failed. They failed above all because the British recognized that their control of India rested upon the army, and that an army recruited from "loyal" provinces and groups, above all Punjab, was more likely to preserve British rule than one recruited from politically more restive provinces like Bengal. So the administration resisted any efforts by Indians to establish elected oversight over the army, for instance blocking a motion by Sapru in March 1936 that would have established an advisory committee on defense.[21] The Indian Army's senior officers were also, as we have seen, still deeply committed to the idea that an army composed of single-class units from the "martial races" was militarily much more effective than one composed from other groups. With the prospect of a European war on the horizon, any sudden shift in policy looked to the military to be very dangerous. The army responded to demands for broadening recruitment in 1933 with the argument that while men from Bombay and Madras might make good soldiers, experience had shown that men from the north and west were better, and "the army must have the best."[22] As the ultimate decisions on all army policy at this time rested with the Indian Army's Commander in Chief, responsible to the Secretary of State and War Office in London, this meant that even had Indian public opinion been unified in its opposition, a vote taken in the Indian legislature would have still been only of symbolic importance.

And Indian public opinion was not unified. The grossly imbalanced colonial recruitment system created big winners as well as big losers. The winning provinces and communities, overrepresented in a colonial political system that gave the vote disproportionately to minorities, the wealthy, veterans, officials, and the holders of titles and awards, not surprisingly used their political advantages to defend their privileges.[23] At the national level, Jinnah and the Muslim League defended the overrepresentation of Punjab and NWFP because it meant the overrepresentation of Muslims within the armed forces. In doing so, Jinnah seems to have considerably overestimated the Muslim percentage in the army. In a press release in September 1938 (Jinnah 1996, 850–851) he defended Muslims' "65 to 70 per cent" representation, whereas the real figure was 38 percent in 1939— no more than about 45 percent even if we exclude the Gorkhas.[24] At the provincial level, politicians from Punjab, NWFP, and a few other recruiting grounds defended their provinces' special position in army recruitment—as some Punjabi and Rajasthani politicians still do today—as no more than the legitimate reflection of their martial traditions and qualities.[25] Punjab Premier Sir Sikandar Hyat Khan's constitutional proposals for an Indian federation in 1937 even included a clause that "The composition of the Indian Army (as on the 1st day of January 1937) shall not be altered. In the event of a reduction or an increase in the peace-time strength of the Indian Army the proportion of the various communities as on the 1st of January 1937 shall not be disturbed" (Malik 1985, 167–174).

The colonial government, not surprisingly, tried to play on the divisions between "winner" and "loser" provinces and communities in recruitment to weaken the Indian opposition to its policy. During the 1935 debate on army recruitment, the British Commander in Chief, Sir Philip Chetwode, asked P. N. Sapru just why he wanted to diminish the number of Muslims in the army.[26] Despite Congress Party denials that this was the motivation, the Muslim members (as well as Hindus and Sikhs from Punjab and NWFP and the thirteen British members) all voted against the motion, which lost 26–18.[27]

The interprovincial tensions over recruitment came to a head in autumn 1938. Since 1937, the Congress Socialists in Punjab had held over two hundred meetings discouraging army recruitment, a move designed to strike at both the military foundations of the Raj and at Sir Sikandar Hyat Khan's Unionist party. These attempts led Sir Sikandar to ask the colonial government to move a bill in mid-August in the central legislature that would criminalize any public efforts to discourage military recruitment or "incite mutiny."[28] A few days before the debate on the final reading of the bill, in early September 1938, Sir Sikandar spoke up publicly in favor of Punjab's strong representation in the army.[29] Ten days later, after the recruitment bill had been passed following fierce debate, a Bengali nationalist

member of the assembly, Brajendra Narayan Chaudhury, asked the
Defence Secretary to clarify

a) "Whether the attention of Government has been drawn to the
address of the Punjab's Premier, the Honourable Sir Sikandar
Hyat Khan, to his 'brother soldiers' in these words: 'No
patriotic Punjabi would wish to impair Punjab's position of
supremacy in the Army,' as reported by the Associated Press of
India in the Hindustan Times of the 5th September 1938; and
b) Whether it is the policy of Government to maintain the
supremacy of Punjabis in the army by continuing to recruit
the major portion from the Punjab; or to attempt recruitment
of the army from all the Provinces without racial or Provincial considerations?"[30]

In asking this question Chaudhury may in fact have misquoted Hyat
Khan, who while he had defended Punjab's overrepresentation is
not quoted in the newspaper accounts as using the term "position of
supremacy."[31] In any event this intervention sparked a second battle
in the Central Legislative Assembly and in the press in 1938 over
both the recruitment bill and the larger overrepresentation of Punjab and a few other provinces. Bengali representatives, in particular,
were outraged and used the speech as an opportunity once again to
challenge the whole basis of class recruitment.[32]

While individual Congress Party members challenged the
overrepresentation of Punjab and other provinces in public on many
occasions, the very top Congress leadership was not as vocal. We
can speculate that this was probably because the most senior Congress leaders were constrained in their ability to demand change by
the need to keep channels of communication open with the Muslim
League and politicians from overrepresented provinces such as
Punjab and the NWFP as they looked ahead to the complex negotiations over an all-India political settlement.

The Army in Politics

Formally, the colonial army was completely professional and independent from politics. In practice the army was sometimes deeply
involved, especially when it felt that it needed to maintain political
stability and the continued supply of men in its main recruiting ar-

eas, or that intervention was necessary to its organizational cohesion and its operational success. Many army officers served in formal political roles as officers, residents, and political advisors in the Indian Political Service, the cadre that represented British interests to the princely states and their administrations. And the army's military intelligence department both conducted its own investigations and spent money, on which systematic information is perhaps understandably lacking, to buy political support and defeat opposition as well as keep an eye on the political activities and loyalties of the Indian officers and other ranks.

The army intervened in politics and society because at various times it felt it had no choice *but* to be involved in politics—especially in Punjab and NWFP, which supplied most of the army. The two most notable cases, both in Punjab, were over the Punjab Colonization Bill in 1907 and the 1920–1925 Akali agitation (the "Third Sikh War") (Omissi 1994, 126–129). The 1907 case involved the Commander in Chief intervening to veto a land bill in the Punjab that had been passed by the provincial government but was deeply opposed by many of the communities (and community leaders) that sent most troops to the army. Settlers in the Punjab canal colonies, many of them ex-soldiers and the families of soldiers, deeply resented efforts to give them land on terms less favorable than those offered to earlier colonizers, and to deny them permanent title to land (Barrier 1967). The army, after hearing about the depth of opposition to the policy through its own channels, went over the head of the Punjab government to the Viceroy, Lord Minto, who vetoed the bill, a step that was virtually unprecedented.[33] The army also got to appoint—directly, and over the strong objections of the Punjab government that the military should not set policy—one of the three members of the subsequent committee set up to look into the workings of land administration in Punjab (Barrier 1967, 377).

The Akali agitation was even more serious, because it involved widespread and sometimes violent agitation over the control of Sikh shrines, many of which were managed by British nominees—including one at the Golden Temple who, incredibly, honored Brigadier Reginald Dyer for his action after he carried out the Jalianwala Bagh massacre in 1919 (Fox 1985, 84; Omissi 1994, 41–43). The Akali agitation occurred in the army's chief recruiting area and

there were many veterans among the agitators (26 percent of the
Akalis in Malwa and 15 percent in the Doaba were former soldiers,
according to British estimates in 1920) (Fox 1985, 82–83).[34] Things
got so bad at one point that recruitment of Sikhs to the army had to
be stopped temporarily till things cooled down, as several Sikh
units were judged by the army to be showing "signs of contamina-
tion" (Omissi 1994, 128). The British initially responded to the agitation by defending the temple managers, who after all supported
their own authority, before eventually realizing that the scale of the
opposition to the existing system and the magnitude of the rural
rebellion—in which perhaps 25,000 Akalis were involved—was so
strong (and violent) that the military effort to put down the rising
had to be accompanied with some form of political compromise
with the Akalis to address the root of the problem (Fox 1985, 91–
93). The threat posed by the Akalis was so great because of their
high level of military organization and tactics, resulting in part
from traditional Sikh organizational patterns and in part from the
large number of former Indian Army soldiers in the Akali ranks.
Richard Fox's work has shown how the recruiting tactics used by
the Akali *jathas* deliberately emulated British recruiting patterns for
the army in the same regions, including baptism into the Singh
identity (1985, 98–99).

The Defence Department also coordinated with other branches
of the government, such as the Political Department, to alter policies in the nominally autonomous princely states. In the aftermath
of World War II, for instance, Military Intelligence was involved in
close cooperation with the Home Ministry, Intelligence Bureau, and
Indian Political Department (including regular meetings to coordinate policy and exchange information) to try to prevent returned
INA men from taking any positions of responsibility in the police,
princely state armed forces or administrations, or any positions relevant to security more generally. For instance, this involved telling
all the residents in the princely states in July 1946 that they should
make it clear to the state governments that employing ex-INA men
in any security or law and order role was "considered undesirable."[35]

The army also operated its own intelligence networks to influence politics in the main recruiting areas, as well as to keep tabs on

its officers and men. For instance, in 1907 Kitchener sent out the army's own investigators to uncover the depth of opposition to the Punjab government's colonization policy, and their reports were sufficiently worrisome that he was convinced that the government of India needed to block the bill (Barrier 1967, 374). In the aftermath of World War I the army secured INR 50,000 from the Home Department to be spent on "counter propaganda work in the army and the recruiting areas," in part because of worries over the political loyalties of large numbers of soldiers who were coming back from military service.[36] This was felt to be so useful that after 1923 the same amount of money was allocated for these political purposes every year, INR 30,000 coming from the Home Department and the rest from the general staff. This arrangement continued until 1939–1940, after which the general staff paid the entire costs of the "counter-propaganda" effort itself. The lists of exactly who got paid off and what got done are unfortunately (and of course deliberately) lost, though notes in the surviving files indicate that much of the money was "distributed by recruiting officers to local notables and key individuals in the districts on an ad hoc basis to make sure they kept the military informed as well as made sure to counter efforts to suborn recruitment."[37]

And of course the army used a variety of methods to influence local politics in areas where long-term civil unrest was continuing, through conversations with residents and local officials, and through its own direct methods. The main areas where this kind of direct intervention took place were in the NWFP and the Pashtun areas beyond, which combined both a fertile recruiting ground and the ever-ready potential of larger tribal conflicts and risings. The army political officers in this region, often fluent in Pashtu, distributed money and positions and used their influence to try to ensure the stability of the region and the continued flow of Pashtun recruits to the army.

Conclusion

The Indian Army before 1939 was developed to deal with the internal and external threats to the colonial administration. The difficulty for the Raj was that the single-class mix of troops it thought it needed to address the main likely external enemy, Russia, was the one that also seemed to have the greatest potential to create internal law and order problems. To deal with these domestic threats, the colonial government used three strategies. First, the state tried to prevent Indian units coordinating against the British by making sure that they were ethnically diverse and balanced against each other, so that their coordination against the colonial regime would be more difficult. This strategy of creating obstacles to coordination was also extended to military hierarchies (Indians of one group were not posted as officers to a regiment of the same group) and even to creating barriers to coordination in small unit assignments, as we saw with the Pathan Regiment guard duty rules that insisted guards be of different Pashtun subcastes. Second, the colonial regime "balanced" outside the army by deploying large numbers of well-armed British and Gorkha units, which could be deployed very quickly against Indians over the road and rail network that was rapidly expanded after 1857. And last, the military tried to defend its own organizational cohesion by intervening, when it thought it had to, in the society and politics of its most important recruiting regions. One potential problem, though, was how this system, finely balanced as it was between domestic security concerns and external military ones, could respond if the army suddenly had to expand to meet serious external threats that required major expansion and frequent replacements for combat losses, as it would in World War II.

2

War and Partition

Introduction

WARS AND CIVIL wars have often played an important role in helping to "solve" the problem of ethnic imbalance in the military. In colonies such as Burma and Indonesia, invasion by the Japanese during World War II largely destroyed the old colonial armies, which relied on favored ethnic minorities, while the Japanese created new forces during the war, drawn from the ethnic majority populations, to buttress their own hold on power. The existence of these forces at the end of the war—Aung San's Burma National Army and Sukarno's PETA organization in the Netherlands Indies—had two significant effects. First, it accelerated the drive for independence after the Japanese were defeated, as these new forces refused to accept the restoration of the colonial status quo ante. Second, these forces helped ensure that the new "national" armies that eventually emerged in Burma and Indonesia were much more representative of the population than they would have been if the colonial armies had survived intact.

Although only a small part of India was invaded during World War II and the Indian Army suffered no defeat similar to that of the Netherlands Indies Army, the war is often seen as leading to a similar transformation in India, turning a narrowly recruited colonial military into a much more representative force. Many accounts of Indian Army recruitment in World War II, especially those from official sources, describe how the army's belief in a "martial class" structure was "demolished," both by its need to rapidly expand the army in the face of threats from the German and Japanese forces, and by the success in combat of the many new groups the army had been forced to recruit (Prasad 1956; Venkateshwaran 1967, 187).

As I show in this chapter, however, the scale of this wartime transformation has been greatly exaggerated. In fact the army's top generals saw the need to expand rapidly to fight a strong external enemy as the main reason *not* to change the martial composition of the frontline army.[1] So when the army was forced to expand beyond the traditional recruiting areas, it did so throughout the war in a way that tried to keep the most "tested" and loyal groups in the key frontline roles and to make sure that the newly recruited "nonmartial" groups got the maximum publicity and were allowed to make the minimum impact on the front line. This strategy set an important precedent for how the Indian Army would respond two decades later, when forced to expand rapidly in the face of the Chinese threat in the 1960s.

India's colonial political leadership was also deeply concerned at various times during the war with how the composition of the army might either enable or limit its political freedom of action. The War Department consciously tried to broaden support for Britain and the war effort in the early years, despite the resignation of the Congress provincial governments, by creating and heavily publicizing several new regiments with men from lower castes and the northeast whose leaders might be potential allies. And in 1942, when the British government was debating how to respond to the threat of the 1942 Congress "Quit India" campaign—with massive repression or with negotiations and a deal offered by Sir Stafford Cripps—the British political leadership checked with the (British) senior officers in the Indian Army to see if the minority units and others in the army could be expected to stay loyal if the politicians decided to make peace with the Congress Party and announce a deal.[2]

The Need for Troops

The British declaration of war in September 1939, the need to garrison Southeast Asia as well as send troops to the Middle East, and then the cataclysm of defeat in 1941–1942 and threat of invasion each in turn created a massive need for military manpower. Britain,

under threat itself and stretched near to the breaking point, looked
to India to add to its forces in the Middle East and East Africa, as
well as to take the major role in containing the Japanese forces in
Southeast Asia. The Indian Army, which in 1939 had been expanded
from its prewar level of 120,000 to just over 200,000 men, grew to
343,740 by October 1940, to 735,490 by October 1941 (a few months
before the fall of Southeast Asia and Singapore), and to 1,274,440 by
October 1942.[3] By the war's end, as we can see in Table 2.1, there
were more than 1.65 million Indian men in the Indian Army, with
15,700 Indian officers (including medical doctors) and hundreds of
thousands more recruits serving in auxiliary roles, making for a total strength of 2.285 million.

The conventional story about this massive expansion, the one reprinted in the multivolume *Official History of the Indian Armed Forces
in World War II (Second World War)* published in the mid-1950s and
in many secondary sources, is that it "exploded" the martial races
policy, because the number of recruits that could be obtained from
the traditionally recruited groups was simply insufficient for the
enormous wartime manpower demands of the army (Venkateshwaran 1967, 187).[4] As Anirudh Deshpande puts it, a combination of
manpower shortages and good experiences with the many newly recruited classes "proved the 'martial races' theory wrong" and "on
the whole the shifts in recruitment were considerable" (1996, 183–
184). The *Official History* reports that due to the "exhaustion" of traditional sources of recruits, the army looked instead to people from
Madras, Bengal, and elsewhere in India: "How widely the recruiting
net was cast in an effort to get over the difficulty of class composition is illustrated by the raisings of new infantry regiments which,
geographically, were drawn from the four corners of India, such as
the Madras Regiment, the Ajmer Regiment, the Mazhabi and Ramdasia Sikh Regiment, the Assam regiment, and the Bihar Regiment"
(Prasad 1956, 84–85). The *Official History* reports aggregate recruitment data from 1939–1945 that show that, indeed, some underrepresented provinces' recruitment went up dramatically: recruits from
Madras went up from 3 percent of the pre-1939 army to 17 percent of
wartime recruits, while recruits from Assam went from 0 percent to
3 percent. It goes on to say that "few problems arose," and "it was

Table 2.1. The Wartime Expansion of the Indian Army, 1939–1945

	British Officers	Indian Commissioned Officers	B.O.R.s	Viceroy Commissioned Officers and Indian Other Ranks	Noncombatants Enrolled	Civilians in Military Employ	Total
September 1, 1939	4,585	1,115	5,262	161,658	18,954	19,082	210,656
April 1, 1945	36,438	15,741	54,342	1,650,805	384,200	144,410	2,285,936

Statement showing the Comparative Strengths of the Indian Army in India and Overseas in 1939 and 1945, India Office Records, British Library, London, L/WS/1/707 "Indian Army Morale and Possible Reduction 1943–45." The Indian Territorial Force consisting of officers 534, IORs 15,354 is included in the September 1939 figures. . . . The Burma Army (strength 22,000) and civil labor units (strength 256,354 civilians) are not included in the April 1945 figures.

discovered that 'vested class interests, bogus caste prejudices and parochial minded B.O.s [British Officers] and V.C.O.s [Viceroy's Commissioned Officers] have endeavored unsuccessfully to maintain the narrow class composition on which most of the pre-war Army was based'" (Prasad 1956, 85). The history cites an undated memo from the Adjutant-General saying that "It is most necessary that the prewar conservative system of enlisting from only small subareas and favoured sub classes should not be allowed to creep in again. Every effort should be made to keep in areas and all classes and sub-classes 'ticking over' in peacetime in the recruiting field" (Prasad 1956, 88).

However, the view that the war changed things completely ignores the fact that different ethnic groups in the army were assigned very different roles in the war, with troops from the traditional "martial classes" areas assigned to most of the important combat roles (Marston 2003).[5] The fundamental challenge, as the British military officers in senior command saw it, was how to expand the Indian Army's manpower while not diminishing its fighting quality and loyalty, both of which were perceived to rest upon the disproportionate recruitment of men from the "martial races." The Indian Army therefore initially tried, as it had done in World War I, to expand by recruiting only from the martial classes, particularly from the favored provinces of Punjab and the North West Frontier Province (NWFP), and the hill districts of U.P. and Jammu. In June 1940 the Government of India authorized eleven new battalions for the Punjab Regiment, the Frontier Force and Frontier Rifles, and the Sikh Regiment, all regiments that recruited from the NWFP and Punjab, by combining new recruits with men "milked" from existing battalions. The army also authorized nine new Gorkha battalions to be raised by October 1940.[6] Table 2.2, below, shows the breakdown of the 418,000-man army of January 1941, about double the size of the force that had existed in 1939, and as we can see the composition at this time was still very much in line with the prewar balance shown in Table 1.3.[7]

But the strategy of relying only on the martial classes ran into problems in the next year and a half for several reasons. First, many of the agricultural families from which the army recruited, and the landlords and other notables who encouraged this recruitment, were reluctant to send more sons away to the army with a booming

Table 2.2. Indian Army Composition, January 1941

	Muslims	Hindus and Other Religions	Total	Percentage of Total
NWFP	35,253		35,253	8.5
Punjab	96,826	104,919	201,745	48.0
Uttar Pradesh and Bihar	5,245	33,587	38,832	9.5
Central India	6,559	21,689	28,248	7.0
Bombay	5,399	18,703	24,102	6.0
Madras	2,603	19,320	21,923	5.0
Nepal		46,185	46,185	11.0
Central Provinces		267	267	0.0
Other Districts	3,352	18,624	21,976	5.0
Total	155,237	263,294	418,531	

Source: Table 'A' Grand Total Indian Army 1st Jan 1941 (SECRET), in "Class composition of the army in India 1909–42," L/WS/1/456 Publications (GI).

wartime agricultural economy at home. In the Attock district in Punjab, for instance, which was a leading producer of "Punjabi Muslims" for the Indian Army (and still is for the Pakistan Army), recruitment started off well but then slowed down substantially in 1943, because booming wartime agricultural prices made the locally dominant *zamindars* (landlords) loathe to encourage their tenants and laborers to sign up.[8] Second, the British became nervous about recruiting too heavily from one of the major groups, the Sikhs, after several small mutinies among Sikh units in the first year of the war. Third, news of the defeat of British forces in 1941 and 1942 made the position of the British themselves seem less secure to potential recruits, as did the 1942 Quit India campaign of massive civil disobedience. By late 1942 the Adjutant General of the Indian Army was telling the Commander in Chief and the India Office that "The pre-war classes are becoming exhausted and further expansion of them is only possible to a very minor degree, and then at the expense of the maintenance of existing units. In these classes I include P.M.s, Jats, Mahrattas, Pathans and Rajputs. Dogras are now unable to meet maintenance demands through exhaustion, whilst Jat Sikhs are not coming forward well."[9]

The India Office sympathized with this bleak assessment. The Military Secretary at the India Office, Major General G. N. Molesworth, wrote that "During Great War I, by various means amounting to 'press gang' methods we managed, under the 'voluntary' system, to get about 850,000 good <u>fighting</u> men over 4 years. We did not spread our net very much wider than the execrated 'martial classes', but we drained those to the last drop." In remarks that combined the class and caste bias of the stereotypical Indian Army officer, he went on to say that "In other words we exhausted Fortnum and Mason, without tapping Marks and Spencer or Woolworths to any great degree. I believe that under any system, excluding Gurkhas, that remains (850,000) India's figure for really good troops."[10] The problem, from the army's perspective, was that India needed to recruit around two million troops and auxiliaries. So where were they to come from?

The Indian Army developed three strategies to meet this challenge. First, it continued, as it had in World War I, to press recruitment of the traditional martial classes as hard as it possibly could, though recruitment bounties to agents and increased payments and other incentives such as the remission of land taxes and gifts of watches, swords, turbans, and special pins to recruits (Deshpande 1996, 182–183). In some cases in Punjab, village officials were pressured to produce recruits by being threatened with suspension or other penalties (Talbot 1988, 145–146). In other cases agents used a variety of unscrupulous tactics to get men to sign up. This mix of strong-arm tactics and a lot of incentives was largely successful, and the army recruited a total of around one million men from its traditional recruiting areas between 1939 and 1945. The Punjab as a whole provided over 700,000 recruits, 31 percent of the entire recruiting total; the NWFP provided another 100,000 (4 percent) (Prasad 1956).[11] In Attock district more than 43,000 men had signed up by January 1944, with the best recruiting tehsils sending 12–16.5 percent of their young men into the forces.[12] In the adjacent Rawalpindi district, 1,420 families each sent three or more sons to the armed services (Talbot 1988, 145–146). By war's end (see Table 2.3), by pressing the traditional groups in this way, the Indian Army estimated it had recruited close to a third (30 percent) of all estimated possible

Table 2.3. Patterns of Class Recruitment during World War II

	Fit Males of Recruitable Age	Serving Prewar	Recruited from September 3, 1939, to October 31, 1945	Total Enrolled Prewar and during the War	Percentage of Recruits to Eligible Members of Each Class
HINDUS					
Ahirs	469,715	2,121	39,349	41,470	8.8
Assamese	106,690		3,041	3,041	2.9
Bengalis	607,017		23,052	23,052	3.8
Bhils	24,505		283	283	1.2
Brahmans	388,960	793	72,684	73,477	18.9
Chamars	388,215		12,853	12,853	3.3
Dogras	94,696	10,570	30,297	40,867	43.2
Garhwalis	50,820	3,816	19,412	23,228	45.7
Gujars	65,874	1,029	16,048	17,077	25.9
Chirts	6,510		389	389	6.0
Gurkhas	280,000	18,000	109,952	127,952	45.7
Jats	153,561	9,390	72,275	81,665	53.2
Kabirpanthis	1,000		491	491	49.1
Kalis	9,600		1,203	1,203	12.5
Kumaonis	39,600	2,364	20,150	22,514	56.9
Kamhars	51,225		1,256	1,256	2.5
Lodhis	51,466		1,545	1,545	3.0
Mahars	120,560		10,835	10,835	9.0
Mahrattas	346,800	4,771	61,266	66,037	19.0
Meghs	1,030		582	582	56.5
Rawats and Minas	30,980		3,963	3,963	12.8
Oriyas	182,953		3,877	3,877	2.1
Rajputs	335,143	5,832	75,979	81,811	24.4
Shilpkars	12,617		1,790	1,790	14.2
Others	2,684,947		226,136	226,136	8.4
	6,504,484	**58,686**	**808,708**	**867,394**	
MUSLIMS					
Pathans	128,200	6,048	68,606	74,654	58.2
Assamese	80,565		3,247	3,247	4.0
Baluchis	11,780	57	1,549	1,606	13.6
Bengalis	764,720		70,896	70,896	9.
Dekhanis	156,478	164	20,654	20,818	13.3
Punjabis (including Hazariwals)	1,087,450	33,935	348,620	382,555	35.2
Hindustani	450,848	654	32,981	33,635	7.5
Meos	17,300	384	2,811	3,195	18.5
Katats	1,300		1,061	1,061	81.6

	Fit Males of Recruitable Age	Serving Prewar	Recruited from September 3, 1939, to October 31, 1945	Total Enrolled Prewar and during the War	Percentage of Recruits to Eligible Members of Each Class
Rajputana and Central Indian	53,760	1,001	10,123	11,124	20.7
Ranghars	28,160	1,857	7,722	9,579	34.0
Others	161,040		54,278	54,278	33.7
	2,941,601	**44,100**	**622,548**	**666,648**	
SIKHS					
Jats	165,625	17,156	45,828	62,984	38.0
Mazbhi and Ramdasia	35,000	1,303	34,175	35,478	101.4
Others	127,579	4,211	36,103	40,314	31.6
	328,204	**22,670**	**116,106**	**138,776**	
CHRISTIAN					
Assamese	1,642	—	1,145	1,145	69.7
Others (excluding Madrasis)	51,769	—	38,788	38,788	74.9
	53,411	**—**	**39,933**	**39,933**	
MADRAS CLASSES	**2,843,280**	**4,010**	**453,225**	**457,235**	16.1
MISC.					
Hos, Oraons, and Mundas	47,740		5,299	5,299	11.1
Santhals	60,630		1,223	1,223	2.0
Coorgs	6,070		NA	NA	
Assamese Tribals	72,400		NA	NA	
	186,840		**6,522**	**6,522**	
OTHER CLASSES			147,748	147,748	
NCs ENROLLED			107,509	107,509	
IPC (details by classes not available)			233,549	233,549	
GRAND TOTAL	**12,957,811**	**129,466**	**2,535,848**	**2,665,314**	20.7

Source: Calculated from Appendix H in Bisheshwar Prasad, ed. *Monographs, Adjutant General's Branch* (Interservices Historical Section), 140–142.

recruits (men between eighteen and thirty years old) from the Dogras (30 percent), Punjabi Muslims (30 percent), and Garhwalis (36
percent), and close to half of all potential recruits from the Jats (45
percent), Pathans (49 percent), and Kumaonis (49 percent). The
army also recruited an astoundingly high 92 percent of its estimate
of the potential recruits from the Mazhabi and Ramdasia classes,
perhaps a reflection (as we also see in the case of Punjabi Christians)
of the lack of other remunerative economic opportunities in those
lower-caste Sikh communities.[13] It is important to bear in mind, of
course, that the whole concept of "recruitable" population was not
an independent measure of the total number of young men in a province, but a combination of demographic data with the army's own
view of which classes within a group were suitable for military purposes. That explains why the total estimated "recruitable population" in Punjab was around the same size as that in the much more
populous province of Bengal.

Second, the definition of "martial" as far as frontline infantry and
cavalry regiments was concerned was broadened a little, and new
class infantry regiments were raised from groups such as the Mahars,
Biharis, and Assamese. Some of these groups were not in fact new to
military service at all. The Mahars had at one time been heavily
recruited in the Bombay infantry, where they accounted for 15 percent of all troops in 1875. But they had lost out in the whole "martial class" and Punjabi drive of the 1880s and early 1890s, and they
had then been excluded altogether from the Bombay Army in 1892
(Constable 2001, 464). They were recruited again to a new "Mahar
Regiment" in World War I, after their community leaders peti-
tioned the government to rescind the ban on Mahars serving, which
it did in February 1917. But after the war was over, caste prejudice
led to that regiment being disbanded in 1922. This time, though,
the community had a strong advocate in the shape of B. R. Ambedkar, the important Scheduled Caste political leader, and a man who
had grown up hearing stories from his soldier uncles and other community leaders about the great wrong done the community when
the regiment had been disbanded. Ambedkar's own father had served
in the Mahar infantry in Bombay until 1892, and then tried unsuccessfully with other veterans to get the unit reestablished (Cohen

1969; Constable 2001). In World War II, Ambedkar was appointed a member of the Defence Committee on the Viceroy's council, and due to his persistent prodding, as well as the community's previous military record and the desire of the colonial government to create allies where it could, the Mahar Regiment was one of the first new class regiments to be formed after the outbreak of war. It was joined by the Assam Regiment, the lower-caste Chamar Regiment, the Sikh Light Infantry (which recruited lower-caste Mazhabi and Ramdasia Sikhs), the reraised Madras Regiment (which had been demobilized in 1928), and the Bihar Regiment, each representing communities that had been largely excluded before.[14]

These newly raised class regiments, however, despite being very heavily publicized by the army and government as evidence of the army's increased inclusiveness, in fact added only thirty thousand or so recruits to the infantry during the whole war. This was less than a tenth of the troops that Punjab province alone contributed to the army, and the new troops therefore did not move the army's overall ethnic composition very much. By mid-1945, there were only 17,232 troops in the five new regiments, less than 5 percent of the total infantry strength of 366,473, and less than a quarter the number of men in the Gorkha regiments at the time. Several other class regiments, the Mahratta Light Infantry, the Baluch Regiment, and Rajputana Rifles, on their own, were each larger than all of these new units combined.[15]

Third, and much more important from the overall perspective of meeting the army's total manpower needs, the army recruited around a million men from underrepresented provinces, princely states, and regions; in particular, men from Madras, U.P., and Bengal. By war's end over 475,000 men from Madras and 120,000 more from nearby princely states such as Mysore had been recruited into the armed forces, where they constituted 24 percent of the total. Bengal, which had been excluded from the army completely since World War I, supplied 176,000 men, 7 percent of the total recruits. And Uttar Pradesh and Bihar supplied 360,000 and 94,000 recruits, 15 percent and 4 percent of the total (Prasad 1956).

It is important to understand, however, that the raising of a few new martial-class units and the large-scale recruitment of troops from underrepresented regions did not fundamentally change the ethnic composition of the frontline Indian Army or challenge senior officers' preconceptions about which recruits made good combat soldiers. Although General Sir Claude Auchinleck, while Commander in Chief in 1941, had envisaged all these new troops being widely deployed, as soon as he left in June 1941 the traditional views of the rest of the senior officer corps reasserted themselves, and the deployment policy towards these new units did not change substantially even after Auchinleck—who had far fewer biases against "untried" classes than his peers—returned as Commander in Chief in mid-1943 (Marston 2003, 50; Connell 1959, 757–778).[16] The new recruits were shunted into auxiliary and support roles in the army, leaving "martial classes" to continue to occupy the vast majority of the frontline roles. This division of different people into hewers of wood and drawers of water was never acknowledged publicly, and casual readers of the official histories of the Indian Army in World War II—which show the recruitment totals of large numbers of men from Madras and Bengal without showing the units to which they were recruited or how these units were deployed—have therefore quite reasonably drawn the conclusion that the class recruitment policy was substantially weakened under the demands of war. This misperception was freely encouraged by the Army and the government of India, which was anxious to broaden support and deflect criticism of its recruitment policy. During the war the government generally refused to provide accurate data to politicians who asked about class recruitment in the Legislative Assembly, on the grounds of "security."[17] General Auchinleck banned the Army from using the term "martial classes" in official correspondence so as to reduce political opposition to the policy.[18] And when asked questions about whether bars still existed to the recruitment of some castes, such as Scheduled Castes, the defense spokesmen dissembled and gave answers such as "there is no discrimination at present against scheduled classes and there will be none" (Marston 2003, 220). This was a half truth at best: there was no army-wide policy against employing Scheduled Castes, but most infantry and armored units recruited only from martial classes, which led to the same result as if there had been a formal policy.

The fact that the essence of the martial-class policy had not been dismantled, though, was admitted in secret correspondence between the Indian Army and the India Office in response to Winston Churchill's May 1943 proposal to shrink the size of the Indian Army. Churchill proposed this in part because of his worries over the Army's allegedly diminishing "martial class" composition. In an August 1943 file submitted by General Auchinleck to resist the cuts, a note presumably prepared by the Adjutant General of the Army Lieutenant General W. M. G. Baker reassured the India Office that while the Indian Infantry and Armored Corps had expanded by 325 percent and 115 percent, respectively, since the beginning of the war, the Armored Corps was still "composed entirely of men from [the] prewar 'martial classes'" and the Infantry nearly so, with "all but 14 active and 4 Garrison battalions [out of 255] drawn from prewar "martial classes."[19] The note made clear that *none* of the 18 infantry battalions out of 255 that comprised nonmartial classes was posted in a direct combat role: "Such battalions are filling roles on L. of Cs [Line of Controls], internal security and a few on N.W. Frontier Defence." It was a similar story in the Indian Artillery, which expanded 615 percent during the war. Baker reassured the Indian Office (and Churchill) that the "Indian Field and A/T [antitank] regiments are almost all pre-war martial classes," while the huge new influx of Madrassis had been deployed well away from the front "in static A/A regiments engaged on protection of bases." Following through the individual service histories of new regiments confirms that this is exactly what happened. If we look at the history of the Mahar Regiment's wartime deployment, for instance, we find that one battalion was stationed on patrol in the NWFP, two battalions were used to guard POWs, and one was deployed in a support role in Burma (Longer 1980, 32–34). In fact all the new units recruited from the nontraditional classes were held in reserve until the very end of the war (Marston 2014, 78).

Of course, the fact that the newly recruited groups were not assigned to significant combat roles until the last days of the war meant that it was much easier later for the top officers to maintain, as they had done earlier with other groups, that only the traditional castes had proven themselves in combat. The 1945 Army Reorganization report, when considering the future class composition of the army, stressed that "no class [should in the future] be included in an arm for which its suitability has not been proved in action beyond reasonable doubt (Willcox Committee, 1945, 1:110). The term "catch-22" had, unfortunately, not yet been invented.

World War II, then, provided no real institutional shock to make the Indian Army rethink its commitment to the martial classes as the cornerstone of its recruitment policy. The bulk of the recruitment shortages of frontline troops, as in 1914–1918, were largely met by intensifying the recruitment effort among the traditional "martial class" groups, and by recruiting men from other groups so as to release these "martial" troops from less important support, logistics, and guard duty roles. The army's internal reviews did acknowledge, however, that there were some significant problems with the policy. The first one was the difficulty for frontline regiments of securing the necessary number of recruits of each class at the right time, especially when large combat losses or a slowdown in recruitment back home at the unit's regimental center in India caused either a sudden increase in demand or a decrease in supply (Prasad 1951). This introduced sometimes serious delays in combat readiness, as units waited for recruits of the right class to be sent up to them from their training centers. Major General Enayat Habibullah, who served in the cavalry during the war, describes how this caste-based system led to problems in North Africa and Italy: "As the war went on, the question became more acute until in the armoured corps, no tank formations could be deployed in the western theatres because of the problem of reinforcement through Indian reinforcement camps. All that the Indian armoured regiments did was making tracks [sic] in Arab deserts and over Arab sand dunes. A few armoured car regiments that went up got no further than southern Italy" (Habibullah 1981, 92). The class policy apparently caused even bigger problems in Southeast Asia, where an Army monograph reported that the "main reinforcement problems of HQ, ALFSEA 2nd Echelon were caused by caste and community basis on which most Indian units are recruited. This prevented reinforcements being pooled beyond a limited extent and tremendously increased detailed staff work on the part of the reinforcement section of 2nd Echelon, besides being expensive in men." The author recommended mixed-class recruitment as the cure for the problem (Prasad 1951, 10–11).

The second significant problem the class policy in World War II caused was in promotions and hierarchies within battalions. The issue was that if a certain NCO position needed to be filled by a Rajput, for instance, in a mixed battalion of Rajputs and Punjabi Muslims, in order to keep the overall company and battalion mix of NCOs in balance, then that promotion might block the path of more deserving members of the other class. This could especially be an issue where, because of combat losses, the available promotion candidates from one class were less experienced and hence fitted for promotion than that of another. The Army therefore recommended that future promotion lists be regiment-wide to provide greater opportunities to deserving candidates who might otherwise be blocked by the fact that their battalion had no vacancy for a promotion in "their" class (Prasad 1951, 10–11).

Despite the problems that class recruitment created, the 1945 Willcox Committee, set up by General Auchinleck in late 1944 to look into the whole future organization of the postwar Indian Army, was unanimous that it still made sense in terms of military effectiveness. This committee had five British officers, including Brigadier Enoch Powell, who drafted some important sections and was later to achieve notoriety as a British politician with extreme views on immigration, as well as one senior Indian officer, Brigadier K. M. Cariappa, later to become independent India's first Indian Commander in Chief (Willcox Committee 1945).[20] The committee examined the whole question of class recruitment and recommended, not surprisingly given the conservatism of the army, that it preserve the status quo of class regiments subject to some small changes, such as (1) the updating of the caste handbooks, which had been largely unchanged for forty years, and (2) not recognizing in future the various subclass distinctions (for example between the seventeen tribal subclasses of Punjabi Muslim and the nine types of non-Jat Sikhs and three types of Jat Sikhs) that had at one time played a role in assembling units at the platoon and company level but that had been increasingly ignored over time in any case (Willcox Committee 1945, I:221).[21] In 1946 a number of army orders were passed to implement these changes, for instance one that expanded the areas from which Pathans could be recruited, abolished separate platoons organized by Pathan subclass, and announced that "His Excellency the Commander-in-Chief has decided that in future all Pathans serving in Indian infantry regiments will be mixed in sub-units."[22] The committee spent many pages on this issue of class recruitment, knowing that it would be controversial and would likely be challenged by an elected Indian government. It began by acknowledging that there were three main objections to the policy: that it was "anti-national," "anti-democratic," and the result of an insidious divide-and-rule policy. "It has been asserted that the degree of national unity attained by India under British rule implies and demands that there should be no recognition in the Indian Army of any internal distinctions and divisions. There is a feeling, too, that it would be inconsistent with a democratic constitution, such as that given to the Provinces in 1935 and now advocated for the Centre, if any Indian citizen were not free to enter any arm or corps of the Indian Army for which his physique and education qualified him. The allegation is even made that class differences in the Indian Army have been recognized, fostered and perpetuated by the British for their own ends on the principle of 'divide and rule.'"

The report tried to knock each of these objections down in turn. The divide-and-rule allegation was completely "baseless," it said, because "the breaking down of no-class organization in the Bengal Army before the Mutiny, and in the Bombay Army after it, was much more the work of the men themselves than of their officers or the Government. There is no doubt that a no-class system would be bitterly disliked and resented by the present-day Indian soldier, whose happiness and contentment, like that of all soldiers, is greatest when he can live and fight with those of his own kind whom he most resembles." The antinational and antidemocratic arguments were also wrong, it said, for several reasons. First, the idea that there were no divisions in the wider society was simply wrong; "Politically, it would be impossible to dispute that the antipathy of the communities, far from having diminished, has been greatly intensified in the past decades." Second, the army, far from accentuating these divisions, actually helped to diminish them. The army, it claimed, was in fact "a phenomenon unique in India for the complete absence of communal hostility and the unreserved cooperation of men of different communities in a cause transcending communal interests." A focus on particular identities, in other words, did not prevent national loyalties. Third, and perhaps most importantly for the long term, the committee claimed that class regiments were desirable because they were the most effective militarily: cohesive ethnic and class backgrounds produced more effective and cohesive units for fighting purposes (Willcox Committee 1945, I:216–221).

There was no necessary conflict between national identity, democracy, and class composition, the committee argued. The fact that Britain had the Scots, Welsh, Irish, and Coldstream Guards and Highland, Lowland, and regional regiments did not seem to hamper either democracy or unity, and greatly enhanced operational effectiveness. In fact, after reviewing various militaries around the world, the committee concluded that "no army of a major power can be found that does not have features, which, after due allowance for conditions peculiar to India, correspond more or less closely to the class composition of the Indian Army" (Willcox Committee 1945, I:216–221).

There was an obvious risk, according to the Willcox Committee, involved in bringing new and "untried" classes such as Bengalis into the army.[23] Of course, the report said, that was desirable as a long-term goal in the (very distant) future. But in the meantime, for the sake of security and operational effectiveness, it was surely better to stick with the tried and tested classes. It was therefore not a good idea, the committee argued, to introduce class regiments of groups that had little frontline experience, or that had "not performed well" during the war, too soon. The irony of all this, of course, in an echo of the 1879–1880 debate over the future of the Madras regiments in the army, is that caste and regional biases were constantly being used to steer particular groups away from frontline roles in World War II and then these groups' consequent lack of frontline experience was used to justify their noninclusion in the army. The definition of a unit "not having performed well" also seems to have been very malleable. Communities the officers wanted to keep were deemed to be performing well, and decisions to exclude groups were justified by citing a litany of past problems. The committee took an especially hard line with Bengalis, who were perceived as politically disloyal and therefore militarily unsuitable. After describing records of poor military performance, court-martials, and disciplinary problems of various units, the committee argued that "in view of this record, which corresponds closely with the career of the 49th Bengalis in 1917–1920, and evidences the unsuitability of Bengalis for service in homogenous units or sub-units, we cannot recommend that any units or sub-units of Bengalis as such be included in the Army, except that Bengali pioneer companies [construction battalions similar to the US Army's Seabees] should be maintained." These same disciplinary reasons could of course easily have been given to justify the nonrecruitment of the Dogras (a unit of which had mutinied in 1930), the Sikhs, or many other communities that were in the army.

The Indian National Army

One other issue that might have substantially altered the composition of the Indian Army and the States Forces as independence approached was the question of whether to reintegrate the survivors of the twenty thousand Indian soldiers who had joined the nationalist "Indian National Army" (INA) after the Japanese invasion and conquest of Malaya and Singapore at the beginning of 1942. From the INA soldiers' perspective they too were Indian patriots, and with freedom approaching many of the INA veterans as well as their political supporters felt that they ought to be reintegrated into the army. However, most senior Indian Army officers—Indian as well as British—viewed the men as having betrayed their comrades, many of whom had suffered a great deal in captivity, and also worried about the effect on unit cohesion, loyalty, and morale if the men were allowed to rejoin the army. The serving friends and relatives of INA men, such as INA leader Captain Mohan Singh's brother-in-law and good friend Captain Hardial Singh, had been placed under special observation during the war because of worries they might cause problems in their units.[24] The Home Ministry was also determined to prevent INA men from being employed in any security capacity, either by Indian provinces or by administrations in the princely states. The military and Home Ministry largely succeeded in this campaign, partly by agreeing not to press on with large-scale prosecutions and punishments of the INA men after the politically disastrous attempt at a show trial of three officers at the Red Fort in

November 1945 (Bayly and Harper 2010, 78–90). The government persuaded Congress in late 1945 and 1946 not to press the issue, which turned out to be easier than it thought because Congress leaders themselves were worried about introducing factionalism and indiscipline into an army that would be needed very soon in a free India (78–80). In the aftermath of the Royal Indian Naval mutiny in Bombay in February 1946, Sardar Vallabhai Patel wrote to a fellow Congress leader that "discipline in the Army cannot be tampered with. . . . We will want Army even in free India" (Sarkar 1983, 425).

The colonial government used a variety of methods to block the INA men from employment in the security forces, especially the ones termed "blacks" and "greys" who were judged to have been most disloyal to British interests while fighting for the INA and alongside the Japanese. In Punjab, district-wide lists of these ex-INA men were drawn up in late summer 1946 to prevent them from getting any position seen as threatening to state interests.[25]

The Impact of Partition

In early 1947, with political negotiations that might have kept India united having collapsed, a few of the most senior Indian Army officers were instructed to start considering, in secret, the question of how the army might be divided along religious lines should partition take place. In June, once partition was decided, the work began in earnest. The method of partitioning the army between India and Pakistan kept the system of unit class composition intact; only individual officers and minority units recruited from within either India or Pakistan had the right to declare for either country. For example the "Hindustani Musalman" units in the cavalry, which were recruited from India, got the choice of going to Pakistan or staying behind in India.[26] As most regiments in the Indian Army had a fixed composition before independence—for example, with two companies of Hindus, one of Muslims, and one of Sikhs in a battalion—the army first allotted a regiment to India or Pakistan based on its overall Hindu or Muslim or Sikh proportion; the eight infantry regiments with 50–75 percent Muslims were allotted to Pakistan and the remaining eighteen regiments allotted to India. The eight regiments allotted to Pakistan were 56 percent Muslim overall, and the eighteen regiments allotted to India were composed of 78 percent Hindus, Sikhs, and Christians and 22 percent Muslims from Punjab, NWFP, Uttar Pradesh, Rajputana, and Bihar.[27]

Once a regiment was allotted to either India or Pakistan on the basis of its majority community, the next step was to transfer out the remaining minorities in each unit. So Indian regiments that were majority Sikh or Hindu sent all their Muslim companies off to join Pakistani regiments (unless the minorities were recruited from Indian territory, in which case they got the choice whether to stay or go), while Pakistani regiments sent back their Hindu and Sikh companies to fill in the gaps left by the departing Muslim units. The numbers of each group in and out did not balance, however, so that some classes and regiments got bigger and others smaller. The Jat Regiment, for instance, lost around 2,440 Muslim personnel to Pakistan's Frontier Force and Punjab Regiments and got only 900 Jats back from these units in return, while the Dogra Regiment received so many Dogras from Pakistan's Frontier Force Regiment and Baluch Regiment that it had to add two extra battalions (Ross 1967, 401; *The Gallant Dogras* 2005, 91–92).

The only exception to this religious unmixing was in the case of troops from Madras, where a diverse number of communities, including Muslims, Christians, Adi-Dravidas, Kapus, Malas, Reddis, Vellalan, and others, had long been recruited into the army and mixed together as "Madras Classes" (Mouat 1929).[28] Because these groups were so mixed at the company and platoon level, it was simply impossible to unmix them while retaining unit discipline and cohesion, as had been done with the other units. So a decision was made to keep the Muslims, who numbered 12 percent of the Madras Classes, together with their fellow Indian soldiers.

The partition violence and ethnic cleansing was, as is well known, horrific and on a massive scale. From the perspective of thinking about civil-military matters it raised two big issues. First, the partition demonstrated some of the very real problems of a class recruitment policy based on only one or two regions. One reason that the violence was especially bad in Punjab and NWFP was precisely because there were so many ex-soldiers living in these areas, trained in the use of military tactics and weapons and with tight organizational bonds that allowed them to quickly mobilize against the rival community, when they felt threatened. The involvement of military veterans in the ethnic cleansing has already been widely noted in the historical literature on the partition, but there is always a question of course as to whether these are isolated incidents or indicative of a wider trend. So in a recent research project Saumitra Jha and I looked at the quantitative evidence for veteran involvement in ethnic cleansing during the partition, which we identify as the product of organizational skills (as well as skills in fighting and tactics) gained through frontline service in the army. To begin with we identified just where the home districts were of all those Indian troops serving during World War II, as well as the average amount of frontline combat experience (in months) the soldiers from each district had been exposed to during the war. Then we gathered data on the degree of ethnic cleansing and out-migration in every district of India and Pakistan during the partition period (1941–1951). This allowed a test of whether the numbers of ex-soldiers in a district or the number of soldiers with frontline experience was related to the level of ethnic cleansing, controlling for all the obvious counterarguments such as the demography of a district, its previous level of crime and communal violence, or its economic characteristics. We found that there was a robust relationship between whether there was a large number of veterans with combat experience in a district and whether there was a lot of ethnic cleansing: an additional average month of combat experience among veterans in a district was associated with a 1.1 percentage point reduction in the minority population (17,000 people, in the average district) by 1951, due to killing, conversion, or migration (Jha and Wilkinson 2012).

The second important aspect of the partition violence was that it demonstrated the potentially very real problems that the army faced in trying to use force against the groups from which most of its own troops were recruited, especially in an environment in which these troops had heard of atrocities committed against Hindus and Sikhs by members of the Muslim community they were now being asked to protect. The internal army reorganization report in 1945 had recognized this issue, but took the optimistic view that "cases in which this condition occasions any difficulty will be rare" (Willcox Committee 1945, 1:216). However, the events of 1947 in north India showed that the risks could be very real and widespread where, as in Punjab and the NWFP, the army was asked to control violence in its home districts. By late August 1947, many of the units recruited from these areas had become unreliable in protecting members of the opposite community and unwilling to go on the offensive against members of their own community who were involved in the violence. General Auchinleck, the Commander in Chief, reported on August 28 that the commander of the Punjab Boundary Force had told him that "owing to the extraordinary circumstances in which they found themselves situated and the very great strain imposed upon them by the circumstances in which they were being called upon to act in aid of the civil power the Indian Officers and men had become inevitably affected with the communal virus. He anticipated that this deterioration would increase rapidly and stated his considered opinion that he would be unable to guarantee the reliability and general impartiality of the troops under his command beyond the middle of September."[29] Because of this, the Joint Defence Council had been obliged to pass new rules requiring that after September 1, 1947, only Muslim soldiers would protect Muslims en route to Pakistan and only Hindu and Sikh soldiers would protect Hindus and Sikhs en route to India.[30]

The *Daily Telegraph* correspondents Colin Reid and Douglas Brown, who traveled widely in Punjab at the time, reported several instances of troops refusing to protect or being lax in protecting refugees of the other community—for example by firing over the heads of attackers—and of the frantic insistence of refugees that they be protected by members of their own group.[31] In perhaps the most notorious instance, men of the Baluch regiment took an active part in the ethnic cleansing of Hindus and Sikhs in Sheikhpura district (Singh 1972, 126–127). One officer complained in a secret dispatch to Sir Francis Mudie, the new Governor of the Pakistani province of West Punjab, that

> the non-Muslim troops do not provide adequate protection for the trains or columns. They are adequate for minor attacks, which they appear to beat off, but for any planned attacks on a large scale they are very conveniently away from the place of

attacks. I have heard allegations of their joining in shooting or subduing any resistance, but I cannot corroborate this. I have noticed that whenever marching columns, trains or MT convoys are escorted by Muslim troops in sufficient strength, all such convoys get through without any incidents or only long-range sniping. I am, therefore, of the opinion that even if the non-Muslim troops do not take part in shooting, they certainly are in the knowledge of large-scale planned attacks, and conveniently deploy themselves in places where there is no trouble or arrive on the scene after the damage is done. This does not apply to Gurkha or Garhwali troops, or to certain non-Punjabi troops, but if they are commanded by a non-Muslim officer— other than a British officer, then their action is also not as vigorous as it should be.[32]

Sir Francis Tuker, a senior general at the time, noted that on the Indian side of the border Hindu and Sikh troops "inflicted very few casualties" and that "the most effective troops were Muslim or non-Punjab Hindu," especially the tribals in the Bihar Regiment and the lower castes in the Mahar Regiment (Tuker 1950, 449). Tuker suggests that after the first few incidents in which troops did not act strongly to prevent massacres, the Muslim refugees would just vote with their feet and leave a train if they saw an all-Hindu or all-Sikh guard (449). We can get some idea of just how worried the Indian Army was about the reliability of its Hindu and Sikh troops from north India by the fact that when communal violence broke out in Delhi in early September 1947 the Indian government decided to rush in Gorkhas (5 Gurkhas) and troops from southern India (4 Madras) to stop it rather than use units recruited from the Punjab and Western Uttar Pradesh.[33] The Gorkhas were from Nepal and the Madras regiment was a mixed-class regiment in which Hindus and Muslims and Christians of various castes served together at the battalion level. To some observers, incidents like this in 1947 might have seemed a strong argument for substantially broadening the regional and group composition of the Indian Army. But any decision on that would have to wait until after independence.

3

Protecting the
New Democracy

The Inheritance

THE INDIAN ARMY that emerged from partition was very different
from the one that had existed at the beginning of 1947. First, it was
now a truly *Indian* Army. The British regiments had all left by the
beginning of 1948, and only a few hundred British officers remained
behind by mid-1948 to help with the transition, most of them in
training and technical roles. This loss of most of the army's officer
corps obviously required huge adjustments, as none of the Lieutenant Generals, only one of the eight Major Generals, only 5 percent
of the brigade and subarea commanders, and fewer than 10 percent
of the regimental and battalion commanders had been Indian at independence.[1] However, the Indian Army was able to cope with this
massive loss of European officers much better than armies in most
of the other Asian and African colonies at independence. This was
because even the very grudging and partial "Indianization" of the
officer corps from 1919 to 1939, followed by the large-scale emergency recruitment of Indians in World War II, left India with more
trained officers at a more senior level than these other colonial
armies. In Ghana, for instance, there were forty-seven Ghanaian
officers at independence in 1957, one-sixth of the total, but all of
these men had been commissioned only after 1950, so they were at
very junior ranks and not ready to move into command positions
(Gutteridge 1962, 42–45). The Belgian Congo, a country of 14 mil-

lion people, was even worse off when it got independence in June 1960. The colonial government there had only just started training fourteen Congolese officer cadets the month before, and these men were not due to graduate from the Belgian military academy as second lieutenants until 1963. Crawford Young describes the result after the *Force Publique*'s entire thousand-strong European officer corps left the Congo in a panic at independence: "Overnight, the whole of its officer corps disappeared. Soon thereafter, the political fragmentation of the country was reflected in the emergence of four separate armies. Leaderless bands of mutineers committed atrocities without number in 1960–1961; the new Congolese officers had a daily battle to regain control over the troops and to restore discipline to the army" (1965, 442–444; Young 1966).

In India, though, the slow process of Indianization begun in 1919 had created a high-quality pool of several hundred middle- and high-ranking Indian officers by mid-1947; Lieutenant Colonels, Colonels and, at the top, ten Indian Brigadiers. Muslims accounted for 36 percent of these senior officers, somewhat higher than their 25 percent percentage in the prepartition Indian population (Rizvi 1988, 31).[2] In both India and Pakistan, these officers could now be promoted very quickly to fill the gaps left by the departing British Lieutenant Generals, Major Generals, and Brigadiers. In India, S. M. Shrinagesh, who was commissioned in 1923 and had just received his promotion to Colonel in August 1945, was promoted to Brigadier in 1947 and to Lieutenant General and General Officer Commanding (GOC) of the entire Western Command in 1949, a position that preindependence would have taken him almost a decade longer to reach (Issar 2009, 116, 182).[3] In addition to the fifty or so Indian King's Commissioned Indian Officers (KCIOs) who trained at Sandhurst between 1919 and 1934, and who were the most senior and ready to move into the top command positions, there was also a larger pool of several hundred officers who had been trained at the Indian Military College from 1934 to 1939, including such future leaders as Sam Manekshaw and Harbaksh Singh. The highest ranked of these IMC-trained officers were now Lieutenant Colonels and Colonels. Finally, the massive expansion of the army during World War II had also led to the hiring of around nine thousand Indian emergency commissioned officers, who combined with the Indian officers recruited from 1919 to 1939 accounted for around 20 percent of the total officers by late 1945 (Sharma 1996, 184). The existence of these officers allowed the new, much smaller postwar Indian Army much more flexibility, because the best thousand of them could now be offered regular commissions to fill some of the gaps left by the departing British (182–183).

It is important not to overstate the value of this reserve from the perspective of India's future military effectiveness, however, because the slowness of Indianization and a British determination to keep political control of the army had excluded Indians from many of the key battlefield, military planning, and intelligence roles (Marston 2014, 253). Only one senior Indian officer, Brigadier (later General) Thimayya, had ever commanded a brigade in combat during World War II. Likewise no senior officer had wartime experience in military operations or military intelligence, areas that had been reserved for British officers (Lehl 1997, 47).[4] This dearth of officers with senior-level wartime experience would not show itself immediately, but would be felt severely in 1962.[5]

The second big difference, of course, was in the army's communal composition. Before 1947, Muslims had constituted one-third of the army's other ranks and almost a quarter of its total number of officers.[6] Now, as a result of the transfer of the Muslim regiments and companies to Pakistan and their replacement by Hindu and Sikh units, these men had almost all left. Minority officers on each side of the border had been given an individual choice to opt for either India or Pakistan. But whether because of a deeper commitment to Pakistan, fears of discrimination for themselves or their children, or the better chances for advancement in a short-staffed and majority Muslim army, almost all of India's Muslim officers ended up leaving (Cohen 2006, 59–60).[7] By 1951 only a handful of senior Muslim officers remained: Major General Anis Ahmed Khan in the Service Corps, Brigadier Enayat Habibullah in the elite Sixteenth Cavalry, Brigadier G. Shahbaz in the Rajputana Rifles, Brigadier M. K. Sheriff, and Colonel M. M. Badshah in the Sikh Regiment.[8] These five Muslim officers accounted for around 2 percent of the senior officers (Lieutenant Colonels and over) in the army, and the proportion dropped even further in 1955 when Major General Khan left for Pakistan in a setback for Muslim officers anxious to prove their loyalty to India (Khalidi 2002, 533).[9]

Among other ranks the Muslim proportion was, because of the transfer out of all the homogenous Muslim units, even smaller than in the officer corps. So the few Muslim soldiers that remained were in units, in particular the Madras Regiment, that were so mixed at the company and small-unit level that it was impossible to easily separate out troops of different communities. The last available manpower report before partition counts 5,158 "Madras Classes" in the Third Madras Regiment in January 1946 and 539 nontech combatants, with no Madras classes in any other Infantry regiment.[10] If we assume that the 12 percent Muslim proportion in the Madras Regiment units all remained behind in India after partition, even though some probably did not, then the overall Muslim proportion to the total strength of the Indian Infantry and Armoured regiments after the division of the army would have been around 0.6 percent. Some more Muslims who had been recruited to clerical and service roles in other regiments (Muslims were often employed as cooks, mechanics, and the like) and also stayed behind would have to be added to this number to get a more precise figure, but any estimate much higher than 1 percent Muslim troops in the Infantry in 1947 seems highly unlikely. Given the somewhat higher Muslim representation in the Armoured Corps, which had several units that included "Kaimkhani Muslims" and "Hindustani Muslims" as well as a couple (Eighth and Sixteenth Light Cavalry) with "South Indian Classes" that included Muslims, I estimate the total Muslim share of the Infantry and Armoured Corps battalions (excluding Kashmiri units) as 1.5 percent in the late 1940s.[11]

The third big difference after 1947 was in the overall provincial and class composition of the force. And here one central fact that should be emphasized is that just as Dr. Bhimrao Ambedkar had predicted, partition substantially reduced the degree of ethnic imbalance, and hence the political threat, in the part of the army that had been left to India compared to the army that Pakistan inherited (Ambedkar 1941). The Punjab and North West Frontier Province (NWFP) were, as we have seen, the two most overrepresented areas of India in the pre-1947 army. And the large, populous territory

of East Bengal was, together with the rest of Bengal, the most underrepresented large province in all of India. So by losing Punjab,
NWFP and the most populous part of Bengal the degree of ethnic
imbalance in the Indian Army that was left went down quite substantially, while in Pakistan it went up. In Tables 3.1 and 3.2 I use the
Indian Army's 1946–1947 *Manpower Report* to estimate the class and

Table 3.1. Estimated Class Composition of the Postpartition Indian Infantry,
December 1947

Class	Total	Percentage
SIKHS	24,159	17.2
Non-Jat Sikhs	*1,796}*	
Mazbhi and Ramdasia Sikhs	*3,536}*	
Sikhs	*18,827}*	
Punjabi Hindus	606	0.4
DOGRAS	23,429	16.6
Dogras	*17,666*	
Dogra Brahmins	*5,763}*	
Garhwalis	6,762	4.8
Kumaonis	6,539	4.6
Jats	22,441	15.9
Ahirs	3,914	2.8
Gujars	4,976	3.5
Brahmins	2,276	1.6
Rajputs	13,904	9.9
Madrassis (including 12% Muslims)	6,928	4.9
Assamese	3,923	2.8
Biharis (including Adivasis)	3,120	2.2
Chamars	994	0.7
Rawats	1,651	1.2
Minas	646	0.5
Katats	717	0.5
Mahars	3531	2.5
Mahrattas	10,546	7.5
Total of Troops from India	**141,062**	100
Non-Indians (Gorkhas)	18,500	–

Source: Calculated from Column 10, "Total Assets" in *Tenth Indian Manpower
Review (1 Jan 1946–31 March 1947)*, Appendix I: Infantry Non-Tech Combatants—
Summary by Regiments by Classes. Indian Office Records, British Library, London
L/WS/1/1613 Manpower. Gorkha numbers calculated by taking 1946–1947 manpower
estimates for the six units allotted to India (1,3,4,5,8,9 G.R.) but exclude 1947–48
optees and new units, which would raise the Gorkha percentage closer to 20%.

Table 3.2. Estimated Provincial Composition of Indian Infantry, December, 1947

Province	Troops	Percent
Bombay	14,077	10
Punjab	44,876	32
Uttar Pradesh	25,516	18
Madras	6,097	4
West Bengal	0	0
Rajputana	13,904	10
Assam	3,923	3
Bihar	3,120	2
Orissa	0	0
Jammu and Kashmir	17,666	13
Others / Not Clear	11,953	8
	141,132	

Source: Calculated from Column 10, "Total Assets" in *Tenth Indian Manpower Review (1 Jan 1946–31 March 1947)*, Appendix I: Infantry Non-Tech Combatants— Summary by Regiments by Classes. Indian Office Records, British Library, London L/WS/1/1613 Manpower. Slight differences in totals between Table 3.1 and Table 3.2 due to the difficulty of assigning some groups to specific provinces.

provincial composition of the Indian Infantry immediately after partition, after subtracting those Muslim troops that we know were sent to Pakistan from the different branches of the Infantry and adding in the various groups of Sikhs and Hindus who were transferred from the Pakistan regiments to India.[12] Some units such as Sikhs and Mahars are easily assigned to particular provinces. In the case of other groups, such as the Jats and Rajputs, I allocate them to different provinces based on their known pre-1947 recruiting proportion from each province.

As we can see from Tables 3.1 and 3.2, the rank and file of the Indian Army in 1947 was still, as before independence, very heavily drawn from the state of Punjab, and also from the traditional "martial classes" such as Sikhs, Dogras, Jats, Marathas, and Rajputs. Six Gorkha regiments had also been absorbed into the Indian Army, and in addition so many individual Gorkhas had opted for service in India rather than stay with their British units that a whole new Gorkha regiment (11 Gorkha Rifles) had to be created and several new battalions added to the existing Gorkha regiments (Palit 1997, 297–308).

Despite this overall "martial caste" majority, the most important
fact to stress is that the loss of so many Punjabi Muslims to Pakistan
meant that the share of Punjabi representation in the Indian infantry had now been reduced to just a little less than a third (32 percent), compared to 54 percent of all troops (and 60 percent of Indian
troops) before the outbreak of World War II in 1939. So unlike in
1939, no single province in India now had anything like a majority of
the army. And within the largest single group, men from Punjab, it
is important to remember that the salience of these soldiers' regional
and linguistic identities was crosscut by significant caste and religious
cleavages. Troops from Punjab had different religious identities
(18 percent Sikh, 14 percent Hindu), and within the Sikh units there
were also substantial cleavages along caste lines: roughly three-quarters
of the total were from Jat Sikh communities and the rest were from
other Sikh communities, including the lower-caste Mazhabi and
Ramdasia Sikhs who had been recruited to the new Sikh Light Infantry regiment during the war. So in terms of the rank and file, India
inherited an ethnically imbalanced army; but the imbalance was a
lot less serious in India in 1948 than it had been in 1939, and it was
also a lot less serious than it was in Pakistan (which also suffered a
rise in terms of its overall imbalance because it had retained none
of the Hindu Gorkha troops that acted as an additional hedge against
the high representation of Punjabis). In Pakistan after partition, one
province with 25 percent of the population, Punjab, now had 72 percent of the army, and a province with 55 percent of the population,
East Bengal, had basically no representation in the entire army in
1947 (Rizvi 1974, 176).[13] And in Pakistan, unlike in India, the Punjabi
troops' identity was not crosscut by major religious or caste cleavages.

Offsetting this relatively good story in terms of the army's overall degree of ethnic imbalance, however, was the fact that India's most
senior officers were still quite a bit more ethnically homogenous than
the troops they commanded. This reflected the fact that the British
had recruited officers disproportionately from Punjabis, Pashtuns, Jats,
Dogras, Rajputs, Kumaonis, and a few other groups.[14] In Figure 3.1
I show the composition of the middle- and senior-ranking officers in
the army in 1951, based on a detailed name analysis and coding of the

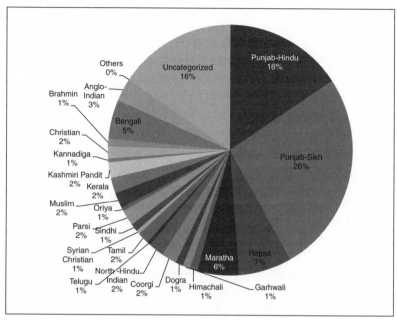

FIGURE 3.1 Estimated group composition of senior officers (colonel and above) in Indian Army 1951

1951 Indian Army List.[15] As we can see, fully half of all the senior officers (at the rank of Colonel and above) in 1951 were from Punjab; Sikhs alone were 26 percent of all officers, followed by Punjabi Hindus (16 percent), Rajputs (7 percent), and Marathas (6 percent). The traditional "martial" groups were around 75–80 percent of the overall officer corps altogether.[16] This clearly posed some potential political problems from the perspective of coup proofing, not least because, as Hiranyappa Venkatasubbiah pointed out at the time, "with the exit from the army of most of its Muslim and British officers in 1947 the ascendancy in its higher ranks was gained by Sikhs and Punjabi Hindus—two groups most vehemently opposed to partition" (Venkatasubbiah 1958, 16–17).

Things were made even worse by the fact that the senior officer corps, as well as being ethnically much more homogenous than the rank and file, was also small and very tightly knit. The fifty or so remaining Indian King's Commissioned Officers (trained at

Sandhurst over the period 1919–1934) had largely been selected on
the basis of their common attributes—their martial class origins, the
fact that they and their families were loyal (or not obviously disloyal)
to the Raj—as well as their social and cultural fit with British values
and norms. For instance, General K. M. Cariappa, who became
the first Indian Commander in Chief in 1949, was famous for his
inability after three full decades in the army to speak comprehensi-
ble Hindustani—one enlisted soldier famously responded to a question from Cariappa in Hindi by apologizing that he did not speak
English—as well as his habit of formally dressing for dinner even
when dining alone (Chaudhuri 1978). After their initial selection,
the Indian officer candidates after 1920 were all sent to Sandhurst,
where they were concentrated in a few platoons, to alleviate home-
sickness as well as to accommodate British biases. After Sandhurst
each young officer spent a year with a British regiment, after which
he was posted to his "permanent" Indian regiment. All the Indian
officers were sent to just eight "Indianized" units, a tenth of the total
number of battalions, as a result both of British prejudices about
serving with Indians and British officers' ill-founded doubts about
Indians' leadership abilities (Verma 1988, 17).[17] So the links between
these KCIO Indian officers were much tighter than if they had been
spread across all the units of the Indian Army at the beginning of
their careers. To take an example, consider the careers of the ten
Indian officers, one each year, commissioned from 1920 to 1929
into just one of these eight units, 1/14 Punjab Regiment, a unit that
was later merged into the Pakistan army in November 1947. These
ten officers ate and drank together, trained together, often went on
leave together, and served in the field together. By 1951, of the six
who were still in service (one had retired the year before because of
ill health), there were three of India's twenty-two Major Generals
(Sant Singh, Dewan Misri Chand, and S. P. P. Thorat) as well as Vir
Singh, the Colonel of the elite Sixteenth Cavalry Regiment,[18] not to
mention, on the Pakistani side, the Pakistani Commander in Chief
and future military dictator Ayub Khan and the first postindependence governor of the NWFP, Sahibzada Mohammad Khurshid
(Sharma 1996, 237–239). If we add in the further strong bonds among

India's senior officers from their training at Sandhurst (where, for example, future Chief of the Army Staff General Thimayya and future Lieutenant General Shankarrao Pandurang Patil Thorat were in the same company) and the various staff colleges, as well as the tight bonds forged in military operations in World War II, it is easy to see why India's civilian leadership might have been worried.

The Push for Change

Together with worries about the loyalty and potential political threat posed by the army, the Congress Party leadership and the army both faced pressure for radical reform of the armed forces. There was the widespread feeling among many Congress members that the army officers had been "brown sahibs" more loyal to the British than to their own countrymen and needed to be taken down a peg. There was also a broader attack on casteism and communalism, of which the army structure with its class regiments seemed a symbol. As we saw in Chapter 1, Congress elites had attacked colonial policies for years as accentuating caste and religious divisions through what Nehru described as a "policy of poise and counterpoise." The Congress Party leaders who had criticized these policies were now, at last, in clear control of the country, and were engaged from 1947 to 1949 in the dismantling of many of the "divide and rule" aspects of British government. Separate religious electorates and job reservations for Muslims and several other minorities were dismantled in most provinces from 1947 to 1948. In 1949 the Constituent Assembly voted to abolish religious and caste reservations at the national level as well, with exceptions only for the Scheduled Castes and Tribes, and even these were expected to remain in force for only a short time. In 1948 the Dar Committee recommended that the government of India and the census no longer maintain the sort of caste data that allowed for caste reservations to be implemented.[19] Many questions were asked in parliament about when army recruitment, too, would be opened up to all Indians and reflect India's democratic values. Many argued that World War II had "exploded" the myth of martial classes, and demonstrated that Indians from all castes and regions were qualified to serve. H. V. Kamath demanded in parliament in March 1948 that

there be a true "nationalization of the Army," by which he meant
"not merely the replacement of British by Indians, but throwing open
the Army to all classes and communities of the nation and not merely
confining it to certain aristocratic classes or certain so called martial
classes."[20]

There was also pressure from MPs from regions and castes with
a very low share of army recruitment to employ much larger numbers of Bengalis, Oriyas, Madrasis, Andhras, etc., as well as lower
castes and tribals. In 1948 one article by S. P. Roy Chowdhury in the
Modern Review spent seven pages reviewing the proud martial history of the Bengalis, from the Ramayana and battles in 500 BC to the
present, to prove that Bengalis "possess the true martial spirit" and
should be in the army. There were many questions asked in parliament about the army's composition, and provincial leaders from
underrepresented states also began to put pressure on Nehru and
Deputy Prime Minister Patel to act swiftly to repudiate "martial
class" recruitment and provide more jobs for their constituents.
MPs from Andhra asked about the number of Andhra officers being
recruited and about the steps being taken to ensure "adequate representation" of Andhras in the armed forces; in February 1948 the
Bombay politician P. S. Deshmukh complained about the declining
proportion of Marathas in the army; and MPs from Bengal and
Orissa asked about steps to employ more of their people. In August
1948, Ravi Shankar Shukla, the powerful Chief Minister of the Central Provinces (later renamed Madhya Pradesh) formally proposed
to Nehru that the army raise new regiments that were identified with
particular provinces, and recruited only from those provinces.[21] It
was obvious that the issue was not going away. When in late 1948 it
was announced that now-General Cariappa would soon replace Sir
Roy Bucher as the first Indian Commander in Chief of the army, the
pressure on the army to clarify its recruitment policy intensified.

Finally, there were the continuing Congress leadership worries,
expressed publicly since the mid-1930s, that a massively unrepresentative army with a tight-knit officer corps might be a threat to the
new democracy. These worries had been somewhat eased by the
partition of the army and the departure of Punjabi and Pathan

Muslim troops for Pakistan in late 1947. They had also been eased by the army's good performance in Kashmir in 1947–1948 and the top generals' apparent responsiveness to the political leadership. But Nehru, Sardar Patel, and highly placed civil servants, in particular H. M. Patel of the Indian Civil Service, Sardar Patel's confidant and the first Defence Secretary from 1947 to 1953, and his successor M. K. Vellodi, Defence Secretary from November 1953 to June 1957, were still worried enough about the military that they felt some kind of structural change was necessary.

Challenges to Reform

This problem of how to politically neutralize the army as well as respond to demands for more inclusion was made even more difficult by three things. First, and most obviously, the 1947–1948 war with Pakistan over Kashmir, continuing instability in some parts of the country, and the military action in Hyderabad in 1948 made a large-scale restructuring of the army seem a lot riskier in 1948 or 1949 than it had looked when Nehru first sketched out his plan for reorganizing the army in September 1946. This was also true, even more so, in Pakistan, which was in a militarily weaker position, as a country with no "strategic depth" and fewer troops and supplies than it needed to defend its very long new borders.

The restructuring of the army was also made more difficult by the fact that most politicians' aim immediately after independence was not to expand the army, which could have helped solve the problem by creating lots of new positions that could have been given to excluded groups and regions, but instead to shrink it. The budget for India's armed forces consumed around 50 percent of India's total central government expenditure, and as early as 1946 the prepartition government had decided as a long-term goal to try to reduce that cost by around half, to Rs. 100 crores (1 billion rupees) INR 1 billion. From the average Congress MP's perspective, large-scale cuts in the army, as long as they could be done without endangering security, were the obvious place to look to provide money for provinces with deep financial problems, and to finance India's long-term development. In a 1949 debate on the constitutional clauses that

divided federal and provincial revenues, one MP from Orissa complained that army expenditure was still INR 1.48 billion even after
partition, much of it paid by the jute duty (produced in the east, especially Bengal), and that he could not "see why the Government of
India should grab the wealth of the provinces and dispense it in the
way they like. . . . Sir, on behalf of the provinces, particularly the undeveloped provinces of Bengal, Bihar, Orissa and Assam, I plead before this august House for justice for the undeveloped provinces."[22]

Nehru acknowledged the trade-off between defense spending and
development. He pointed out that every cut of ten thousand men in
the total strength of the army would save INR 30 million that could
be used for other purposes—to develop the country's industry and
infrastructure, build schools, and pay for better medical facilities.
But for what he tactfully called "obvious reasons," he said that he had
been unable to cut the army at all in the first few years of independence.[23] He was prodded into this stance by Deputy Prime Minister Sardar Patel, who wrote several letters to him in 1950 in which
he urged the "reconsideration of our retrenchment plans for the
army in light of . . . new threats" posed by Pakistan, Burma, and
especially by Communist China.[24] So that meant that the most obvious solution to the demands of underrepresented states—to quickly
add new units to the army from underrepresented states without
demobilizing existing units—was largely off the table for financial
reasons.

The other major obstacle to the fundamental reform of the army's
ethnic structure was very strong resistance from the senior officer
corps itself. The army commanders were adamantly opposed to
major changes in their traditional regimental structure and recruitment practices, especially when India seemed likely to go to war
with Pakistan again and the country was still unsettled. Some also
saw the major Royal Indian Navy mutiny in Bombay in February
1946 as proof that a service recruited broadly from across the country might be more prone to indiscipline than one that used the traditional class recruitment model. The senior leadership's commitment to the class regiment system is shown quite well by the views
of General K. M. Cariappa. Cariappa was commissioned as one of the
very first batch of KCIOs in 1919, and in several decades of service

with two class regiments, the Dogras and the Rajputana Rifles, he fully absorbed the army's beliefs about the combat effectiveness of class regiments compared to mixed units. He also served a period as Adjutant for the Rajputana Rifles, the officer in overall charge of class recruitment for his regiment. Far from opposing the class regiment policy, as a Brigadier and the only Indian officer to serve on the 1944–1945 Indian Army Reorganisation Committee, he pressed instead for the conversion of the five proposed post-1945 mixed regiments to single-class regiments in order to increase their military effectiveness. The report noted that "Brigadier Cariappa considers that the advantages of class company units are sufficient to justify the adoption of the system throughout, in infantry as in armour, artillery, etc.; in view especially of the factors of inter-class feeling and of reinforcement difficulties in war" (Willcox Committee 1945, 1:216). This portrayal seems to be an accurate statement of his views, because Cariappa's own copy of the report, which survives in the National Archives of India, contains notes in his hand that show his strong opposition to other measures, but has nothing to indicate disagreement on this point. He is also known to have not been shy, in other circumstances, in speaking out in public where he disagreed with his superiors, a habit that periodically got him into trouble.[25]

Cariappa's support for the existing class-recruitment system was, we know, shared by most of the other senior Indian officers at the time. General Thimayya, the Chief of Army Staff (COAS) from 1957 to 1961, told his biographer in the 1950s that "soldiers perform better when their units are not mixed. . . . This has been proved. Also, the officers of a 'pure' battalion are apt to be more careful about expending their men, and this always improves morale" (Evans 1960, 285). General J. N. Chaudhuri (COAS 1962–1966), when writing anonymous military columns for the *Statesman* in the 1950s, perhaps came closest to sounding like the prewar supporters of the martial classes when he sang the virtues of the infantryman who "has always come from solid, stolid, yeoman farmer stock. This breed produces a type who is strongly built, used to hard work and adverse living conditions, observant and wise in fieldcraft. He has individuality, but is not over-imaginative, too much imagination being a handicap when faced with the machines of destruction" (column 3 December

1951, reprinted in Chaudhuri 1966, 32–35). Chaudhuri's autobiography also describes his class cavalry regiment (Seventh Light Cavalry) with its Jat Sikhs, Jat Hindus, and Punjabi Muslims as one of the two great loves of his life (Chaudhuri 1978, 61, 207).

This is not meant to imply that these officers adopted all the British officers' martial-class prejudices wholesale. They did not. Cariappa, for instance, had opposed the senior British officers' denigration of some "non-martial" groups' military qualities when on the army reorganization committee in 1944–1945. His own surviving copy of the report contains marginal notes emphasizing his disagreement with the British officers' negative views of the martial qualities of Bengalis and other groups during the war. Cariappa's own copy of the report highlights various portions that were negative about the Bengalis' war experience and recommended their nonrecruitment, next to which Cariappa wrote "These are NOT my views" in ink at the side.[26]

But these officers did all share the view that long regimental traditions and the attachment of particular groups to the regiment paid dividends in terms of fighting effectiveness. And they shared the belief that any attempt to put recruitment on a different basis was positively dangerous for India, given the security threat the country faced from Pakistan and potentially from China. The generals could make the point, quite truthfully, that the division of the army in 1947 had been an enormously wrenching experience from which the army as a whole was still recovering. The division of the army had left many Indian regiments looking for new home bases and barracks— many of the Indian Army's pre-1947 barracks and bases had been located on the northwest frontier and were now in Pakistan—and had forced the army to found a new staff college at Wellington to replace the one at Quetta inherited by Pakistan (Patel 1963, 17). The senior Indian officers felt that the army needed a period of calm and consolidation, not a hurried restructuring that threatened its very core. Of the many senior officers' memoirs that exist from officers commissioned before 1939, only one—by Major General D. K. Palit, written well after he and all the other officers had retired—criticizes the class regiment and recruitment strategy (Palit 1991, 12–13).

Strategies for Coup Proofing

As Stephen Cohen rightly points out, "The present, compatible re-lationship between the military and India's democracy did not just happen. Nehru, Patel, and other Indian politicians, as well as their civilian advisers, had a clear idea of which elements of the 'British tradition' they wanted to keep and which they wanted to discard" (Cohen 1990b, 99–100). The clearest statement of Nehru's thoughts on civil-military issues is the letter he sent to the Defence Secretary as well as General Auchinleck (Commander in Chief) in September 1946, just a week after the new national government had been ap-pointed, and before an Indian Defence Minister had even been appointed (Nehru 1946).[27] In that letter, he raised the general issue of the need to make the army firmly responsible to India's elected representatives in the future, which meant that the army's leadership had to be fully Indianized and not influenced by British policy con-cerns. He also insisted that there was a real need to make the Indian Army a truly national army, drawing on the whole country, and that the distinction between martial and nonmartial races "must disap-pear." Finally, Nehru raised the issue of the use of the army to quell domestic disorders. He recognized that using the army extensively for this purpose was bad for the army and (presumably because it drew the army into domestic politics) for the country, so he recommended that "it would be desirable, wherever necessary, to increase the Police force or to form special peace preservation corps for this particular purpose so as to relieve the army from this distasteful duty."

The Congress leadership was clearheaded on the issue of what to do about the military in part because of the genuinely broad and representative character of the Congress Party, which made the un-representative nature of the army from a distributional and fairness perspective much more of an issue than it did for the more elitist Muslim League. But the Congress Party's sensitivity and sure-footedness on the issue also reflected its broad national composition (including many underrepresented provinces and communities), and its own long history of opposition to British rule and planning for independence (Oldenburg 2010, 10). Congress members had written many articles and working papers on the need to construct a national army, participated in various parliamentary debates on the army, and had a variety of more informal conversations on the issues, sometimes with serving army officers (Chaudhuri 1935).[28] The Congress Party leadership clearly saw three main issues with the army: first, its lack of representativeness, both of Indians relative to British at the higher ranks, and in terms of regional representation; second, the army's potential threat to democracy; and third, the huge cost of the military, which necessarily posed a threat to other important parts of the party's agenda, such as improving literacy and health. The Muslim League's leadership, on the other hand, once the issue of Indian versus British personnel had been addressed, seems to have largely thought about the military through the much narrower lens of defending its high degree of Muslim, Punjabi, and Pashtun overrepresentation. The classic instance of this is Jinnah's September 1938 press release defending Punjab's role in the military and Muslims' over-representation in the army (in fact, the number was closer to 25 percent) (Jinnah 1996, 850–851).

The Congress therefore took a number of steps in the first few years that, as a whole, represented a coordinated and effective effort to restructure civilian relations with the military. In taking these measures, the political leadership was helped both by its own clear political legitimacy in the country and by the fact that from December 1948 to January 1949 the Commander in Chief (General Sir Roy Bucher) was still British, as were the heads of the Air Force and Navy. These top British officers knew that, as non-Indians, they could now be sent home for any reason, as General Sir Bruce Lockhart, the previous Commander in Chief, had been in December 1947 when he was seen as not fully "on team" over the government's Kashmir policy. General Bucher, on the other hand, was viewed by many of his fellow officers as pliable and eager to do almost anything to keep his job and please H. M. Patel, the new Defence Secretary (Khanduri 2000, 60–61).

Nehru decided to set the new tone early. When senior officers were obstructing Congress's plans for the Independence Day celebrations in August 1947 he wrote a stern letter to the Commander in Chief, with copies sent to several other senior officers (including

mander in Chief and the creation of three new chief positions on the services at a meeting in early 1953, at the instance of H. M. Patel, who had a long-running feud with General Cariappa. This was, not coincidentally, just the day after General Cariappa had left town (Mukherjee 2012, 35–36). The Ministry of Defence claimed that the policy had the prior approval of the three chiefs (Pizey was clear that it did not) and gave the services only two days' notice to lodge objections before it became official policy. The three service chiefs—in the case of the army and air force, still British officers—scrambled quickly to block it, and they were able to extract a promise from Nehru that it would not be implemented immediately. But this was only a temporary victory, and in 1955, after the retirement of General Shrinagesh, India downgraded the position of the Commander in Chief to "Chief of Army Staff" (COAS), which was then made coequal with two newly created positions, Chief of the Naval Staff and Chief of the Air Staff (Chari 2012, 183).

The policy has been blamed by senior military officers on Patel or his successor Vellodi, but it could not have happened without the strong backing of Nehru and other senior leaders. Admiral Pizey wrote to Admiral Lord Louis Mountbatten in February 1955, when the decision on the chiefs was implemented, explaining that "We think that certain high-ups in the Party feel that the Commanders in Chief have got, or are getting, too much popularity and, perhaps, power. We believe that in certain quarters there is a feeling of danger if the Services' Chiefs get too much in the public eye as they may follow the same 'practice' as certain Service Chiefs in other countries have done!"[35] When Lloyd Rudolph and Susanne Rudolph interviewed the prime minister in February 1963 and asked him about the downgrading of the Commander in Chief position to COAS, he told them plainly that "As far as the demotion from Commander-in-Chief to merely Chief of the Army Staff was concerned . . . yes that it certainly was a deliberate decision to reduce the role of the military on the Indian Scene."[36]

Nehru also recognized the potential danger of letting senior generals stay in their positions too long, in case they got too secure and developed political ambitions. This was a particular issue because

due to the rapid departure of British officers in 1947–1948, the most
senior Indian officers had attained their ranks at comparatively
young ages, when in peacetime they might have still had seven or
eight years of service ahead of them: Cariappa retired in 1952 at the
age of 53, Thimayya and Thorat at 55 (V. K. Singh 2005, 47). These
officers, not unnaturally, were quite frustrated at having to retire
when still in the prime of life. Cariappa in particular spent much of
the two decades after leaving the service in 1953 going round high
officials to offer his somewhat eccentric policy ideas and reassure them
that he was ready to serve the nation in any capacity.[37] But Nehru was
determined not to extend the generals' tenures, and in 1955, on the
retirement of Commander in Chief Shrinagesh, the normal tenure
was in fact reduced from four to three years. Nehru also refused to
bring generals into Indian politics at a high level as state governors.[38]
The method of sending senior officers that had been employed
with Cariappa far away lest they create trouble at home was also
used with several others: General Thimayya was given a UN peace-
keeping role in Cyprus on his retirement, and (after Nehru's death)
General J. N. Chaudhuri was called in unexpectedly by Defence
Minister Chavan to be told that after his retirement he was going to
be posted as High Commissioner to Canada (Chaudhuri 1978, 195;
Guha 2007, 749).

Another important step was to rein in the military intelligence
services. Prior to 1947 the military had its own very active Military
Intelligence department (MI) that monitored internal as well as
external threats. In a different environment this might have developed into a real problem for India's politicians. One of the main
reasons it did not was that the British, given their suspicions of
Indians' loyalties, had staffed the higher positions in MI entirely
with British officers until just before independence. The huge loss
of senior British MI personnel and expertise in 1947 and the negative
association of MI's domestic intelligence functions with colonial
attempts to defeat India's freedom fighters left the military unable
to perform this domestic intelligence role. The military's domestic
intelligence functions—though not initially their monitoring of external threats—were transferred over to the Home Ministry's own
Intelligence Bureau.[39]

The generals quickly learned to adapt to the new system. Many of the generals had spent twenty or twenty-five years in a system in which they had been given considerable leeway to speak their minds on service matters and had paid little heed to what politicians thought. But in the new India that was the quick route to being passed over for promotion. When Major General Rajendra Sinhji (later COAS) took over as General Officer Commanding (GOC) Delhi and East Punjab (1947–1948) in late 1947, he told Brigadier J. N. Chaudhuri (later to take over as COAS after the China debacle in 1962) that "I want to brief you about all these new people now in charge here, whom I have met but you have not. Your very direct ways of dealing with all and sundry won't work in this set up. You will have to be a little more circumspect in your method of dealing with the politicians of your own country. . . . You have to be more of a courtier."[40]

Compositional Strategies

The Congress leadership's other big effort was to use what Horowitz terms compositional strategies to prevent any ethnic group within the military from being large enough to coordinate against the political leadership (Horowitz 1985, 534–536). The British had done this in several different ways: by only employing reliable (that is, British) officers in key military roles, by hedging the risk from Indian troops with large numbers of Gorkha and British troops, by recruiting officers disproportionately from martial class and "loyal" groups, and through the use of fixed company compositions that balanced different castes and religions within a battalion against each other.

The new Indian state continued some of these strategies, and developed new compositional strategies of its own. One important step here was to open up future *officer* recruitment to members of all regions and communities, not just to members of the "martial classes." This had been done initially as a temporary step by the British in 1940, to encourage Indians to take up emergency commissions, but Defence Minister Baldev Singh confirmed the policy as permanent in 1947. Several well-informed defense analysts and former high officials have pointed to the political coup-proofing value of developing a diverse officer corps. Former Defence Secretary S. S. Khera pointed out that "The heterogeneous mixture of officers from different parts of the country is represented throughout the structure of the officer cadres, and right up to the high command. They would not hold together for long, if they participated in an attempted coup" (Khera 1968, 85). The influential security writer and advisor K. (Krishnaswamy) Subrahmanyam, reflecting in the early 1980s on the reasons for India's success in keeping the military out of politics, also highlighted the important role of this ethnic diversity among the officer corps:

> The Indian armed forces have developed as national forces with their personnel drawn from all over the country. The officers too are recruited from all the states. . . . The same type of territorial distribution applies to the Air Force and Naval chiefs as well. The officer corps of the Indian Armed Forces does not run the risk of being drawn from a restricted area or predominantly from one or two ethnic groups. It is only when the officer corps is drawn from restricted areas and ethnic groups and they are trained and passed through a single training institution that it tends to develop a degree of cohesiveness and like-mindedness and the Army tends to develop political ambitions. . . . Therefore, there is no risk of a cohesive, like-minded officer corps from the landed gentry posing a threat to the Republic. Today's officer is from the lower middle class and organized working class and he shares values and aspirations with the rest of the country. (Subrahmanyam 1997, 12)

Consistent with the desire to maximize the number of different places and streams producing officers, a new National Defence Academy was opened near Pune in Maharashtra in 1954, far from the main Indian Military Academy at Dehra Dun where it had originally been planned. Enayat Habibullah, the academy's first commander, reports that the original idea was hatched by Sardar Patel and N. V. Gadgil, a powerful politician from Maharashtra, together with Defence Secretary H. M. Patel, over the strong objections of the top officers (Habibullah 1981, 98).

Another very important step that was taken, consistent with this desire to limit the ability of the officer corps to coordinate against the state, was to make sure that India's top army officers were much more diverse than the officer corps as a whole. As Figure 3.1 shows, the Punjabi Hindu and Sikh communities occupied around half the top positions in the officer corps in 1951, and therefore posed the biggest potential threat to the regime, should they coordinate. So from 1947 to the late 1970s, the strategy seems to have been to make sure that no chiefs were chosen from Punjab. All but one of the Army COASs were from outside the traditional Punjabi heartland of the army: a Coorgi from Mysore (Cariappa, 1949–1953), a Rajput (Rajendrasinhji, 1953–1955) a Maratha (Shrinagesh, 1955–1957) another Coorgi (Thimayya, 1957–1961), a Bengali (Chaudhuri, 1962–1967), a Tamil (Kumaramangalam, 1967–1970), a Parsi (Manekshaw, 1969–1973), a Kannadiga (Bewoor, 1963–1975), and a Kashmiri (Raina, 1975–1978). The only exception to the implicit "no Punjabis" norm, General Thapar (1961–1962) was appointed out of turn, alledgedly, because of his perceived pliability by Defence Minister V. K. Krishna Menon (Verma 1988, 122).[41] There is of course no publicly available document that states why any of these appointments were made, as the COAS and the Prime Minister discuss the selection verbally, and each individual decision could no doubt have been justified on several grounds. But it seems very unusual that in an army whose senior officer corps was around 50 percent Punjabi during these years, a Punjabi was in the top job for only a year out of India's first two and a half decades. Sardar Surjit Singh Majithia, Deputy Defence Minister 1952–1962, was frank in telling Stephen P. Cohen in 1964 that Krishna Menon "did attempt to cut down the number of Punjabis in the military, [he] felt that there were too many of them."[42]

That is certainly the way that many Sikhs saw it and continued to see it for several decades.[43] The Sikh Akali Dal organization protested to Nehru and the President of India as early as 1953 about the "discriminatory allocation of high area commands and promotions consequent to the retirement of General Cariappa [that] have given the rudest shock to even the most complacent of Sikhs."[44] And in

1957 Sikhs again complained loudly when Lieutenant General Thimayya was selected as COAS to replace General Shrinagesh, ahead of two very successful and well regarded Sikh generals, Lieutenant General Sant Singh (Eastern Command) and Lieutenant General Kulwant Singh (Western Command). This decision prompted Sant Singh, who had been favored by many for the position, to retire immediately from the army (Thorat 1986, 173). Nonetheless, from the perspective of ethnic hedging against potential political risks, the steps that the Indian government took to diversify its top generals made a lot of sense.

Another compositional issue that had to be decided was the place of Muslims in the new army. Should the army replace the Muslims from the units which had been transferred to Pakistan? The decision here, reflecting the more general sense in the 1950s, was that there should be no overt ban on Muslims but no special help for them either, especially as reservations for Muslims were seen as having been part of the divide-and-rule politics that had led to partition. Without reservations, however, the proportion of Muslim officers declined steadily over the next few decades with the emigration of many of the elite and professional Muslim families who had once sent their sons into the army. The few Muslim officers who remained in India after partition, though, got high-profile positions meant to demonstrate the army's and the country's aspirations to inclusion: Major General Anis Ahmad Khan was appointed the independent country's first Muslim Major General in September 1949, to wide press coverage and served as director of supplies and transport from 1950 to 1953.[45] Major General Enayat Habibullah served as the National Defence Academy Commandant from January 1953 to December 1958. And Major Mohamed Mirza commanded the prestigious President's Bodyguard in the late 1950s. It is perhaps worth noting, though, that these positions, important though they were, did not involve the active control and direction of the most strategically important corps or frontline units (Khalidi 2002).

Balance Outside the Army

Before 1947 one of the major strategies that had been used to hedge any potential risk from Indian troops was to "balance outside the army," using large numbers of British troops and twenty battalions of Gorkhas from Nepal to hedge the risk of Indian troops rebelling (Horowitz 1985, 534–536). This policy was expensive, because India paid for this "insurance" by diverting scarce foreign currency to pay for more expensive European troops and officers, as well as the money for wages, pensions, and recruitment activities that went to Nepal. The British troops were now, of course, all gone. The Indian government apparently heard in April 1947 that the British were trying to monopolize recruitment of Gorkhas after independence, and Sardar Patel intervened to make sure that he and Nehru's close Indian civil service confidant Girija Shankar Bajpai and a senior Indian Army officer (Brigadier A. A. "Jicks" Rudra) were on hand to represent the Congress position, which was to offer Nepal and the Gorkhas as good terms as those the British were offering (and in the case of opportunities for Nepalis to get commissions, better terms) (Palit 1997, 297–308). The initial agreement was hashed out in May 1947, and the final agreement signed on November 9, 1947, allocated six regiments to India and four (the Second, Sixth, Seventh, and Tenth Gurkha Rifles) to the British forces. Whether the immediate motivation for this was to preserve a future loyal hedging force for India's political leadership or primarily to prevent the British from monopolizing Gorkha troops that they could use throughout Asia in a way that might be contrary to Indian interests is still unclear, as there is no detailed discussion of the topic in the Nehru or Patel archives. In any event, India got far more Gorkhas than it bargained for, because the Nepalese government insisted that each man have a free choice as to whether he wanted to serve with the regiments that had been allotted to India or those allotted to Britain. Most of the Gorkhas, much more willing to serve under Indian officers than the British had presumed and unwilling to go off to Britain's next overseas adventure after having been on overseas deployments almost continuously from 1939 to 1947, opted for service in the Indian Army. Only 1,900 of the 6,000 men whose votes are recorded at the time of partition opted to stay with British units (Des Chene 1991, 205–207). So the Indian government, unexpectedly, had to accommodate a much larger and considerably more expensive Gorkha force than it had anticipated. On the other hand this force, with close to a fifth of

India's infantry battalions after partition, did act as an additional hedge against any short-term problem with the rest of the army.

Defending the Army's Recruitment Structure

The Congress Party and India's politicians, as we have seen, reined in the army in many ways, but had not dismantled its core regimental structure and class-recruitment policies. The army's leadership was determined to preserve these, because it saw them as crucial to its effectiveness and cohesion. At least four of the army chiefs in the 1950s and 1960s—Cariappa (1949–1953), Thimayya (1957–1961), Chaudhuri (1962–1966), and Manekshaw (1969–1973)—as well as several other senior generals are on record as supporting class recruitment to the army.[46] The generals therefore walked a delicate line, publicly proclaiming their determination to broaden the colonial army into a true national army, while arguing privately against any large scale structural change on the grounds that this would endanger the country's security. The army dealt with the political pressure to broaden its recruitment base using all the methods that had been developed by the colonial state over the previous decades, especially those techniques used to blunt political criticism during the 1939–1945 war: publicly maintain that the army was open to all, even if that was not the case; raise a few new units with members of underrepresented groups and give these new units a lot of publicity; and conceal as much information as possible about actual levels of representation and recruitment on the grounds of national security.

First, a few weeks after taking office in January 1949, the first Indian Commander in Chief, General Cariappa, passed an Army Order that stated that "recruitment to the Army will be open to all classes (and) no particular class of Indian nationals is to be denied the opportunity of serving in the Indian Army" (Khanduri 2006, 216–217). This order was released to the press, reiterated by the Defence Minister in parliament, and given very wide publicity.[47] On his many trips around the country during 1949 General Cariappa hammered the message home that there had been a decisive break with the past, telling a press conference in Calcutta in March 1949, for instance, that he found the theory of martial and nonmartial provinces "horrible" and "nauseating," then going on to tell audiences in

Bangalore and Lucknow that the Indian Army now recognized only one province and one class: Indians.[48] Just how the army could preserve class regiments that mandated the recruitment of specified caste and religious groups in each battalion on the one hand and not recognize caste, province, and class on the other was not, however, made clear. The second thing that the Indian Army did, just as it had done with the creation of the "49th Bengalees" [*sic*] in World War I and the Mahar, Assam, and Bihar Regiments in World War II, was to establish a few new units from excluded groups to demonstrate that it had become more inclusive. These new units, small though they were in the overall context of army recruitment, were then given the maximum amount of publicity. In April 1949, on his second public visit to Calcutta after taking office, Cariappa announced to a receptive audience that the Infantry was going to recruit a new company of Bengalis which, it was hoped, would help train future Bengali units.[49] This unit was given very extensive press coverage, out of all proportion to its 120 recruits, and Cariappa lost no opportunity to mention it at every stop. Cariappa also made serious efforts to reassure regional politicians that their provinces' men were doing well under the new recruitment norms, telling Bengal's Irrigation and Home (Defence) Minister Bhupati Majumdar in October 1949, for example, how impressed he was with the fine performance of the new Bengali troops he had enlisted in the Territorial Army.[50] And in 1957 a second company of Bengalis was added to the second battalion of the Parachute Regiment (Praval 1975, 338–341). To support the idea that recruitment had changed in a large way and reduce pressure from politicians, new recruiting *melas* were also held in Bihar, Madras, Orissa, and other provinces that were underrepresented.

Cariappa's publicity masterstroke was the new Guards regiment that was formed in April 1949. This new elite regiment, given wide publicity by the army and in the press as Cariappa's "special project," recruited only six footers to its elite first battalion and was the first infantry regiment to explicitly draw on recruits from across the country.[51] The Guards regiment represented the unity of India, and the regiment was given the highest rank in the order of precedence of the infantry regiments, again symbolically showing that the larger Indian collective was superior to the individual martial classes.

Cariappa had been posted to the British Guards Regiment earlier in his career, so the usual explanation given for his interest in forming an Indian Guards regiment is that it stemmed from that experience. But the first formal proposal for an Indian Guards regiment was in fact made during World War II by none other than Winston Churchill, who thought of it as an integral part of the British Household Brigade, and as a way of bringing India and Britain closer together.[52] In any event, by the end of Cariappa's first year as Commander in Chief, the army could now point to a new declared policy, a new high-status regiment, and a number of new army companies that manifested its real commitment to change, even if all these new units together represented only a handful of battalions out of the army's total strength of 166 battalions of infantry and armored corps units.

In private, though, the army leadership continued to emphasize that any radical shift in recruitment policy would greatly threaten its ability to defend the country. Cariappa blocked a request to consider the reemployment of ex–Indian National Army men by writing to Nehru that "We appreciate their part but by forsaking their oath of allegiance they had breached the ethics of a soldier. . . . By including them back the very fibre of Army's discipline will be disintegrated. I recommend their employment elsewhere" (Historical division archives, cited in Khanduri 2000, 56). In the late 1950s, Defence Minister Krishna Menon, prodded by some Congress and opposition MPs, asked the army why it was not implementing the reservation policy that applied to Scheduled Castes and Scheduled Tribes in other branches of government (Khanduri 2006, 216–217). The COAS at the time, General Thimayya, was the proud product of a class regiment, the 4/19 Hyderabad, later renamed the Kumaon Regiment, and he like other officers opposed any significant change in recruitment policy. So in a letter back to Menon, he first emphasized that there had already been a lot of substantial changes since independence. The January 1949 order abolishing caste, religious, and regional discrimination in the armed services and opening up recruitment in every branch outside of the Infantry, Armored Corps, and Artillery had been an important change, he said. Thimayya also pointed to the new mixed-class units that had been created, as a result of which 10 percent of the armored corps and artillery units now had mixed classes (he was very careful not to mention the proportion of mixed units in the infantry, which I estimate as only 4 percent at this time), and expressed the hope that things would improve even further in the years ahead.

Then Thimayya got to the real point, his argument that changing the army too much risked endangering India's security. "It is laudable," he wrote, "that a break has been called to be made to the present class composition: however, care should be taken to see that the new proposed arrangement should under no circumstance impair the fighting qualities and cohesiveness of units based on intimate sense of kinsmanship and traditions." He went on to say that "It is easier to take an academic view of this matter but it would not give the quality to the army that we must have. Equally, we need to see that the Indian soldier is deeply imbued with regional, linguistic and social ties. Any radical departure from the present concept of class composition in the fighting arms is, therefore, fraught with grave danger and I do not recommend it" (Khanduri 2006, 216–17).[53] Krishna Menon and the civil servants apparently accepted Thimayya's points, and they left the core of the class recruitment system in place. Krishna Menon was certainly prepared to push the army in many other matters, so it seems that either he was convinced by Thimayya's arguments or he did not feel that the issue of class composition was important enough to push compared to his other goals for the armed forces.

If, despite public declarations of nondiscrimination and substantial change in policy in response to political pressure, the practice or recruitment was pretty much the same, it was obvious that any widespread release of information about the ethnic composition of the army, as was routine before 1939, would lead to big problems. So the army and Ministry of Defence decided to continue the policy of secrecy about the army's actual force composition that had been introduced during the war. For instance, in 1940 Pandit Kunzru, P. N. Sapru, and others had complained in the Council of State that they were not being given figures they had asked for on the composition of the army, particularly in terms of the British-Indian balance among new officers.[54] But the army continued to ignore requests for information. For instance, in 1942 the Government of India had emphasized in secret telegraph correspondence with the India Office on the composition of the army that "we are not repeat not giving publicity to these figures in India in spite of requests in the Assembly and elsewhere to do so."[55] The Ministry of Defence's consistent post-1948 approach to questions about ethnic imbalances or the exclusion of particular groups has been the same: to restate the general principle of nondiscrimination to which the army was committed in all new units, and then to deny all requests for more detailed information on the grounds that it is a security threat or not in the public interest to provide such data.[56] Deputy Prime Minister Patel replied to an MP's question about discrimination in recruitment, in a statement that was clearly misleading, because it ignored the army's insistence on class units, that "recruitment . . . is open to all personnel of Indian domicile irrespective of class, creed or religion, who satisfy the conditions laid down as regards age, physical standard and educational qualifications."[57] The usual parliamentary replies to questions about class recruitment to this day combine some part of General Cariappa's 1949 order that "all *new* Infantry and Armoured regiments now open to members of all provinces, and 'recruitment to the Army will be open to all classes (and) no particular class of Indian nationals is to be denied the opportunity of serving in the Indian Army,'" with Defence Minister Baldev Singh's February 1948 and (March 1949 statements that recruits would no longer be classified as belonging to "martial" or "nonmartial" classes, and recruitment to the army would "henceforth be open to all Indians, specifically including Scheduled Castes, Muslims, and members of other regions and communities that had been excluded."[58]

Nehru could take all these early and important steps, crucially, because the Congress Party was a strong, broad-based national party with wide legitimacy, capable of governing the country and resolving most significant political controversies within the party. This altered the balance of power between the military and civilians in India from 1947 to 1957 when compared to Pakistan, even if it did not in itself guarantee that the Congress Party would (as it did) carry out specific defense reforms that would permanently reduce the threat of a coup. In Pakistan, by contrast, the fundamental weakness of the Muslim League (about which more in Chapter 6) compared to the civil service and military increased the leverage of the latter, as the party failed to agree on a constitution for the best part of a decade and gradually disintegrated. The corruption of politics and the inability of the League to govern effectively—every Pakistani province had been placed under emergency rule for at least some time by the early 1950s—gradually made the army think that military rule might not be a bad option. This naturally occurred to some officers earlier than others. As early as 1951 General Ayub Khan apparently told one of his senior Pakistani colleagues that "This Army has a much greater and wider role to play than people realize. The C.-in-C., in fact, is a more important man than the P.M. in our country as the situation stands today" (Pataudi 1978, 132).[59]

In India, by contrast, the Congress Party was an effective governing party, which provided no opportunity for the army to contemplate "improving" things by intervention. The party-stability aspect of this has been well covered by Weiner, Hardgrave, Kohli, Oldenburg, Tudor, and others, so there is little point in repeating that here. But sometimes overlooked, and perhaps just as important as the overall strength of the Congress Party, were the specific policy decisions over caste, language, and religion that Nehru took in the late 1940s and early 1950s in the nonmilitary realm. These decisions were vital because, as Horowitz points out, "To understand ethnically based military coups, civilian and military ethnic politics must be viewed in tandem. Perhaps the two spheres are not quite a seamless web, but they are at least a single web" (Horowitz 1985, 459–460). If India had not made the right decisions on religious and ethnic politics in the 1950s, in other words, the consequences for civil-military relations might have been profound, as they were elsewhere.

Two of these decisions—on caste and linguistic states—were at first opposed by Nehru, but he had to reverse his stance because of deep opposition from the south. In a more hierarchical and less institutionalized party, such as the Muslim League, this regional opposition would not have been crucial. But in an internally democratic party like Congress, in which there were many strong regional and national leaders, even Nehru sometimes had to bend with the wind.

One very important early decision, enshrined in the constitution, was to defuse the power of two macroidentity conflicts—religion and north-south—that might have dangerously divided the country and the army. The Constituent Assembly decided, first, that religious claims for political reservations or jobs in public employment were not legitimate in the new secular state, and second, not to make an immediate decision that would have divided the country on the question of an official national language.

In addition, more as matter of good fortune than a well-thought-out strategy, the Congress was forced in 1951 and 1952 to concede to the demands of two big popular mobilizations in the south. The first of these, in Madras in 1951, demanded the continuation of job reservations for the "backward classes," which had just been ruled unconstitutional by the Madras High Court on the grounds of caste discrimination. Nehru, who was initially opposed to conceding reservations (which he hoped would die out), ultimately changed his mind after pressure from Congress politicians in the south, where backward caste reservations had been in place since the 1920s. So in 1951 parliament passed an amendment to the constitution, providing that measures to help "backward classes" would not be invalidated by the antidiscrimination clauses in the constitution. The practical effect of this loophole over the years, especially when combined with the ban on religious discrimination, has been to encourage many different groups in society to mobilize along "backward class" lines rather than along, say, lines of religion. The advantage of caste mobilization, from the perspective of introducing crosscutting cleavages into the polity, is that caste is much more a state-level identity group than a national one. So the hundreds of different "backward class" mobilizations also help to crosscut larger north-south and religious macroconflicts. That has been enormously helpful from the perspective of conflict moderation.

The second movement in the south, again in Madras, was a mass mobilization in late 1952 to secure a separate state of Andhra for Telugu speakers, who felt overshadowed by the Tamil-speaking majority in the state. The Congress had for several decades been committed to the idea of linguistic states, and seriously considered creating Andhra and other linguistic states in the Constituent Assembly after independence. But in the aftermath of a bloody partition the party ultimately decided not to, mainly because of worries that it might weaken national identity as well as lead to separatism. The Dar committee, which considered the issue, pointed out that "Not only the groups whose cases we are considering, but many other linguistic groups in so-called homogenous provinces, as also many other communal groups, who have as strong an individuality as these linguistic groups possess, are not happy in their present surroundings. And if once this principle is recognized, it will set the ball rolling for the disintegration of the entire country. And we do not think that case is any further advanced by the fact that these groups are not only discontented groups but also linguistic groups."[60]

In a speech in mid-1952 Nehru admitted that he had "never been very enthusiastic about linguistic provinces," and that "Any decision that might come in the way of [national] unity should be delayed till we have laid a strong foundation for it. Because of that, I for my own part have frankly—and I should be quite frank with the House—not taken any aggressive or positive step in regard to the formation of linguistic provinces" (Nehru 1963).

But after the death of a leading Andhra activist, Potti Sriramalu, in December 1952 after a long hunger strike in pursuit of a separate state, and the widespread riots that followed, Nehru and the Congress Party leadership again decided that it was better to concede the demand than stand firm. Important here, as with the decision on reservations, was that the Congress Party had many strong leaders from the south who could pressure the leadership to reverse course. The Congress Party set up a States Reorganisation Committee to consider the whole question of whether more linguistic states should be carved out after Andhra; the committee sanctioned several new states and created a framework for satisfying future demands. Like the institutionalization of "backward class," the institutionalization of language as a legitimate identity to make political demands has also helped to undercut larger cleavages that might otherwise have been very damaging.

The recognition of Andhra in 1952, the formation of the States Reorganisation Committee, and the backing down on the issue of caste reservations were all proof that Congress was committed to a federal India—as long as it was understood that it was also the Union of India—and that Congress itself had a federal structure that forced the party to pay attention to regional pressures. Nehru certainly did not want any sort of federal structure in the army, however. When Ravi Shankar Shukla spoke up in 1948 in favor of provincial regiments, which would benefit his own underrepresented Central Provinces, Nehru was quick to shoot down the proposal, arguing that creating regiments with a purely provincial label would only encourage provincialism and even separatism (Parthasarathi 1985, 175–187).

But federalism did help to "coup proof" the new country in two very important ways. First, the federal structure together with the broad legitimacy of the party helped reduce the ethnic fissures in the country at large, which meant that the army never felt obliged to step in to "save the country from the politicians" as in Pakistan. Second, a genuine federal structure with multiple poles of authority— Delhi, Mumbai, Bangalore, Calcutta, Bhopal, Ahmadabad—also made it much harder for the military to seize power quickly and easily. Federalism itself, in other words, created big coordination problems for potential coup makers. Defence Minister Chavan, when interviewed by the Rudolphs in February 1963 about why India had not had a coup like Pakistan's, answered that "The federal structure of the country . . . made it very unlikely that the kind of takeover which was possible elsewhere would be possible here. Particularly he mentioned Pakistan. He thought it would be very difficult to carry out the coup in India as happened in Pakistan. He specifically mentioned the state centers of power and said at one point something like that Delhi could not so easily control them."[61] Other senior politicians interviewed by Stephen P. Cohen from 1963 to 1965 also mentioned India's heterogeneity and regional diversity as an important factor in preventing a coup. In 1963 Frank Anthony told him that the "Indian Army was too big, too diverse for a coup. [There are] too many communities."[62] Lieutenant General S. D. Verma thought that the Indian Army was too diverse with too many classes to have a coup. And Aruna Asaf Ali, interviewed in January 1965, told Cohen that India would not go the way of Pakistan because "the Army will not function on an All-India plane, very severe pulls exist on an all-India basis."[63]

Conclusion

It is easy for many Indian observers to persuade themselves that the Indian military, in terms of its willingness to intervene, was just different, more professional and committed to civilian oversight than the generals in Pakistan. But there is little discernible difference, in terms of broad political attitudes and culture, between those officers recruited between 1919 and 1939 who opted for India and those who opted for Pakistan. As a read through the confidential reports of Indian cadets at Sandhurst in the 1920s shows, these men had many common traits, and had also been through powerful assimilative experiences, at British-style public schools, at Sandhurst, and later in their regiments.[64] When the opportunity presented itself, in the late 1960s and early 1970s, at least a few of these Indian officers were quite open—in a way reminiscent of their Pakistani Batchmates— about the corruption of domestic politics and the need for some firm leadership, perhaps to be provided by some former army officers. General Cariappa, most famously, suggested at various times in the mid-1960s and again in 1970 that political parties ought to be disbanded for a time, that the vote should be restricted to the educated, that students should be prohibited from political activities, that the country might benefit from a period of (constitutional) army administration, and that the fourth general elections might be postponed until "law and order" were restored by the president.[65] This followed on his earlier approving remarks about the 1958 coup in Pakistan, as well as his suggestions in 1965 that president's rule might be imposed on the country for a few years until law and order was restored (Guha 2007, 749).[66] When Cariappa's 1970 statements were condemned by Congress politicians, and Cariappa talked of entering politics himself, he was supported at a press conference by several retired military officers, including Lieutenant General S. P. P. Thorat, Air Marshal Ranjan Dutt, Rear Admiral S. G. Karmarker, and a bevy of retired Brigadiers and Colonels, who told journalists that they "felt that the General's entry into politics would provide an element missing in the Indian political scene."[67] So it is not hard to imagine that with a major political crisis similar to that in Pakistan in the 1950s, some of India's most senior officers might, like their Pakistani colleagues, have been tempted to think that intervening in politics might have provided some necessary stability to the country.

That India's army officers never organized a coup in this way is the result of several factors. The fact that Congress was a strong, legitimate, and broad-based party meant that there was no festering political crisis in which the army felt it had to intervene. In addition, Nehru and Congress, in part because the army had long been identified with alien rule, were determined and skillful in using their strong position to rein in the military as soon as they could, and the measures they took from 1947 to 1955 helped ensure that any future Indian generals who might have thought of a coup would find it much harder to implement than their former army Batchmates in Rawalpindi and Karachi. The Congress Party leadership in the country also implemented new policies that helped ensure that the most divisive cleavages in the country were crosscut by new identities of caste and language. And last, Nehru, Patel, and others refused to allow new regiments and units to be created that would have institutionalized in the army the same cleavages that were most controversial in the country at large.

The news was not all good, however. Politicians and bureaucrats in the 1950s, in retrospect, had put too much emphasis on the benefits of command and control, and had not thought enough about the costs. Krishna Menon's bullying and interference in military decision making and the military's internal hierarchy and organization—for instance by cultivating his own links with favorite officers and encouraging juniors to inform on seniors—was deeply destructive (Thorat 1986, 175–178, 190–191; Verma 1988, 100–121). Several senior officers such as Lieutenant General S. D. Verma were either forced out or retired early in disgust. In 1959 the COAS, General Thimayya, tendered his own resignation. Nehru encouraged Thimayya to withdraw the resignation with promises that he would help to prevent Krishna Menon's interference and restore the balance, but then he publicly criticized Thimayya in parliament, and Thimayya's failure to resign a second time meant that the army's moment of leverage was lost (Thorat 1986, 176–178).

The restrictions the politicians were putting on the army and the various coordination challenges they were introducing, though functional in terms of coup proofing, were also preventing the army from coordinating and planning effectively against an external enemy. This was especially dangerous because the country's politicians were pursuing a foreign policy from 1959 to 1962 with regard to China that was premised on assumptions about Krishna Menon's ability to deal with China diplomatically and about the Indian military's preparation and capacities that bore increasingly little relationship to the facts on the ground.

4

From 1962 to Bluestar

Introduction

INDIA'S CIVILIAN leadership worked hard after independence to reduce the potential threat the army posed to democracy, with strong civilian oversight and policies that created significant coordination challenges for any officers tempted to follow the example of their Batchmates in Pakistan and launch a coup. This policy worked well from the perspective of making sure the civilian leadership was firmly in control. But it was not good for India's military preparation and effectiveness, especially when the civilian leadership pushed an aggressive "forward policy" on the frontier with China without checking with the generals first as to whether the army was strong enough and sufficiently prepared to follow through (Maxwell 1970, 171–256). Despite periodic warnings from several high-ranking officers about the threat from China and the dangers of the forward policy, Prime Minister Nehru, his intelligence chief B. N. Mullik, Defence Minister V. K. Krishna Menon, and several of the generals that they promoted to senior positions were convinced that there was no serious danger (Dalvi 1969). They were wrong. In October 1962, Chinese troops invaded and quickly overwhelmed Indian Army units in the northeast, shocking the political leadership and the country as a whole.

This chapter examines the three major challenges to civil-military relations in the decades after 1962. First, in the aftermath of defeat, India faced a major challenge to the civil-military control strategies it had evolved since independence. The country was now forced to expand the army rapidly to meet the threat from China, and as I show, most of this expansion was done by recruiting heavily from the existing "martial classes" in the infantry and armored corps, rather than by forming new all-India units as politicians had been led to expect in 1949. The obvious concern, from the politicians' point of view, was that the generals might, as General J. N. Chaudhuri later put it, "get ideas above their station." There was no great difference in political outlook, as we have discussed, between the pre-1939 commissioned officers on the Indian side of the border who were now in command of the army and their former Batchmates in Pakistan. When Lloyd and Susanne Rudolph interviewed General Chaudhuri in February 1963 and asked him about his former Sandhurst batchmate Ayub Khan's 1958 coup in Pakistan, "He said that he thought what must have happened was that Ayub Khan, finding Iskander Mirza playing *ducks and drakes* with the political situation in Pakistan had felt obliged to move in and 'put things right.' "[1]

So how could India avoid a situation in which the senior generals felt that they had the freedom of action to "put things right"? The most important thing that had already been done, as we have discussed, was that the Congress Party provided stable government and that important decisions over linguistic states reorganization, religion, and caste in the late 1940s and early 1950s had helped to prevent the sort of conflicts that drew the army into politics in Pakistan. But the politicians were still understandably worried, by the Congress Party and Nehru's loss of legitimacy after the China debacle, by growing challenges to Congress on national and state politics, and by the strategic need to double the size of the army and provide more operational autonomy to the top generals.

The political leadership and bureaucrats in the Ministry of Defence dealt with these worries in several ways. First, despite persistent pressure from top army officers they refused to change the main elements of the command and control structures they had introduced from 1947 to 1955, such as having three nominally equal service chiefs rather than a Chief of the Defence Staff drawn from the army and having many important decisions approved by a parallel Ministry of Defence bureaucracy. The government also continued to diversify the ethnicity of the top generals and lieutenant generals as it had done in the 1950s, and to keep tabs through the intelligence services on what these officers were up to.

As time went on, the government also implemented several new measures to deal with the potential threat of this new larger army as well as specific worries about the loyalty of particular groups such as the Sikhs and Nagas. The main strategy employed was to "balance" the army with large new paramilitary forces drawn from a much wider cross-section of the Indian population.[2] India's paramilitary forces, which were only 29,000 strong in 1961 just before the China war, grew to 202,000 a decade later, to 258,000 by 1980, and to more than 497,000 by 1990.[3] This balancing was not intended to provide a direct military hedge against the regular army, as was the Saudi National Guard (Quinlivan 1999) or the General Service Units in Uganda and Kenya (Horowitz 1985, 546–547). The paramilitaries did provide some sort of hedge in and around the capital, New Delhi, where they outnumbered the infantry, but in training, equipment, and capacity they were clearly no match for the regular army. Their more important function was as an indirect hedge, standing in for the army in delicate and politically fraught internal policing duties, thereby relieving the army from these roles and making it less likely that it would be drawn into politics.

Beginning in the 1970s, the Ministry of Defence also finally began to do what it had promised to do in 1949; seriously start to increase the number and proportion of mixed units in the infantry and armored corps. Finally, the army seems to have specifically hedged the risk from several groups it was most worried about, such as Sikhs and Nagas, by changing the location of their bases and deploying them in barracks adjacent to other army units, in the same way that the British had done.

A second challenge, after the death of Nehru in 1964 and the struggle for succession in the Congress Party, was political. With the breakdown of the "Congress system" and the increasingly authoritarian policies by pursued Prime Minister Indira Gandhi in the 1970s, was it possible for the army to remain above the political fray, even as government and opposition political leaders might look to it for support? The army's leadership, very concerned about the threat political involvements might pose to its organizational structure and military effectiveness, was determined to stay out of politics, avoiding calls both by the government to play a more supportive role in the emergency and by opposition figures to disobey what they claimed were illegal instructions from government. By and large, as I show, the army's top officers did a good job in insulating the force from these threats.

The third challenge, perhaps the most serious threat of all to the army's historic regimental structure, was the Sikh militancy of the late 1970s and 1980s. This militancy demonstrated again the potential dangers of class regiments for internal security and threatened for a while to lead to a major transformation in the army's regimental and recruitment systems. In the end, though, for both operational reasons (traditional class units were still viewed as more effective) and the strength of the "class regiment" constituency within the army, these attempts to fundamentally reform the regimental structure were beaten back.

Defeat and Expansion

The disaster of the 1962 India-China war highlighted several general problems with the military structure that had been put in place since 1950.[4] Most of these problems were identified in the inquiry carried out in response to parliamentary pressure immediately after the war, headed by Lieutenant General T. B. Henderson Brooks and Brigadier Prem Singh Bhagat. Though still officially classified despite several right to information requests, extracts from the inquiry report have been extensively leaked by former *Times of London* correspondent Neville Maxwell, both in his book *India's China War* and in a 2001 article in the *Economic and Political Weekly* (Maxwell 1970, 2001).

The biggest problem the war exposed was that the various steps taken in the 1950s to reduce the army's autonomy as an institution, prevent interservice and interintelligence coordination, and keep the top generals away from the big meetings at which policy was decided had been only too effective.[5] Krishna Menon was asked in March 1963 about "how he would account for the Indian military not playing the same role in public life as a good many other developing areas. He said that partly this was due to him. That he had kept a 'tight rein' on them while he was in Government."[6] Krishna Menon had in fact superseded, bullied, and marginalized several of the army's most capable officers, and this and his control over access to Nehru had weakened the army's ability to respond to threats, communicate with politicians about military realities, and protect the country. Even H. M. Patel, the former Defence Secretary who had introduced many of the command and control measures from 1947 to 1953, complained in March 1963 that "What appears to have let our men down was the absence of sufficient previous planning, of the necessary strategic and tactical thinking, and the failure of the civil authority to put the most experienced and capable military leaders in charge. In addition, there may well have been much interference by high civil authority in spheres of purely military concern. . . . There comes to mind immediately a fact which has never been satisfactorily explained, why such a number of senior officers were allowed to retire or resign during the very years when every effort, one would have thought, would have been made to retain them" (Patel 1963, 6).[7]

The top military intelligence officers and officers on the ground had in fact realized several years before the war—and definitely after the 1959 Kongka Pass skirmish—that the "forward policy" risked a major war that India was ill prepared to fight (Maxwell 2001).[8] As early as 1951 a committee headed by Major General M. S. Himmatsinghji had suggested the government strengthen defenses against China after its invasion of Tibet the year before. But the ascendancy of a faction closely allied with Defence Minister Krishna Menon and interference with promotions, ensuring that the diversity of views among the few top generals who had access to the political leadership became narrower and narrower, severely limited the prospects of the political leadership learning anything about the strategic risks they were running. When the Kaul faction within the army took over after General Thapar's promotion as Chief of Army Staff (COAS) in May 1961, there was no longer anyone to challenge the views of Nehru and his intelligence chief B. N. Mullik that the forward policy held no risks. At a meeting on November 2, 1961, the top political and military leadership ordered the army to establish forward posts in areas disputed between the Indians and Chinese.

By mid-1962, the army officers who actually had to implement the policy on the ground were writing memos, as diplomatically phrased as they dared, pleading that "It is imperative that political direction is based on military means. If the two are not co-related there is a danger of creating a situation where we may lose both in the material and moral sense much more than we already have. Thus, there is no short cut to military preparedness to enable us to pursue effectively our present policy" (Maxwell 2001).

The Chinese invasion and defeat of India in 1962 forced India to massively upgrade its military capacity and the size of its army to counter the Chinese threat. As Neville Maxwell says, "Stinted for years, the armed services, and especially of course the Army, were now given almost a blank cheque" (Maxwell 1970, 439). Prior to the Chinese invasion, the Indian Army had nine infantry divisions, one armored division, and a number of miscellaneous brigades, for a total strength of 458,000.[9] As a result of the Indian defeat in late 1962, the government decided to increase the number of infantry divisions from nine to sixteen, with an additional five new reduced-strength divisions and a number of specialized brigades for a total strength of 825,000 men. By March 1963 the army had already recruited 200,000 new officers and men, and had grown to 659,000. This expansion was very expensive, however, and defense spending rose dramatically from INR 2.81 billion in 1961–1962 to INR 3.76 billion in 1962–1963 to INR 8.67 billion in 1963–1964.[10] Recruitment and spending rose sharply every year for the rest of the decade, until the army hit its target of 825,000 just before the 1971 war with Pakistan that led to the independence of East Pakistan as the new state of Bangladesh.[11]

To pay for all this military expansion, other development spending was put on hold, new taxes were imposed, and senior figures flew to Washington to secure promises of $100 million in military aid (Maxwell 1970, 439). Krishna Menon, the powerful Defence Minister who had humbled and bullied many of the top generals, was forced to resign on November 7, 1962, after the senior Congress Party leaders made it clear to Nehru that either Krishna Menon had to go or Nehru himself might be forced out of office.[12] The new attitude of the public and many MPs was that political meddling in the army had been disastrous for the country, and that the military had to be given everything it needed to defend the country from China and Pakistan.

The obvious problem, from the perspective of the politicians and bureaucrats, was how to prevent this newly expanded and well-equipped army from getting too big for its boots, especially now the costs of the previous overaggressive supervision of the military were clear to see. As General J. N. Chaudhuri, the new COAS, put it, now that the army had been doubled to 825,000 men "Would [the generals] get ideas above their station?" (Chaudhuri 1978, 193). Neville Maxwell quotes a personal letter from Nehru to Bertrand Russell in late 1962, the month after the cease-fire, in which Nehru worried about the "danger of the military mentality spreading in India and the power of the Army increasing" (Maxwell 1970, 440). The army leaders and a few politicians were also, in a post–Krishna Menon world, pressing for a reversal of some of the changes made since 1947. They wanted a unified defense command with an (Army) Chief of Defence Staff (CDS) coordinating things, greater access to policy making so that they would no longer suffer from the politicians making promises that the army could not fulfill, and a greater ability to gather and share intelligence across the services. Major General P. S. Bhagat, who as a brigadier had been one of the two chief investigators into the China debacle, wrote a very diplomatically worded but widely read book in 1965 that highlighted the two central problems many senior officers believed had led to the defeat; first, a militarily inefficient command and control structure, including the lack of a coordinated defense staff with a chief drawn from the army, and second, the development of military policies and strategies by civilians in New Delhi without involving the generals in a timely way to think through their implications (33–37). The classic example of this was Nehru's answer to the press in an interview while returning from Ceylon about the timetable for evicting the Chinese from their forward positions, which sparked off a dangerous war fever in the country at large (Maxwell 1970, 342–343). General Bhagat made a strong plea that in future "Whatever the circumstances, it should be clear that at no stage should political objectives be fixed which are beyond the military means of the country" (1965, 33–34).

Many other serving and retired officers, as well as some politicians, joined Bhagat in the 1960s in calling for the reform of the system and the appointment of a CDS, and many others, including several retired COASs, have spoken up in favor of reform since.[13] The government ultimately decided, however, not to do away with any of the main control strategies that it had developed in the 1950s: bureaucratic control and the division of the armed forces into multiple commands that provided obstacles to army coordination against the state, the close monitoring of top generals, and the policy of ethnically diversifying the top generals. A few efforts were made to improve coordination within existing institutions, with more intelligence sharing and new committees at which people from different branches would be brought around the same table more often. But despite army pressure there would be no new CDS to take the place of the three chiefs and coordinate the armed forces as a whole. And there would be no new military intelligence infrastructure that could make up for the many failings of the civilian Intelligence Bureau's advice on military intelligence before the China war. To balance the growing size and power of the army, there was also a decision to improve the "coup proofing" plans in New Delhi and to greatly increase the size of the country's paramilitary forces.

Expanding the Indian Army

What did the greatly expanded post-1962 Indian Army look like? In Figure 4.1, I show the fixed/single versus mixed composition of the army's infantry and armored battalions from 1947 to the aftermath of the India-Pakistan war in 1972. This graph therefore captures the massive expansion of the army as it doubled in the 1960s, in response to the threats from China and Pakistan (for data sources, see Chapter 5). The top line shows the total growth in battalions as the army doubled in size: the other lines show the growth in fixed units, single-class units, and all-India mixed units.[14] As we can see, the dramatic expansion of the army in the five or six years after 1962 was not achieved by creating lots of new all-India units, as we might have expected given Cariappa's 1949 promise about all "new regiments" being mixed. This was because the army wanted to raise new high-quality units as quickly as possible to confront the threat from

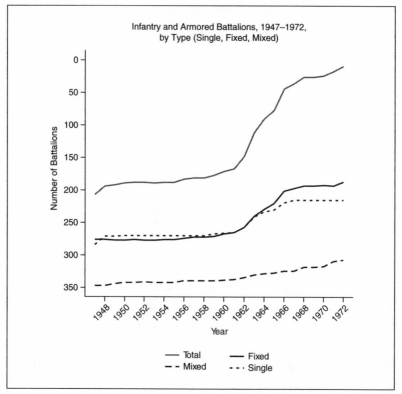

FIGURE 4.1 The expansion of the army 1947–1972, showing the number
of fixed, single-class, and mixed battalions

China, and the easiest way to do this, as in World War II, was to add
new battalions to existing class regiments. The absolute number of
"mixed" units did increase, but as we can see in Figures 4.2 and 4.3,
which show the growth of the army as well as the proportional shares
in class composition from 1947 until after the 1971 India-Pakistan
war, the proportion of these mixed units (labeled "All-India" in the
chart, though some were recruited on a zonal mixed basis) did not
dramatically increase. In Figure 4.3 we can see that the number of
all-India mixed units was around 10 percent of the total by 1972. There
was also some growth in "other classes" during the mid-1960s expansion, which includes "new classes" such as Gujaratis, Oriyas, and Bengalis; as we can see in Figure 4.3, this category had increased to
around 15 percent by 1972. But overall most of the growth in the

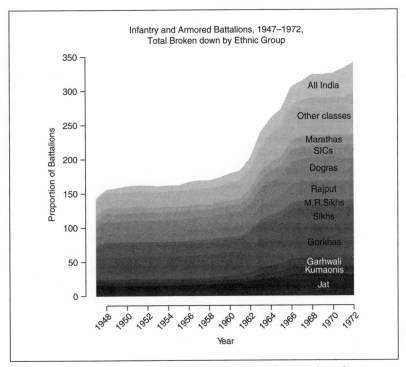

FIGURE 4.2 The expansion of the army 1947–1972, showing battalion-equivalent numbers of each class

Source: Wilkinson data. I count all the companies of each class and then aggregate these into battalions, so these totals represent the battalion-equivalent representation of each group rather than the total number of battalions in which, e.g., Sikhs, Dogras, or Rajputs might be represented. For more details on data see Chapter 5.

army's most dramatic period of expansion in the 1960s, as in World War II, was achieved by raising traditional single- and fixed-class composition units, which started with a core of men "milked" from existing battalions in each regiment and used well-established regimental training structures. To create a ready-made feeling of history and fighting spirit, the new battalions were often reraisings of specific numbered battalions that had been disbanded between 1945 and 1947, whose battle honors and traditions could be used to inspire the men. The Punjab Regiment for instance added eight new battalions to its existing nine battalions between 1962 and 1967, and all these new units were single-class companies with a mix of Jats and

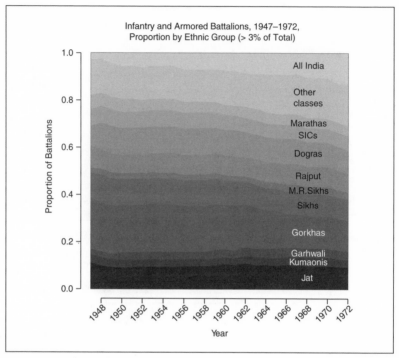

FIGURE 4.3 The expansion of the army 1947–1972, showing different class
percentages over time

Source: Wilkinson data, based on the battalion-equivalent representation of each
group rather than the total number of battalions in which, e.g., Sikhs, Dogras, or
Rajputs might be represented. For more details on data see Chapter 5.

Dogras (Raghavan n.d.). The Rajputana Rifles similarly increased
in size, adding seven new single-class company battalions (typically
50 percent Rajputs and 50 percent Jats) to its existing eight battalions between 1962 and 1966 (Sethna and Valmiki 1983).[15] And the
Kumaon Regiment added three new single-class battalions (two 100
percent Kumaoni and one 100 percent Ahir) to its strength from
1963 to 1964 (Praval 1976, 255–256).

As in World War II, the army also raised a number of new class
units from previously underrepresented groups, to enlarge the base
of recruitment and to get the country as a whole involved and supporting the war effort. Of the twenty-two new infantry battalions
raised in 1964, several recruited groups had previously been largely

excluded, such as Oriyas, Gujaratis, and Bengalis. In the Maratha Light Infantry, the new 8th MLI recruited "Mysoreans" for the first time when it was raised in 1963 (*Valour Enshrined*, 1971, 70). And the 8th and 9th Rajputana Rifles, raised in 1963 and 1964, each recruited a company of Muslims from north India and Gujaratis from Saurashtra. Bengalis and Oriyas were also recruited to 7th Para Parachute Regiment when it was raised in 1964 (Praval 1975, 338–341). In most of the class regiments, though, these new recruits, though given a lot of publicity, did not greatly alter the existing balance. In the case of the Mahar regiment, the addition of two new battalions in 1964–1965, 11th and 12th Mahar, which added companies of Oriyas, Bengalis, and Gujaratis, only intensified a change towards a mixed all-class composition (with substantial Mahar representation) that had already begun in 1956 (Longer 1980, 78; 120–121).

This massive expansion was hugely expensive and demanded sacrifices from all parts of the country in terms of taxes and lost development spending. As part of a wave of national solidarity and patriotism after the Chinese invasion, men from every state applied for emergency commissions and to join the armed forces. In West Bengal the state legislature passed a motion in January 1963 urging the army to create a Bengali regiment to help in the effort.[16] The army and Ministry of Defence wanted to harness this energy, without, however, upsetting the existing regimental compositions too much, which they felt would have a bad effect on these units' fighting capacity. Adding new battalions of less-well-represented groups clearly went some way to achieving this. The other thing that was done, very skillfully, by the new Defence Minister Y. B. Chavan, who had taken over from Krishna Menon in November 1962, was to announce that recruitment was henceforth to be based on each state's "recruitable male population" (RMP), the percentage of likely good recruits in each state (10 percent of all men). The Ministry of Defence report for 1963–1964 clarified that this new policy would, however, be implemented "in such a manner as to ensure that there is no lowering of efficiency and battle potential of the various Arms."[17]

This seemed very straightforward and fair, but behind what seemed like a clear new policy there were obviously some things that were a little hazy to anyone who understood military recruitment and wondered about the semantic difference between the phrases "on the basis of RMP," and "according to RMP." What would happen to the existing class units? Did the principle of RMP recruitment apply to the whole army or just to those units that did not already have a fixed class composition? And what if a state did not achieve its RMP quota for a given year? Would the proportion of a state's quota that was not met be reallocated to another state? And was the state identity of an applicant to be judged by the state of birth, of schooling, of language, or of residence?

In fact, as the answers to several parliamentary questions made clear, the new RMP policy was initially applied only to those new units and branches that did not already have a defined class composition rather than to the bulk of the infantry and armored units, which already did. In 1975, for instance, Minister of Defence Sardar Swaran Singh responded to a question by clarifying that "due to historical reasons and on grounds of tradition, certain class compositions are still continuing. However, recruitment to the major part of the Army is on the basis of the recruitable male population of States, between the age group of 17–25 years."[18]

Defence Minister Chavan, who presided over the army's biggest surge in growth in the 1960s, could have altered recruitment patterns substantially had he been determined to do so. But he did not push on that, partly because of the need to smooth the waters with the military after the tensions of the Krishna Menon years and to focus on the major strategic challenges and defense buildup, partly because, as someone from the main Maratha recruiting districts, he was also much more receptive to pleas about the value of class-composition units. When interviewed by Lloyd and Susanne Rudolph in March 1963 and asked about recruitment policy,

> he said that he personally didn't believe in any such thing as martial races. However, he said, there were certain traditions in the army which couldn't be changed without affecting morale and the unity of units. There was something to be said not so much for the martial races but for homogeneity in units, because men from certain areas sharing a certain language simply understood one another better.

He said this was particularly true in tank units or infantry units where men had to fight under stress and be able to communicate with each other immediately. He said that this was in marked contrast to technical services such as electronics or to the newer services like the air force and much of the Navy.[19]

Only after the 1965 and 1971 wars, with India having defeated Pakistan and the fear of China having receded a little, was the issue of army recruitment opened up a little. Jagjivan Ram, during his terms as Defence Minister (1970–1974, 1977–1978), made efforts to increase the number of Scheduled Castes in the Army as well as the number of new mixed units, something he had previously pressed for when a member of the cabinet.[20] The Defence Ministry consistently denied this, but a statement by Ram in March 1974 that recruitment was being reduced in Punjab, Himachal Pradesh, and Haryana because of overrepresentation in these areas, though quickly retracted after protests from Sikh leaders and Punjab, suggests that he was concerned with carrying out a prudent rebalancing of the force's composition.[21]

In an interview, Lieutenant General Sinha, who as a Brigadier had been appointed Deputy Adjutant General by General Manekshaw in March 1972, recalled Defence Minister Ram's efforts to open up the army to Scheduled Castes:

In 1972 I was Deputy Adjutant General, and Manekshaw was Chief and Jagjivan Ram was Defence Minister. Jagjivan Ram looked over the roll of IMA cadets being commissioned and raised a query re the list sent by the commanding officer of IMA. How many SCs were on the list? I checked up and said 1%. He wrote a strong note to Manekshaw. Jagjivan Ram wrote to Manekshaw saying that government had decided that there should be a SC reservation of 15% and one for the STs of 7.5%. Why is this not being observed?

Manekshaw sent for me. This DM has gone mad, he said, but we have to draft a reply. He knew Jagjivan Ram and I were from Bihar. I found in the files a note that said that when reservations were introduced there was a clause that said that this would not apply to the army.

So in my reply I said that this was the case. But that as far as ranks below officers were concerned we have more than 15% Scheduled Castes already in the army. We have the Mahar regiment, and every battalion has 75–100 depressed classes as sweepers, cobblers, dhobis etc. In terms of officers we had hardly any SCs in 1947 but we are making progress and now have 1% and it will grow further.

Since 1947 we have had continual conflicts and preparations for conflict. Under these conditions we cannot compromise national security. I accept it if the Minister wants to take action against me.

As Sinha told the story, "But of course [with Manekshaw] the hero of 1971, with these reasons, and as the hero of the war, there was little Jagjivan Ram could do."[22]

In the officer corps, the recruitment did broaden at the junior level. And as a result of the creation of several new training academies in the 1950s and 1960s and an increase in the ways officers could join up, new officers now came through many different streams, which further lessened the chances that they would coordinate on the basis of common ties and affiliations. But at the senior level, as in 1951, the force was still very much dominated by Punjabis and other members of the traditional "martial castes." In Figure 4.4 I show the composition of the top officers (colonels and above) in 1981, and as we can see there is, at this stage, no dramatic difference from the 1951 composition shown in the previous chapter.

Command and Control

To ensure that the army did not get "ideas above its station" the political leadership continued to implement several of the same strategies that it had used in the 1950s in the 1960s and 1970s. First, it retained the existing command-and control-procedures, in which there were separate chiefs for each of the three services and uncoordinated intelligence and procurement policies. For a time, after India's success in the 1971 war, it seemed that the prime minister might make the COAS, General Manekshaw, CDS, but the proposal foundered on traditional worries about making the military too

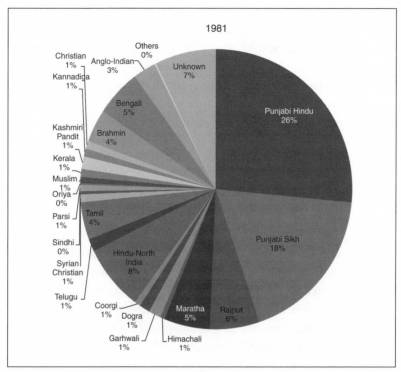

FIGURE 4.4 Estimated group composition of senior officers (colonels and above) in Indian Army, 1981

powerful. The bureaucracy successfully killed the proposal by making its implementation conditional on support from the three service chiefs, which they knew would not be forthcoming; the Air Force Chief, P. C. Lal, would never agree because he had a difficult personal relationship with Manekshaw and shared his service's traditional concerns about being dominated by the army in the decision-making structure. Former COAS General Chaudhuri, writing a year later in a military yearbook, argued that the CDS proposal foundered because of politicians' fear that "their own fissiparousness will make the CDS a credible candidate for military dictatorship."[23]

A second coup-proofing measure that was retained was to diversify the ethnicity of the top generals to prevent too great a concentration of any one group, especially Sikhs. Sikhs in particular and Punjabis in general never seemed to get the big promotion to COAS once they had achieved one or two (and it was never more than one or two) of the big lieutenant-general area commands. Lieutenant General Harbaksh Singh, the Sikh head of Eastern Command, looked to be in line in 1969 for the top post when General Kumaramangalam retired as COAS in June. But his promotion was blocked by a Defence Ministry decision to increase the seniority of Lieutenant General Manekshaw on the grounds that his earlier promotion had been delayed by an unfair political witch hunt conducted against him under Krishna Menon.[24]

In January 1974, similarly, the decision to extend the tenure of General Bewoor for a year had the effect of blocking the appointment to the top job of Lieutenant General P. S. Bhagat VC, who then had to retire before Bewoor stood down as COAS. Both Bhagat's daughter and Lieutenant General S. K. Sinha speculate that this decision might have been because Bhagat—who had earlier coauthored a report on the China debacle that was very critical of the Ministry of Defence and political interference in the military—was seen by the prime minister as too independent and strong a leader, not a "politician's general," especially with the rising opposition to her rule that was to culminate in the emergency in 1975.[25] But Manekshaw's military assistant Depinder Singh—who confirms that Manekshaw had recommended Bhagat to the prime minister over Bewoor, reports that Mrs. Gandhi told Manekshaw that "one reason why Bewoor was preferred over Bhagat was that the latter was pro-Sikh" (D. Singh 2005, 207). There may have been other reasons as well, of course; Bhagat's daughter thinks that it was because Defence Minister Ram and the bureaucrats thought he would not have been pliable and cooperative.[26] One other case of a Punjabi losing out on the top job in the 1970s was Lieutenant General N. C. Rawlley, superseded in 1975 after General Bewoor retired to make way for General T. N. Raina.

Any one of these individual decisions might, of course, have been taken for reasons other than hedging against the risks of a coup from members of particular groups, and no COAS is ever promoted without superseding some senior generals. It is also clear that in a heavily Punjabi officer corps, many of the disappointed aspirants for top jobs would inevitably be Punjabi. Still it is clear that for several decades it was always Punjabis who were losing out for the top job, except in the special case of General Thapar, promoted personally by Defence Minister Krishna Menon so as to block General Thimayya's pick for the job. How effective were such policies of ethnic balance and counterbalance? It is hard to say, but one British visitor to an elite cavalry regiment in the early 1970s, when asking about the possibilities of a coup in India, was told by one officer that if the COAS and Fourth Corps commanders all coordinated the army would follow, but that "the problem was that one of them would be bound to betray the others, hoping for promotion."[27]

The policy was also continued of trying to send senior generals out of the country after their retirement rather than have them sit around thinking of things to do at home. This practice had started with General Cariappa in 1953 (Guha 2007, 748–750). It was continued with General Thapar, who was sent as ambassador to Afghanistan after his resignation in 1962. Thapar's successor General Chaudhuri was then sent as High Commissioner to Canada after his retirement in 1966, despite having shown no previous interest in such a position. And unsuccessful efforts were also made to send Field Marshal Manekshaw, after his retirement, off as High Commissioner to London.[28]

Another aspect of ethnic risk management that seems to have been practiced in the 1970s was to hedge the risk from single-class units, by placing them next to units from other groups or far from their home areas or other locations where they might pose a political threat. The raising of the Naga Regiment in November 1970 had been promised in the peace agreement initially agreed to by the Indian government and the Naga leadership in 1960; part of the justification was that it could absorb Naga militants and provide them employment. But in practice—whether because the army, understandably, did not want to raise a regiment full of former militant "officers" who might chafe at their new lower ranks or because the Nagas did not meet military requirements in other ways—only a small number of Nagas were felt to be suitable for the army. The remainder applied for employment in the Border Security Force, the Central Reserve Police Force, and other paramilitary corps.[29]

But the center, understandably, was still nervous about the potential of a class regiment recruited from a rebellious area to cause trouble in the future. The solution, in line with long-standing army practice, was to hedge the risk by making the Naga regiment 50 percent Nagas, with the balance drawn in equal numbers from Kumaonis, Garhwalis, and Gorkhas. Initially the COAS, General Manekshaw, apparently decided to hedge the risk even more by having each unit completely mixed, Nagas together with the other classes, down to the small section—though for practical reasons the Army later relented and decided to allow separate companies of Nagas and the three "Other Hill Tribes" (Naga Regiment 2009, 44–45). Just for safety's sake, though, and on the ground that there were longtime military ties between troops from the two regions, the new Naga Regiment was then permanently stationed not in its home region in the northeast but instead beside its associated Kumaon Regiment in the hill station of Ranikhet, in what was then Uttar Pradesh and is now Uttarakhand. The cantonment at Ranikhet is approximately 1,300 miles away from Nagaland (Praval 1976, 302–303).

Something similar may also have happened, though it is hard to know for sure, with the two large single-class Sikh infantry regiments, the Sikh Regiment and the Sikh Light Infantry (SLI). In the early 1970s Prime Minister Gandhi seemed to be worried about Sikh militancy, and perhaps for this reason a decision was made to move both Sikh units from their traditional and much-loved training bases at Meerut (the nearest large base to Delhi, just an hour and a half and 51 miles away) and Bareilly (175 miles away). Sikh officers mobilized to try to get the decision reversed through a variety of formal and informal channels, but the COAS at the time, General Raina, was determined to make the shift (Singh 2000, 381). In 1976 the SLI was moved to Fatehgarh in eastern Uttar Pradesh, 205 miles from Delhi, and the Sikh Regiment (as well as the Punjab Regiment), over its strong objections, was moved to Ramgarh in Bihar, 736 miles away from Delhi. The Sikh Regiment's official history notes ruefully that "the 795 acres of land allotted to the Sikh Regimental Centre in 1976 was arid and desolate, in stark contrast to the buoyant and lush environs of the Centre at Meerut, a mere 90-minute drive from the Nation's capital in New Delhi" (Sikh Regimental Officers Association 2010, 220–221).

A third policy that was continued was the practice, which apparently began under Krishna Menon, of keeping the top serving officers and apparently a few retired officers as well under surveillance. Lieutenant General S. D. Verma, who resigned when superseded by Krishna Menon's choice for COAS, General Thapar, in 1961, recalls in his memoirs how in 1959 he was "certain my telephone was tapped and my mail censored under orders of Menon and Kaul. When General Thimayya resigned from the post of Chief of Army Staff after a series of disagreements with Menon, I rang him up to say that we were all with him. That was held against me as it transpired later. Timmy withdrew his resignation when the Prime Minister promised to stop Menon interfering with him, and came to Srinagar. We took a boat into the middle of Nagin Lake to be able to talk about it, as we did not feel safe anywhere else. He was quite bitter about being let down by Mr. Nehru after he had withdrawn his resignation at the latter's request" (Verma 1988, 120–121).

After Krishna Menon's fall in 1962 the surveillance policy continued. Nehru apparently gave Orissa politician Biju Patnaik the job of coordinating efforts to keep the generals in check and prevent a coup (Maxwell 1970, 439–441). According to Maxwell, Patnaik worked closely with Mullik at the Intelligence Bureau and "Senior officers were watched, their conversations 'bugged,' even those of the visiting Chief of the Imperial General Staff, General Sir Richard Hull, according to one of those most closely concerned with this operation" (439–441). Brigadier Khandhuri, in his account of General Cariappa's life, also tells us that Cariappa was placed under intelligence service surveillance by Mrs. Gandhi, almost two decades after he had left his post as commander in chief in 1953. When Lieutenant General I. S. Gill was posted to army headquarters in 1970 he was warned on his first meeting with General Raina about the positive letter he had written to Cariappa congratulating him on his published letter in the *Statesman* excoriating the country's politicians (Khanduri 2000, 76–77).

The really big new effort to hedge against the army's power was the massive expansion of the paramilitary forces, the growth of which is shown in Figure 4.5. These forces amounted to fewer than 20,000 in 1960, less than 5 percent of the size of the army. But after the China war, as the army expanded massively, there was also a massive attempt to ramp up the size of the paramilitary forces, which increased to 200,000 men, 20 percent as large as the army.

These paramilitary forces played several roles. First, the Border Security Force created in December 1965 was to provide a coordinated security force on the borders, as its name suggests, to replace

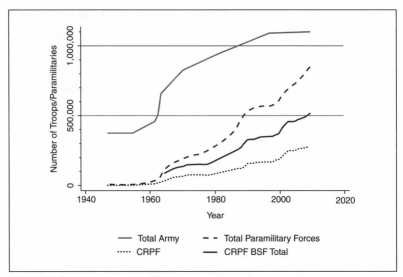

FIGURE 4.5 Relative growth of Indian Army and paramilitary forces since independence

Sources: Paramilitary data from Ministry of Home Affairs annual reports. Total paramilitary forces include AR, SSB, ITBP, BSF, CRPF, NSG, and CISF. Army data from *Jane's Defence*, press reports, and *Indian Defence Plan 1964*. Data interpolated for years where missing.

the previous ill-coordinated state police efforts. Second, and perhaps most importantly, the paramilitary forces, especially the Central Reserve Police Force, were meant to relieve the army of the necessity of deploying large numbers of expensively trained troops on long- and short-term "aid to the civil power" actions. At its peak, in the early 1990s, the Punjab militancy was absorbing seventy-seven battalions of regular troops with a further twenty to twenty-two deployed in Kashmir (Ghosh 1994, 1133). One retired general estimated at the time that relieving the regular army from fighting these insurgencies would contribute three divisions to its strength, and save it 10–15 percent of its budget (K. K. Hazari, quoted in Ghosh 1994, 1133). The problem got even worse by the end of the 1990s, with the intensification of the Jammu and Kashmir insurgency, and by 1998 156 out of the army's 356 infantry battalions (44 percent) were being used for counterinsurgency operations (Rajagopalan 2010, 26). So by increasing the size of the paramilitary forces and the specially trained Rashtriya Rifles (see Chapter 5) the bulk of the infantry and armored corps could be used for the mission it was primarily trained for, to defend the country against external aggression.

This strategy was not always successful. In particular there was always a risk in deploying Indians from one region of the country, particularly police without the training or discipline of the army, to police people with whom they might have little in common.[30] One problem was that long-term deployments in the ethnic periphery of the country by men who did not know the culture of the locals, or regarded them as "the enemy," worked against the prospects of the Indian state successfully putting down insurgencies. This central problem was well identified in a 1970 memo to the Home Minister from B. K. Nehru, the Governor of Assam and Nagaland East, in which he complained about the withdrawal of the locally raised Assam Rifles and their replacement by paramilitaries drawn from other regions of the country.

> The vacuum left by the withdrawal of the Assam Rifles from civil operations and control has been filled through the importation of battalions of Central Reserve Police and Armed Police from other States of the Union. Thus law and order and internal security duties are now performed in NEFA by three battalions of the CRP and one of the Malabar Special Police, whose personnel quite naturally regard themselves as foreigners operating in foreign territory and who are in turn regarded with suspicion as foreign interlopers by the local population. It does not seem to me to make sense at all that a well-respected and well-established local force which was backed by a long tradition should have been withdrawn for the performance of functions which can be performed by others and should have been replaced by a body of people, admirable themselves but disliked by the local people because of their foreign origin.[31]

The second and unstated purpose of the paramilitary forces, in particular the Central Reserve Police Force, which grew from 12,000 before the China War to 80,000 by 1980 (Figure 4.5), was to relieve the army of having to carry out prolonged aid to the civil deployments on riot control, and the possibility that might draw the force into a larger political role.

The third purpose, even less talked about than a general concern with keeping the army out of politically dangerous deployments, was for the paramilitaries to play an explicit coup-proofing role. Major paramilitary barracks were built in and around New Delhi and other important cities, and according to Neville Maxwell, Biju Patnaik and the intelligence services made plans after 1962 to use these units to protect the key political leaders and rush them to safe houses if a coup attempt looked likely (1970, 439). According to Maxwell, "Special battalions of the Central Reserve Police were posted near the capital, plans made to whisk Nehru away to safety in a hiding-place in the old city before the Army could get him" (440). When extra troops were ordered into the capital to help with crowd control in 1964 after the death of Nehru, the Home Minister, Gulzarilal Nanda, was apparently worried enough that he ordered armed police into the city to defend the government against a possible coup.[32] The infantry presence in Delhi also seems to have been kept to the absolute minimum necessary to perform the various ceremonial roles at Rashtrapati Bhawan, the Red Fort, and other central locations; only one infantry battalion of around 800 men was stationed in Delhi at the time the newly commissioned V. K. Singh was posted to the capital in 1970 (Singh 2013, 36). That was far fewer men than the paramilitary presence in the various barracks in the city. The new paramilitary forces were also, unlike the army, ethnically representative of the country as a whole, with the Border Security Force, Central Reserve Police Force, and Central Industrial Security Force all recruited mainly according to state population (Ghosh 1994, 60–70; 92).

The Congress Breakup and Emergency

One major achievement of the army in the mid-1970s was to avoid being drawn into the growing political chaos before, during, and after the emergency. At a time when an authoritarian leader was reaching out to the generals for support in Pakistan, the Indian military was determined neither to support the opposition, which was urging the army to obey illegal orders, nor to give Mrs. Gandhi's regime the more fulsome support it wanted. From the army's perspective, J. P. Narayan and other opposition leaders' call to disobey illegal orders was an invitation to organizational collapse. As General K. V. Krishna Rao pointed out in his memoirs, it would be simply impossible for the average soldier to work out which were the orders that ought to be obeyed and which were not. General Krishna Rao describes how the army officers realized that these calls, no matter how well intentioned, had to be ignored before they ripped the army apart, and he expresses his relief that no officer or unit seemed to act upon them (Rao 2001, 152).

A second danger, after emergency rule was over, was that the Congress Party might be tempted to get the army to support its reimposition. This danger seems to have been especially acute just after the 1977 elections, in which Congress leaders were shocked at the scale of their electoral losses and Sanjay Gandhi in particular seems to have had second thoughts about handing over power to the Janata government. Lieutenant General E. A. Vas, the adjutant general at the time, describes how the COAS, General Tapishwar Narain "Tappy" Raina, was called in to see Prime Minister Gandhi after Congress had lost the election. Her son and political advisor Sanjay then walked in and suggested to General Raina that "there are about 300 districts in the country. One infantry platoon is sufficient to control each district. Thus we can control India by deploying 300 platoons or about 25 infantry battalions; a mere three or four infantry divisions. The Party, supported by paramilitary forces and the police, can deal with other administrative details." Characteristically, Sanjay's assessment was mathematically correct, militarily unsound and politically immature. Mrs. Gandhi had uttered no word and displayed a blank face whilst her son was making this astonishing proposal. Tappy, a seasoned soldier with an impeccable record, was a man of quiet and sober habits. He spoke English and Urdu with a cultivated accent. He had lost one eye and this enhanced his personality, enabling him to always display a controlled and disciplined exterior which gave him an aura of unflappable civilized composure. On this occasion he ignored the young man and addressed his mother, "The Congress Party has ruled the country constitutionally for thirty years. You have held a fair election without any restraints. I am happy that history will record how the Congress under your leadership stepped down from office democratically." The next day a conglomerate calling itself the Janata Party came into power. (Vas 1995, 238)

So the army, while Mrs. Gandhi carried out her quasi-constitutional coup from 1975 to 1977, preserved itself as an institution, and avoided becoming drawn into executive rule in the way that the Pakistan military had done in the 1950s.

The Challenge of Sikh Militancy

The partition violence in Punjab in 1947 had made two risks of heavy class recruitment from one region very apparent. First, there was the difficulty of deploying troops to keep order in the same areas from which they were recruited, especially where members of the troops' own community appeared to be under threat. The second risk was that demobilized soldiers involved in the violence were capable of posing a much more profound threat to the state than ordinary civilians. They were cohesive, they had many links through regimental ties and veterans' organizations, and they were well trained in tactics and weapons (Jha and Wilkinson 2012). The Punjab Boundary Force, meant to keep order in Punjab, found itself being attacked by men in military formation, using mortars, grenades, and submachine guns. And to the north, in Kashmir, the "Azad Kashmir" army in Poonch in September 1947 was estimated to be 90 percent composed of ex-servicemen.

Both of these dangers were realized again in the Punjab militancy of the 1970s, 1980s, and 1990s. This movement was the result of intense factionalism within the majority Sikh community in post-1966 Punjab. In the jostling for position among politicians and leaders of the main Sikh religious and community organization, the Shiromani Gurdwara Parbandhak Committee, different Sikh politicians engaged in what scholars of ethnic politics would term "ethnic outbidding," demanding stronger action against heterodox minorities within the Sikh community (the Nirankaris) or by stronger action in defense of Sikh interests against the center (G. Singh 2000; Singh 1991; Chima 2002, 103–104). To press their positions home, and increase their bargaining power and visible support, the

Akali Dal as well as various separatist leaders organized many large-scale meetings, processions, and protests to emphasize their high levels of support. In December 1982, to put pressure on the center, the leader of the more moderate of the two Akali Dal factions, Sant Longowal, organized a meeting of ex-servicemen in Amritsar as what Chima characterizes as a "warning to the Indian government to compromise or face escalation" (2002, 210–211). This meeting attracted many Sikh veterans, including some who had been alienated by heavy-handed central- and state-government searches and checkpoints designed to stop Sikhs from disrupting the Asian games in 1983. This meeting drew far bigger support from veterans than Longowal had anticipated, with five retired generals (and five more who sent letters of support), 170 officers above the rank of colonel, and over 800 other officers, as well as nine thousand ex-enlisted men *(jawans)* (211). According to Chima, the meeting's strong support for the Akali Dal demands helped push the center back to the bargaining table in January 1983.

However, as extremism rose in Punjab and Hindus bore the brunt of militant violence, the center worried that compromise with Akali demands, even the more moderate demands of the Akali Dal (Longowal) faction, would be seen as a sign of weakness (230). As Chima describes the dynamic, "each time these negotiations failed, it strengthened the hands of Sikh radicals like Tohra and Talwandi, and Sikh extremists like Bhindranwale at the expense of Sikh moderates like Longowal and Badal" (230). Both extremist and moderate Sikhs trained their own groups of supporters for mobilizations and for protection against rival factions and the state, with former officers training men in military-style boot camps (250). In June 1983, for instance, one thousand Akali *marjeeware* (living martyrs) were trained by former military officers and others at Anandpur (250). As Bhindranwale and his militant supporters occupied the Golden Temple complex, the center had boxed itself in, with few other options except force unless it wanted to be seen as weak on separatism and militancy.

In June 1984, Prime Minister Gandhi took the decision to storm the complex, despite reservations among many army officers and politicians about the prospect of a major military attack on the Sikhs' holiest shrine. Reflecting the political sensitivities, there was a media blackout in Punjab and the army picked its units with great care, deploying men from the Bihar Regiment and the mixed-class Guards and Parachute regiments rather than class regiments recruited solely from the Punjab (though there were some Sikhs in these mixed regiments). To organize the attack, and perhaps also to provide some political cover against charges that it was only Hindu officers who were involved in attacking a Sikh shrine, the army selected Major General K. S. "Bulbul" Brar, a Sikh, and several other senior Sikh officers.

The army's attack on the Golden Temple complex succeeded, but with very heavy loss of life on both sides and considerable damage to the temple complex. This was due in part to the fact that the militants' defense of the Golden Temple complex was led by two retired Sikh major generals, Shahbeg Singh and Jaswant Singh Bhullar, with other ex-army men under their command (Singh 1991, 340). The army was only able to retake the complex after several days by bringing in three tanks, which fired a total of sixty shells into the complex. One retired officer estimates that there were one thousand casualties sustained in the storming of the complex, including 336 from the army (Hoon 2000, 80–89).[33]

Given the heavy media censorship of the incident and lack of access to the complex for some months after the attack, it was easier for Sikhs to believe a variety of rumors about what had been done during and after the army's attack on the complex. Sikh units that drew from the Jat Sikhs who had been most involved in the movement were most affected. Sikhs from the Sikh Regiment at Ramgarh, in Bihar, killed their commanding officer and seized trucks in order to drive to Punjab to "retake" the temple, but they were soon captured in Uttar Pradesh and Bihar. Another unit, part of the Ninth Sikh Regiment in Rajasthan, also mutinied, but its troops too were captured and the whole battalion was disbanded in April 1985.[34] Lieutenant General P. N. Hoon also reported smaller mutinies by two Sikh units under his own divisional command at Nagrota, in Kashmir, as well as a mutiny at a corps headquarters (2000, 86–89).

This series of events during and after the army's Operation Bluestar, to retake the Golden Temple complex at Amritsar from Sikh militants, raised two important threats posed by class recruitment. First, it demonstrated that at times of extreme crisis the class-regiment structure, precisely because it engendered greater group loyalty and cohesion, could also allow greater unit mobilization against the state, as it had done in the Sikh unit mutinies. This had been a worry of the British ever since 1857, and they had chosen to hedge against it by mixing companies at the battalion level, so that there might be single-class companies of Sikhs, Jats, and Garhwalis within the same battalion (the Sikh and Gurkha regiments, however, had been exempted from this policy).

Second, the 1984 events demonstrated once again that employing large numbers of soldiers from particular communities might pose a real danger to the country's security if a substantial portion of these communities ever became opposed to the center. The class recruitment policy posed a big problem for the country's external defense, both because Punjab bordered Pakistan and because, as the Western Army commander at the time pointed out in his memoirs, 80,000 of the 300,000 troops under his command were Sikhs (S. K. Sinha 1992, 287–288). Pakistan could supply militants directly across the border, provide a refuge, and create major problems in one of the most strategic Indian states. Several militant organizations also made specific efforts to recruit ex-servicemen and take advantage of their organizational talents as well as their tactical and weapons skills.[35]

In the aftermath of Bluestar, there was mass Sikh militancy throughout Punjab for much of the next decade. One explanation for the heavy concentration of violence and militancy in the Majha region of Punjab is that these districts had unusually high levels of youth unemployment, especially given the reduction in army recruiting. Another is the region's status as a historic heartland for the Sikhs and its local tradition of resistance (Human Rights Data Analysis Group 2009, 32–33; Pettigrew 1987; 1995, 1–7; 65). But what is most striking to anyone familiar with military recruitment patterns is that this region also has the three most heavily recruited army districts in the country: Amritsar, Gurdaspur, and Tarn Taran. These districts have more than one hundred thousand army veterans and thousands more serving army *jawan*s and officers even today. Even if no more than 10 percent of these men were sympathetic to the militancy, that still means that there was a substantial stock of well-trained soldiers that could have fought in the militancy.[36]

The Punjab militancy and the Sikh mutinies posed probably the greatest challenge since independence to the army's single-class regiment structures. The COAS at the time of Operation Bluestar was General A. S. Vaidya, who would be assassinated by Sikh militants two years later, in 1986, in retribution for the Golden Temple attack. The Sikh mutinies and the events of 1984 worried General Vaidya sufficiently that he thought of changing the composition of all the single-class regiments, such as the Sikh Regiment, the Sikh Light Infantry, and the Dogras, over to a mixed composition to hedge the risk. This was, of course, exactly what the British had done in the nineteenth century.

In the summer of 1984 Vaidya ordered each of the army's prestigious single-class regiments to start to add mixed battalions, apparently as a prelude to an even wider restructuring of the single-class regiments. One each of these new battalions, which were known within the army as "Vaidya's Battalions," was added to eight infantry regiments over the next year, including the Sikh Regiment (13th Battalion), the Jat Regiment (20th Twentieth Battalion), and the Rajputana Rifles (21st Battalion).[37] What is still unclear, even twenty-five years later, is whether it was Vaidya's own initiative to radically transform the composition of the infantry, or whether the initial pressure came from politicians worried about the army. It seems likelier that the initiative came from Vaidya than the politicians, because the policy changed immediately after his departure as COAS at the end of January 1985, when General Krishnaswami Sundarji took over. Sundarji halted the creation of new Vaidya battalions, though he did not disband the ones that had already been authorized (Cohen 1990a, 210–211).

Conclusion

India's civil-military structure and the army's central recruiting and operational practices survived remarkably intact from the early 1950s to the 1980s. This was despite the major strategic and organizational challenges of defeat by China, two major wars with Pakistan (1965 and 1971), a difficult intervention in the Sri Lankan civil war, the 1975–1977 Emergency, and the major challenge of a long-running Sikh militancy in the army's recruiting heartland. But even in the 1980s and early 1990s, several well-informed analysts were wondering how long India's higher defense arrangements and army structure could survive. Stephen Cohen wondered whether the army's rising levels of corruption, combined with increasing civilian mistreatment and interference, might raise the likelihood of military intervention (1990a, 218). But then he concluded that the heterogeneous nature of the armed forces and their various commands, the political leadership's awareness of the risks, and the measures they took to hedge against these risks made a coup very unlikely (222–223). Both Cohen and Stephen Rosen, a political scientist who wrote a major study of Indian military effectiveness, asked perceptively in the 1990s whether the army's increasing inability to separate itself from the caste tensions, corruption, and political controversies of wider society might pose a fundamental danger to the postindependence structure, as well as to the army's fighting ability (Rosen 1996).

5

Army and Nation Today

Introduction

IN THE PAST few decades there has been no major change in the various strategies the Indian state employs to minimize the risk of military intervention in politics, even though they are now widely regarded, even by many politicians, as an increasing drag on the country's military efficiency and antiterrorist strategies. In the aftermath of the Pakistani incursion into Kargil in 1999, continuing incursions into Kashmir, and major terrorist attacks on the Indian parliament and in Mumbai, these threats seem much more pressing to many MPs than distant worries about the faint possibility of a coup. The bureaucracy continues to resist political and military leaders who push for a more coordinated command strategy for the armed forces, more integrated intelligence gathering, the appointment of a Chief of Defence Staff, and greater involvement of officers in defense planning (Mukherjee 2011).[1] The Kargil Review Committee, in its review of India's defense deficiencies after Kargil, criticized defects in all these areas and pointed out that "India is perhaps the only major democracy where the Armed Forces Headquarters are outside the apex governmental structure." It recommended that the entire civilian-military defense structure that had existed since the 1950s be reviewed and that military officers at the joint secretary rank be placed in the Ministry of Defence to improve information exchange and planning. The Kargil Committee also tried to defuse worries that this would endanger the country's internal stability by pointing out that "Most opposition to change comes from inadequate knowledge of the national security decision-making process elsewhere in the world and a reluctance to change the status quo. . . . In fact, locating the services Headquarters in the Government will further enhance civilian supremacy."[2] The parliamentary Standing Committee on Defence has also pushed for the same measures, emphasizing that "the post of Chief of Defence Staff (CDS) exists in 67 countries including France, Germany, UK and USA [all of course thriving democracies, just to reassure anyone who might be worried about the CDS model . . .] and the system has proved its efficacy in those countries."

But all these changes have been blocked, partly because of the bureaucracy's desire to defend its own turf and partly, presumably, because of its long-standing concerns, since the days when H. M. Patel was Defence Secretary immediately after independence, over any potential threat to civil military relations. The senior political leadership, pressured by MPs and the public to deal more efficiently with external and internal threats, is not necessarily happy about the status quo. Prime Minister Manmohan Singh appointed a new high-level defense committee under former Cabinet Secretary Naresh Chandra in summer 2013 to review the lack of progress and presumably to make some new recommendations. But given the previous history of blocked proposals to change the structure as well as the possibility of a change of government after national elections in spring 2014, it did not lead to significant change in the main decision-making structure.[3] The Ministry of Defence has also blocked the parliamentary Standing Committee on Defense's request that a Chief of Defence Staff be appointed, on the grounds that not all political parties had yet responded to the idea—a step that seems not, however, to be crucial for bureaucratic action in many other spheres.[4]

Despite chafing at the continued problems in higher defense management and coordination, the army has become somewhat more autonomous in at least one important way. First, since 1962 the army has already had a substantial degree of autonomy in terms of planning its own military operations. And as the insurgencies in the northeast and Jammu and Kashmir have increased in their size and intensity over the years, the army's own domestic operations have increased proportionally (Raghavan 2012, 116–118, 127–130). So the army is de facto playing a larger domestic role, one in which it is given a lot of operational autonomy, through this expansion of its counterinsurgency role. This has not been an easy process, because the excesses that troops have sometimes carried out in this stressful counterinsurgency role have created tensions with local populations as well as calls for some of the army's institutional autonomy to be taken away. Civil rights activists and others are particularly upset about the continuing use of the Armed Forces Special Powers Act, which gives the army substantial powers to act outside the normal judicial and police system, in the northeast and Raghavan (2010b).

Perhaps the greatest challenge to civil-military relations now is not over the traditional concerns of higher command structures and ethnic hedging, but rather from the difficulties the army faces in trying to remain a society apart. Party pressures, corruption, and increasing political and societal efforts to interfere in its workings threaten its ability to retain its traditional recruiting structures and hierarchies and lead to strains on what has been up to now one of India's major successes, the clear divide between the military and politics.

The two major political developments in India over the past twenty-five years have been first, the rise of state parties and state leaders to power in national political coalitions (every government from 1989 to the BJP's election victory in 2014 was either a formal coalition or has involved support from outside parties), and second, the rise of powerful backward caste and lower-caste parties and leaders (Jaffrelot 1999). Both of these developments create intense new demands for politicians to be seen to share out the national recruitment pie more equally among different states and communities. Politicians who have risen to the top by skillfully distributing jobs on the basis of caste and community are unlikely to stop when they achieve high office in New Delhi, and they are also unlikely to understand the army's own personnel needs. Mukherjee details tensions between Defence Minister Mulayam Singh Yadav and General V. P. Malik when the latter resisted Yadav's efforts to promote the career of Lieutenant General B. S. Malik; Yadav was only rebuffed when General Malik took the matter to the Prime Minister (Mukherjee 2012, 300–301). He also describes a case in the Air

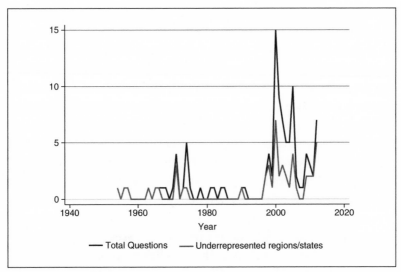

FIGURE 5.1 Parliamentary questions on state and community recruitment
in the army, 1952–2012

Source: Wilkinson data from *Lok Sabha* and *Rajya Sabha* proceedings.

Force in 2002 when a Sikh officer seeking high rank tried to enlist
the Chief Minister of Punjab (whose Sikh party was at the time a
key National Democratic Alliance coalition partner in New Delhi)
for help with his promotion (302). The Congress Party, which has
dominated the United Progressive Alliance coalition since 2004,
also relies heavily on minority and lower-caste voters and its regional party allies, so there has been increasing pressure on the
military to be seen to be fair to these groups in its recruitment
practices—for instance by holding recruitment *mela*s in underrepresented regions and in areas where underrepresented communities
represent a significant share of the population. As we can see in Figure 5.1, there has been an upsurge in parliamentary questions on
the composition of the army in the past decade. Most of these questions are from members of groups or states who feel that they are
underrepresented in the forces, and are either pushing (so far unsuccessfully) for a new unit that will benefit their community or for
information that will make the scale of their underrepresentation
apparent. So we have seen demands for new regiments from tribal

areas, from minorities, and from underrepresented states. MPs from
a variety of tribal, SC, and backward castes persistently ask why,
when Rajputs, Jats, and Sikhs have their regiments, their own Yadav,
Jatav, and Kurmi communities should not have their own regiments.[5]
We have also seen efforts to have more outreach in recruitment, as
well as a relaxation of height and education requirements to allow
particular communities to do better in recruitment.[6] In 1997 Defence Minister Mulayam Singh Yadav revealed that the Ministry of
Defence had received requests from Gujarat, Karnataka, Arunachal
Pradesh, Andhra Pradesh, and Karnataka to raise regiments from
these states, but that "the present policy is not to raise any new Regiment on the basis of caste, creed, religion or region."[7] But there are
also some questions and motions from overrepresented groups anxious to push back and defend the "traditional role" of men from
Punjab, Haryana, Himachal Pradesh, and Maharashtra as well as
particular communities in the army. For example, Jitender Singh, who
until May 2014 represented the very heavy recruiting district of
Alwar in Rajasthan (where his family were formerly the Maharajahs),
asked the Defence Minister in September 2012 if recruitment on
the basis of recruitable male population was badly affecting "candidates from other States who are more suitable for recruitment in
the Army."[8]

Another major challenge has come from the massive economic
development and technological change since liberalization in 1991.
Despite several major pay increases, army officers are still underpaid
relative to many civilian professions. This has a negative influence
on the army and its autonomy from society and politics in several
ways. First, and most directly, the relatively poor pay of officers compared to their civilian counterparts—especially when combined with
the army's promotion structures, in which huge numbers of officers
face being laid off in productive middle age—has led to increasing
numbers of good officers trying to leave the army early in their careers. This "officer deficit," everyone agrees, makes it much harder
for the army to maintain discipline and manage the social and unit
stresses that inevitably emerge, especially during long domestic
deployments. The army's own experts in combat psychology have
emphasized the many problems that can occur in terms of unit co-

hesion and discipline in the many units that have too few officers and too much turnover among those they do have.[9]

Corruption in the army is also a problem, as in other areas of life in India. Just how much of a problem is unclear, because as always it is hard to infer the extent of the problem from those cases that are made public, such as the investigation of a Major General in charge of contracts for army rations in Jammu and Kashmir in 2012.[10] But the size of the sums involved in the major military procurement projects, combined with the fact that the army—in the midst of India's real estate boom—owns and controls prime land in most of India's major cities, has clearly created lots of opportunities. The fact that lower- and middle-ranking officers see the top brass, or at least some of them, enriching themselves through procurement deals and securing allocations for property in ex-officer developments—most notoriously the Adarsh housing development in Mumbai that came to light in 2011—cannot help but gnaw at the sense of solidarity in the armed forces.[11]

In addition, the spread of mass education, new ideas of rights and citizenship, mass media, and modern cellphone technology have created major challenges to the army's ability to retain traditional military hierarchies and remain a society apart. In World War II 82 percent of all infantry *jawan*s were illiterate, whereas today virtually all soldiers have been through at least a few years of secondary school.[12] The "narrowing" of the social and educational gap between officers and men while the military hierarchies and pay differentials between officers and men have remained constant has led to some obvious strains. The Indian Army's loyalty to civilian rule over the years has in some ways stemmed from successful efforts to keep it a highly disciplined force apart from society. But in an age of mass literacy, with the now ubiquitous mobile phones making the *jawan*'s village and all its issues just a moment away, it has been much harder for the army to remain a society apart.

There have been an increasing number of incidents that reflect these tensions in the past decade. For one thing, the army's own Defence Institute of Psychological Research has found that the level of "fragging" (the killing of officers) and soldier suicides is increasing, and that "perceived humiliation and harassment" is often the trigger.[13] Most seriously, there have been several scuffles and even serious fights between *jawan*s and their officers over alleged abuses. In 2010, according to data released by the Minister of Defence in parliament, there was one "scuffle" between *jawan*s and officers, in the 45th Cavalry. In 2012, there were two reported incidents, one in the 226th Field Regiment and the other in the 16th Cavalry. And in October 2013 there was a fight between officers and men of the Tenth Sikh Light Infantry as the officers tried to break up a scuffle at an intercompany boxing match.[14] Both 45th and 16th Cavalry draw troops mainly from south India, the Sikh Light Infantry is drawn from the Sikh Mazhabi and Ramdasia communities, and the 226th Field Regiment has an all-India composition.[15] Tensions have arisen particularly over the treatment of the army's thirty thousand *sahayak*s (valets), who perform duties that have long since been abolished in most armies but—perhaps because of the sharp relative decline in the pay and position of officers in other ways—have been retained in the Indian Army. There are allegations that many of these *sahayak*s, although they are trained soldiers, have often been asked by their officers and families to perform a variety of household and personal service tasks that are not, strictly speaking, part of their job. The 2012 incident involving 226th Field Regiment at Nyoma was the result of a brawl at an army firing range in Ladakh between officers and *jawan*s, when *jawan*s angrily protested against the alleged fatal beating (in fact the soldier was alive) of one of the *sahayak*s, Suman Ghosh, by five majors. The beating of Ghosh took place after one of the officers, Major Sharma, claimed that he had deliberately walked into Sharma's wife's bathroom while she was taking a shower. When the men heard that Ghosh had been beaten and might be dead, they themselves captured and beat Major Sharma, barricaded themselves in the armory, and manhandled the commanding officer who tried to intervene. As a result of this incident, the commanding officer, three majors, and ten *jawan*s were injured, and disciplinary action against 168 men included a number of court-martials the following year.[16] In an interview after the event, one former officer told a journalist that "In the first decades after Independence enlisted men came from backgrounds which led them to unquestioningly accept feudal attitudes and values. The officers were also products of the same feudal landscape. It doesn't exist any more—but the institutions remain."[17]

A potentially even more damaging way in which societal cleavages and army cleavages can interact is over cases in which ambitious or powerful officers have tried to draw allies from social and political organizations into controversies within the military. There have always been a few cases of political and societal pressure to get members of particular communities appointed to top posts; for example there were reports in the 1970s that the government was under a lot of pressure from ex-Defence Minister Y. B. Chavan to appoint his fellow Maratha General Bewoor as COAS rather than Lieutenant General P. S. Bhagat (D. Singh 2002, 207). There have always been officers who have expressed unhappiness at the promotion of others and their own supersession. But in the past decade there have been a number of allegations that some senior officers are practicing personal ethnic favoritism in promotions, in particular hurting the chances of other officers so as to allow their own favored candidates to have a clear run through in the "line of succession." Because so much of the army runs on seniority in rank, and because many of the most senior officers have to retire if they are not promoted by certain dates, much of the politics of all this takes place through moves to promote some officers to block others, to backdate or advance the seniority of some officers, or to give them particular assignments (for example, to command a corps) or alter their dates of service in order to advance or retard an individual's chances of promotion.[18]

The worst of these controversies came to a head in 2012 when the then COAS, General V. K. Singh, publicly alleged that his birth date had been tinkered with in army records in the mid-2000s in a way that ensured that he would have to retire early. His supporters claimed this was done to ensure a clear promotion path for a (Sikh) candidate allegedly favored by COAS General J. J. Singh (2005–2007), as well as unnamed politicians. Chiefs serve a three-year term once appointed, or until they reach age sixty-two; so depending on whether his birth date was accepted as 1950 or 1951, V. K. Singh's tenure might have been extended by a year, during which some of the leading contenders to replace him might have reached the retirement

age or service limit for their ranks and themselves have been forced
to leave. This controversy—which involved a court case (and which
V. K. Singh lost) and press and television interviews by many of the
main parties—was very bad for the army in two ways. First, it publicized a degree of ethnic factionalism within the army at the highest
levels that was damaging to the force's public image as cohesive—a
place where all were Indians first and members of particular groups
second. There have always been senior officers in the service who
were disappointed with promotions and felt they had been unjustly
treated, but three or four decades ago they resigned quickly and more
or less quietly, rather than having the gory details immediately becoming known in the press and discussed on cable television, as has
happened increasingly over the past decade.[19] This time, the Indian
press and the voracious cable news channels devoted a lot of column
inches and time on the news programs to the "showdown" between
Defence Minister A. K. Anthony and General Singh.

Second, and perhaps even more damagingly for the army, the
controversy sparked a wider political and societal mobilization by
several caste groups in support of General Singh and against what
they saw as a policy of Sikh favoritism, especially those representing
Singh's own Rajput community. Two dozen Rajput MPs mobilized
in support of Singh in parliament, writing a letter to the government supporting his case.[20] This type of complaint is extremely rare
in Indian military history, and when such efforts have been made,
as in the 1950s controversy over the supersession of General Sant
Singh discussed in Chapter 3, the officers themselves tried to stay
studiously above the fray. But in this instance General V. K. Singh
seemed to some to encourage public support in his fight against Anthony. There were also allegations made of caste and family ties
influencing promotions (as well as suspensions and supersessions) to
the army's top commands, which typically predict which general
will be promoted to the COAS position.[21]

The Composition of the Army Today

How diverse is India's Army today? How much has it changed it
since the big expansion in the 1960s? This is a sensitive topic that
the army and Ministry of Defence have typically tried to avoid.

Questions in Parliament by MPs anxious to find out the larger patterns of caste, religious, and regional recruitment are typically met with Ministry of Defence replies that do not reveal very much. This is partly because of a general institutional culture that prides itself on secrecy. But it is also because senior bureaucrats and officers realize that in a country where the distribution of jobs and positions is fiercely contested, releasing too much information about who gets what might create larger fights that will endanger the military's autonomy to manage its own recruitment and training in the way it sees fit. The army and Ministry of Defence therefore typically respond to all parliamentary requests for information on the caste and religious composition of the army with the stock response that the army is open to all, that it is secular, and that there are no caste or community reservations of any kind. When probing questioners suggest that things may not be quite that simple because there are still fixed-caste regiments and fixed-class units within those regiments, Ministers typically respond by reiterating that for historic and operational reasons some older units with a caste composition survive, but that these units are now recruiting from a larger number of communities and that in any case no new caste or religious units have been created since independence, in line with the promise made by General Cariappa in 1949.[22]

Information on regional and state patterns of recruitment is more readily available, despite occasional knee-jerk responses that it is "not in the public interest to disclose this information."[23] However, this information is usually given out in very small portions, never more than a few years of data at once. The army also takes care not to put actual recruitment data together with data showing, for instance, whether a state is getting its proportional share or not. But if we aggregate all the various small pieces of information that have been released and put these together with population data from the census it is nonetheless possible to build up a relatively good picture of the overall diversity in the army as well as how this has changed over the past few decades.

In what follows I use three sources to provide what I believe are the most detailed and accurate estimates of the army's changing composition that have so far been published. First, I use *district-level data* on where army ex-servicemen currently live.[24] This provides a snapshot, likely to be quite accurate, on where most army recruits were from twenty or thirty years ago.[25] Second, I use the aggregate *state-level recruiting data* provided in response to Lok Sabha and Rajya Sabha questions, most of them asked by MPs with axes to grind about their states' or communities' current low or declining share of military recruits. These data are usually given for just a year or two, but they can be aggregated and put together with population data from the census to enable us to get quite a good sense of state-level recruitment patterns and whether states are getting their recruitable male population (RMP) share or not. Third, I use the wealth of *regimental unit data* that we can find in all the available regimental and army histories to build up, from systematic battalion- and company-level data, a reasonably accurate picture over time of whether the majority of units in any particular branch of service are "fixed class," single class, or mixed class, as well as the proportion of different groups within these units.[26] Because we know the typical composition of almost all regiments as well as most of their individual battalions, and almost all of their formation dates, we can use these data to generate estimates in the charts and tables in this chapter and in Chapter 4 of the changing composition of the army through time.[27]

The National Picture

What do these national recruitment data show? First, let us examine the 2008 district data on ex-servicemen (ESM) (Figure 5.2—note the individual state boundaries in this figure are represented by the bold dashed lines), which give us a good sense of where much of the recruitment took place twenty, thirty, and even forty years ago. The heaviest density of ex-servicemen in this map, it is true, is still in the classic "martial class" recruiting districts: the Maratha districts near Pune; the Dogra districts of Jammu; the Rajput recruiting districts; the hill districts of Himachal Pradesh and Uttarakhand/ Uttaranchal (together with Darjeeling, which produces many Gorkha recruits), and the Jat and Sikh recruiting grounds of Punjab, Haryana, and (for the Jats) western Uttar Pradesh. Strikingly, three districts in Punjab with less than half a percent of the Indian popula-

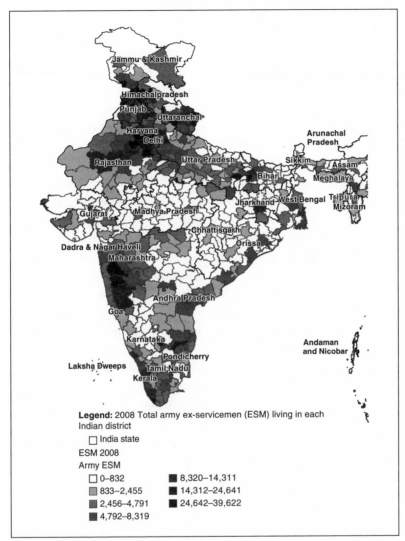

FIGURE 5.2 Total army ex-servicemen living in each Indian district, 2008
(Individual state boundaries in this figure are represented by bold dashed
lines.)

tion according to the 2011 census, Tarn Taran, Gurdaspur, and
Hoshiarpur, had more ex-servicemen in 2008, 97,156, than the states
of Bihar and Orissa combined (12.1 percent of the Indian population,
88,100 ex-servicemen), or the states of Gujarat and West Bengal combined (12.5 percent of the Indian population, 61,706 ex-servicemen).

But already we see some significant broadening of the old patterns, as increasing numbers of recruits are drawn from districts in Kerala, Andhra, Tamil Nadu, eastern Uttar Pradesh, Bihar, and West Bengal. Only Gujarat, Madhya Pradesh, Chhattisgarh, and Orissa, among the traditional "deficit states," have hardly any retired veterans.

Second, we can examine the state-level patterns of recruitment today, which I have been able to aggregate—using official data released bit by bit in the Rajya Sabha and Lok Sabha—for the years from 1998 to 2009.[28] These data can be used to tell two very different stories, depending on whether we focus on the disproportionality of state recruitment—which still continues—or on whether recruitment has broadened and the risks of imbalance have been further reduced, which have occurred. First, let us look at the disproportionality of army recruitment by state, which I show in Figure 5.3. This map simply displays each state's percentage of recruits to the army from 1998–2009 divided by my estimate (using the 2001 Census of India population data) of each state's percentage of recruitable males. Even though the Ministry of Defence maintains in parliament that recruitment is "on the basis of RMP" (10 percent of the state's males), it is clear that this has not yet led to anything like a strictly applied quota in which each state gets only its proportional population share in the army. The most overrepresented states on the map, those with from 2.5 to 6.035 times their estimated RMP recruitment, include the traditional recruiting states of Punjab, Jammu and Kashmir, Uttarakhand and Himachal Pradesh. The traditional recruiting state of Haryana is only slightly behind, with around twice its proportional representation. States such as Maharashtra and Rajasthan fall in the middle in terms of their overall representation, with some districts very heavily recruited and other parts of their states providing very few recruits. Meanwhile states such as Gujarat, Chhattisgarh, and Jharkhand continue to be substantially underrepresented in recruitment, with less than 55 percent of their expected representation on the basis of population. West Bengal and Orissa are doing only slightly better, falling in the band of states that have 55 percent to 76 percent of their expected proportional representation. The flood of Bengali, Oriya, and Gujarati recruits that General Cariappa promised in Calcutta in 1949 has still not fully materialized.

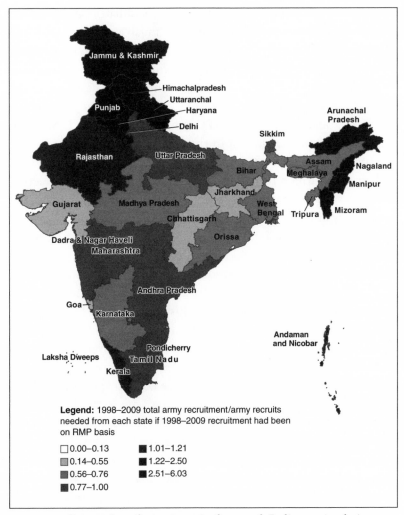

FIGURE 5.3 Proportion of army recruits from each Indian state relative to recruitable male population, 1998–2009 (RMP)

One reason there is a gap between different states' proportion in the army and population is that, in India as elsewhere, men and women from different areas and groups want to join up in different numbers. This is partly due to the presence or lack of a military tradition, and also due to differences in the levels of poverty and other economic opportunities available to potential servicemen in some places compared to others. The recruiting *melas* in Gujarat, which has a booming economy but no strong military tradition, do not yield as many recruits as those in poverty-stricken Chhattisgarh and Bihar or in the traditional recruiting areas in Punjab and Haryana.[29] And even in the traditional recruiting states, growing economic prosperity will probably over time reduce the numbers who want to join up.

There has recently been an important court challenge to the army's recruitment system. A petitioner in a December 2012 Public-Interest Litigation case in India's Supreme Court, Dr. I. S. Yadav, challenged caste recruitment in the army as unconstitutional caste discrimination; he pointed to patterns of recruitment in the navy and air force, which recruit widely and are also militarily effective, as clear evidence that the current class recruitment is unnecessary for military efficiency.[30] Dr. Yadav complained about the fact that the President's Bodyguard, for instance, is composed only of Jat Sikhs, Rajputs, and Jats. The army responded to the Supreme Court that this is purely because "the ceremonial duties demand common height, build appearance and dress for reason of pomp and projection which are important military attributes."[31] Just why it might be that members of lower-caste Sikh or other Hindu communities could not be found who also meet these height and build requirements was not explored in the army's response. But Yadav's argument in the Supreme Court (ultimately unsuccessful, as the case was dismissed by the court in April 2014 on the grounds that it did not want to "rock the army's boat")—that moving to the air force or navy recruiting systems would solve the problem—is also not quite as clear as it sounds.[32] This is because, with a few exceptions, the traditional "martial" states that supply a disproportionate share of recruits to the army also tend to supply more than their share of recruits to the navy and air force, even under those forces' much more open recruiting systems (see Figures 5.4 and 5.5).

The fact that recruitment to the Indian Army does not match the proportions of the Indian states despite the increasing concern with regional fairness and RMP is not completely surprising. The fact is that, for some of the supply and demand reasons above, no nonconscript army in history has *ever* looked exactly like its overall population. The French Army historically recruited disproportionately from the north and east of the country (Scott 1998). The current British Army, with a regional regimental structure very similar to the Indian

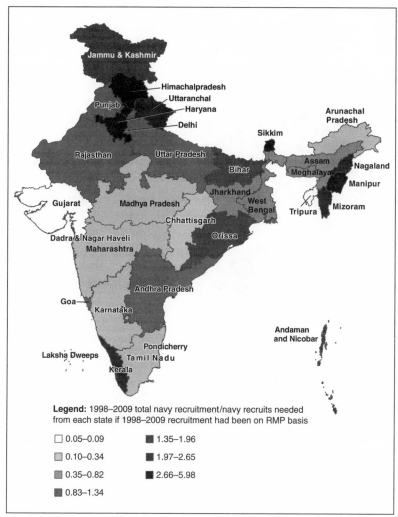

FIGURE 5.4 Number of navy recruits from each Indian state relative to recruitable male population, 1998–2009

Army, has had problems meeting its recruitment quota in some areas (such as parts of Scotland and Greater London) and therefore fills in the gaps with recruits from economically depressed regions such as the West Midlands, the northeast, Wales, and by recruiting men from the Republic of Ireland and from the Commonwealth, which now supplies 10 percent of recruits. The 4,480-strong Royal Regiment of

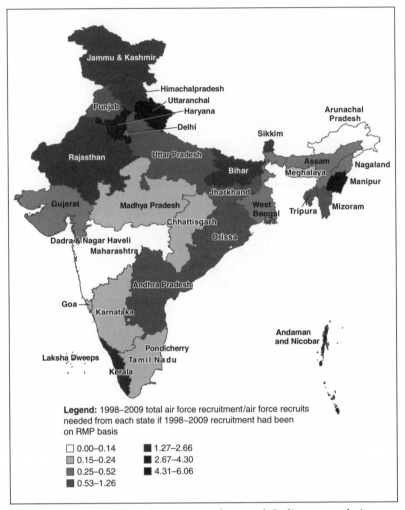

FIGURE 5.5 Number of air force recruits from each Indian state relative to recruitable male population, 1998–2009

Scotland, for instance, which includes such historic legacy regiments as the Black Watch and Argyll and Sutherland Highlanders, now has 250 Fijians, 60 South Africans, 30 each from Saint Vincent and Saint Lucia, and 100 others from India, Ireland, Jamaica, Kenya, and elsewhere.[33] And across the Atlantic, a 2008 study found that the (all volunteer) US Army today somewhat overrepresents whites and African Americans and overrepresents the west and south of the United States compared to other groups and regions (Watkins and Sherk 2008).

The real importance of these differences in the Indian states' level of demand for jobs in the military can easily be seen if we look at patterns of recruitment for the Air Force and Navy, neither of which have class recruitment policies and both of which are supposed to recruit on the basis of RMP. As we can see in Figure 5.4, the two most overrepresented major states in navy recruitment from 1998 to 1999, falling in the band of states on the map with 2.66 to 5.98 times their proportional representation, were the entirely landlocked traditional army recruiting states of Haryana and Himachal Pradesh. The small landlocked state of Sikkim was the single most overrepresented state (5.98 times its proportional representation), and Manipur, the Andamans, and Mizoram also fell into the most overrepresented states category, though, because of these states' very small yearly recruitment figures, the percentage of overrepresentation is not very meaningful. The only other major states with more than twice their proportional share in navy recruitment were the landlocked traditional recruiting state of Uttarakhand (named Uttaranchal for most of this period), and the coastal state of Kerala. These were followed by the states of Orissa and Bihar, with 1.67 and 1.78 times their expected representation, respectively. The coastal states of Tamil Nadu, Karnataka, and Gujarat each had well under half their expected naval recruitment. It is hard to make any sense of these inter-state disparities if RMP is really the major factor in navy recruitment.

It is a similar story (Figure 5.5) in the air force, with Haryana, Himachal Pradesh, and Uttarakhand the most overrepresented states from 1998 to 2009, with 2.66 to 6.06 times their proportional representation. Jammu and Kashmir was only slightly behind with around two and a half times its proportional representation. Only Kerala with 1.6 times its proportional representation and Bihar with 2.38 times its representation are significantly represented in air force recruitment from outside the traditional recruiting states. In both air force and navy recruitment, then, despite the formal differences in recruitment, the overrepresented and underrepresented states are largely the same as in the Army. The traditional recruiting states of Haryana, Himachal Pradesh, Jammu and Kashmir, Punjab, and Uttarakhand are heavily represented, while states such as Assam, Chhattisgarh, Gujarat, Jharkhand, Karnataka, Madhya Pradesh, and West Bengal are all underrepresented.

No army, it is true, ever completely reflects the nation that it defends. What is striking about the Indian Army, though, is the degree of overrepresentation of some groups and states, which continues to be high by international standards. For instance, in the United States the urbanized Northeast is the most underrepresented region, producing only around 60 to 70 percent on average of its expected number of recruits, which is similar to the levels in the underrepresented Indian states. The state of Connecticut has a level of underrepresentation (63 percent of its expected level given its population) similar to that of Orissa, while New Jersey (62 percent) has a similar level to West Bengal. In the United States the most overrepresented state, Montana, has 167 percent of the enlisted recruits we would expect if it were represented proportionately. The other major surplus-recruiting states, rural states like Montana or southern states like Alabama and Texas with strong military traditions, are overrepresented by 122 percent to 150 percent of what we would expect on the basis of their population: Georgia (122 percent), Missouri (126 percent), Idaho (128 percent), Texas, Florida, and Alabama (all 131 percent), Oklahoma and Arkansas (both 132 percent), Maine (145 percent), Oregon (139 percent), and Nevada (150 percent) (Watkins and Sherk 2008). In India, by contrast, the most overrepresented states in recruitment are overrepresented by proportions that far exceed anything we see in the United States: Haryana has 192 percent of the soldiers we would expect on the basis of population, Punjab has 384 percent, Jammu and Kashmir 410 percent, Uttarakhand 480 percent, and Himachal Pradesh has 604 percent. These traditional patterns of recruitment in India have been remarkably "sticky," in part because of the class-recruitment system for regiments with strong regional identities and traditions. For example, the correlation coefficient between the level of state representation in recruitment from 1998 to 2009 and state proportionality in recruitment from 1971 to 1973, three years for which we have good data, is 0.95, which gives an idea of just how slowly things have changed in the past forty years.[34]

So from the perspective of "fair shares" the traditional "martial" states still have a disproportionate share of the total. This is true even for those services—the navy and the air force—that explicitly have no class recruitment and try to recruit on the basis of RMP.

One important point to make, though, is that given the very large populations of the "deficit" states relative to those of the traditional recruiting states, even the moderate increases in recruitment from these states that we have seen over the past few decades have greatly equalized the regional representativeness of the army. We no longer see anything like the dangerous situation we saw before World War II, or after independence in Pakistan (which we still see there today), where one province supplied most of the army while many other large and populous provinces, such as Bihar and Bengal, had no representation at all. In Figure 5.6 I show the absolute number of recruits in the Indian Army from 1998–2009, and, as we can see, this presents a very different picture to the one in Figure 5.3, which emphasized the overrepresentation of traditional states, albeit states that had relatively low populations. As Figure 5.6 shows, the populous "deficit" state of Bihar, in fact, supplied more new recruits to the Indian Army from 1998 to 2009 (38,545) than either of the traditional recruiting states of Himachal Pradesh (21,649) or Jammu and Kashmir (28,275). The "underrepresented" state of Uttar Pradesh, likewise, supplied 98,000 troops from 1998 to 2009, far more than the 58,000 recruited from overrepresented Punjab during these years. Uttar Pradesh is in fact the highest-represented state in current army recruitment, providing around 13 percent of the total army strength, compared to its 16 percent share in the population. So from the perspective of overall ethnic balance, the Indian Army is today probably more balanced than it has ever been, at least among the non-commissioned ranks.

These state-level recruitment data, however, probably somewhat understate the degree of the regional imbalance that remains in the army. As with any system in which state levels of demand for places in the army vary significantly and a quota (the RMP amount) is in effect for at least some of the positions, potential recruits will try to get around the rules. Men from Haryana, Himachal, and other traditional recruiting states where the supply of potential recruits far exceeds their RMP quota sometimes travel to nearby "deficit" states to try to enroll there, as do men from states with high levels of poverty such as Bihar and Uttar Pradesh. Recruits from these states contact touts who can obtain false domicile certificates, ration cards,

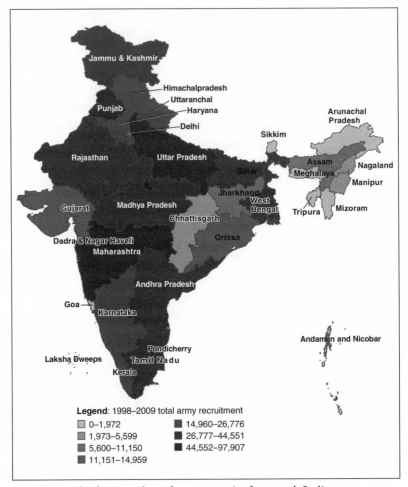

FIGURE 5.6 Absolute number of army recruits from each Indian state,
1998–2009

affidavits, and other verifying information for INR 10,000 and up.
In turn, these touts work in league with army recruiters prepared to
turn a blind eye to large numbers of men from other states who are
trying to enroll in the army under local domiciles. Prosperous Delhi,
as the RMP-deficit state closest to some of the main traditional
recruiting states of the northwest, seems to have been especially heavily affected by such recruiting rackets.[35] But other deficit states have
also seen floods of out-of-state applicants. In 2009, the army's own
audits estimated that 30 percent of the thirty thousand hopefuls

(three times the usual level) who had turned up to a big recruiting *mela* in Ahmedabad, Gujarat, were really from outside the state, mainly from Uttar Pradesh, Madhya Pradesh, Bihar, and Rajasthan.[36] Occasionally there are also press reports and legal judgments in which it is clear that someone from one state has documentation to "prove" he is from another, joins the army under the other state's quota, and then gets found out.[37] But the extent to which men might be subject to this kind of postenlistment verification once they have joined the Army and are performing well is unclear, and one suspects that many of those thrown out may simply have run afoul of their officers or fellow soldiers for some other reason.

The Changing Picture in Terms of Group Composition

In Figures 5.7 and 5.8, I show the absolute and percentage changes in the battalion class composition of the Infantry and armored corps units of the army through time, from the 1940s to the present. This is a "bottom up" way of getting at the same general patterns we see in the state and national data, though given the difficulty of getting complete coverage of accurate battalion composition data and founding dates it is not as complete, even if it allows for a finer-grained sense of composition patterns for the majority of units for which data are available. It is important to bear in mind that the method I use here provides an estimate of the approximate total battalion strength of each group in the infantry and armored corps, rather than the total number of battalions in which members of each group can be found. In other words it is based on a count of the number of companies of each group in each battalion, from which I then estimate the approximate number of battalions of each group in the overall infantry and armored corps. The overall picture these fine-grained data present is still largely the same as the one we get at the broader level; an army that was remarkably resistant to any substantial change in its traditional class recruitment patterns for the first three decades after independence (88 percent of unit strength in the combined infantry and armored corps was still drawn from the traditional pre-1947-recruited classes in the 1960s), but a force that has—although traditionally recruited groups are still the majority—become increasingly broader since the 1970s. Approximately a third of the units in the 2010s, according to my estimates, are a combination of

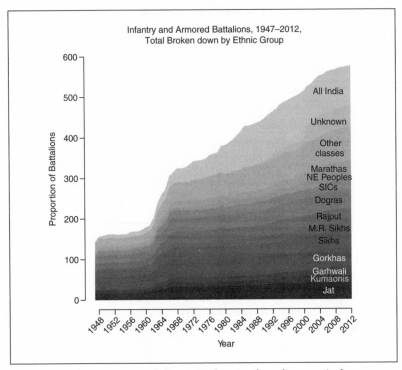

FIGURE 5.7 The expansion of the army showing battalion-equivalent numbers of each class, 1947–2012

Source: Wilkinson dataset estimates.

new classes raised since 1947 (such as Bengalis, Oriyas, and Gujaratis), All-India mixed composition units, and "Unknown," most of which are also likely to be all-India, as they are new units without another specified class composition. The traditional groups are of course still well represented, with around 4 percent Marathas, 7 percent Jats, 8 percent Gorkhas, 7 percent Sikhs, 4 percent M & R Sikhs, and 6 percent Rajputs, according to my estimates. But the share of these groups has in almost all cases been going down, and recent experience suggests it will go down further over the next few decades.[38]

The Officer Corps

The overrepresentation of traditional recruiting states still holds true for the officer corps, as far as we can tell, though it has also lessened over the years. At the very top, one important change that

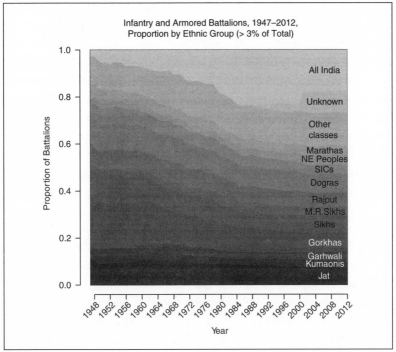

FIGURE 5.8 The expansion of the army showing different class percentages over time, 1947–2012

Source: Wilkinson dataset estimates.

has been made over the past decade has been an end to the apparent glass ceiling, in place since independence, on Sikh officers reaching the very top of the military hierarchy. Six months after the United Progressive Alliance's May 2004 election victory Prime Minister Manmohan Singh, a Sikh himself, appointed General J. J. Singh as the first Sikh COAS, a position he took up in January 2005 and in which he served with distinction until 2007. More recently, in May 2012 Prime Minister Singh appointed General Bikram Singh as the second Sikh COAS. At the end of 2013, India's top military leadership was impressively diverse in terms of minority and regional representation: the COAS is Sikh, Defence Minister A. K. Anthony (2006–2014) was a Christian from Kerala, and the outgoing Chief of Air Staff, Air Marshal N. A. K. Browne, was an Anglo-Indian from Uttar Pradesh, to be replaced by Air Chief Marshal Arup Raha, a Bengali Hindu. More generally, the old civilian strategy of trying to maximize the regional and caste heterogeneity at the top of the army command and minimize the proportion of officers from the traditional recruiting states (especially the states that constituted pre-1947 Punjab) seems to have been largely abandoned. From 2005 to 2014, in fact, all four COASs were from either Punjab or Haryana, and several of those tipped as future COASs are also from these regions. Just before the UPA lost the May 2014 elections to the BJP, the Manmohan Singh government appointed Lieutenant General Dalbir Singh Suhag, from Haryana, as the next Chief of Army Staff, making him the fifth incumbent in a row from the army's recruiting heartland. Although Prime Minister Singh had the final word on these appointments it would be wrong to see them as some kind of Punjabi assertion or a United Progressive Alliance versus Bharatiya Janata Party (BJP) partisan issue.[39] It is more a reflection that in both major coalitions in India there is substantial Sikh representation (the Shiromani Akali Dal is an important member of the BJP's National Democratic Alliance and forms a coalition government with the BJP in Punjab itself), and therefore the old unofficial community bars are no longer sustainable in the new world of finely balanced national coalition politics in which every community's votes are needed.

Below the very highest command ranks, current data on the group composition of officers are not generally available. But the 1981 data on officers above the rank of colonel (see Figure 5.9) that I have collected and coded look remarkably similar in many ways to the 1951 data we saw in Chapter 4. The correlation coefficient between the levels of different groups' representation in the officer corps in 1951 and 1981 is 0.81, indicating a lot of stickiness over these three decades in terms of which groups were heavily represented. Looking at the ethnicity of reported retirements among the most senior officers (at the rank of Major General and above) in the 1990s and early 2000s also yields composition data not too far off from these 1981 estimates—around 16 percent Sikh, 1 percent Muslim, and 2–3 percent Christian.

However, more recent data on Indian Military Academy (IMA) recruits from 1983 to 1987, which likely provide a better guide to the composition of the army officers about to enter the most senior

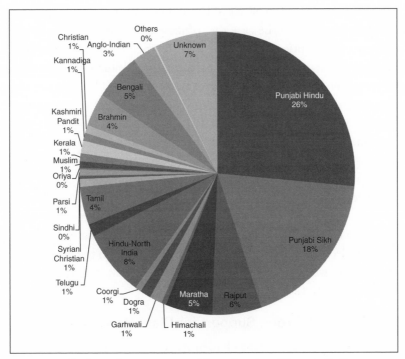

FIGURE 5.9 Estimated group composition of senior officers in Indian
Army, 1981

Source: Wilkinson officer dataset.

command ranks today, show a substantial broadening of recruitment
from the pattern we observe in 1981; officers from prepartition
"Punjab" (Punjab, Haryana, Himachal Pradesh, and Chandigarh
combined) made up 27 percent of the cadets from 1983 to 1987 (Sinha
and Chanda 1992, 254–255). Even if we included officer cadets from
nearby Delhi (9 percent of cadets 1983–1987) in the total—and some
of these are surely not Punjabi—that would still give us a total Punjabi (Hindu and Sikh) percentage somewhere in the low 30 percent
range, which is much lower than in the 1981 (44 percent) or 1951
(42 percent) data, or of the Punjabi proportion among IMA cadets
before World War II, when they accounted for 42 percent of cadets
from 1932 to 1936. Officers from all the traditional "martial" groups
added together probably accounted for around half the recruits in

the 1980s, compared to closer to three quarters at independence. Of
course it may still be the case that officers from the traditionally recruited communities might have a preference for joining the core
infantry and armored units rather than, say, the Indian Army Service
Corps or the Engineers, so the percentage of Jats, Sikhs, Dogras, and
similar groups in these combat regiments might still be somewhat
higher than in the army as a whole.

As many observers have noted, these recruits are also much more
diverse in terms of their class composition and social outlook than
the officers of 1951. Many of them are the children of NCOs and
have been educated at military schools and then at the IMA, National
Defence Academy, or one of the other major officer academies.
They are less elitist in terms of their social and political values, and
perhaps also less likely to want or to be able to retain the clear social
distance between officers and men that was such a marker of the
Indian Army in the past.

Why the Strong Support for Class Recruitment?

There has been significant change in recruitment patterns, as we
have seen. But why has there not been even faster change, given the
political pressures to broaden recruitment? One important reason,
deeply entrenched in the army, is that many senior military officers
are still convinced that there is a lot to be gained in terms of military
effectiveness from deploying men in homogenous units with strong
regimental and battalion traditions. Recruitment from particular
groups, these officers argue, serves a number of military purposes:
the policy helps build a cohesive unit, whose close bonds, common
cultures, and regimental traditions encourage men to fight hard, for
the regiment and for each other. It is easy to portray these views,
as the petitioner in a recent Supreme Court case evidently does, as
simply an unmerited colonial hangover that is unworthy of secular
India. But there is in fact some evidence from outside India that
there is something to this. For instance, the economists Dora Costa
and Matthew Kahn have analyzed patterns of recruitment, ethnicity, and fighting using historical data for tens of thousands of men
recruited in the American Civil War (1861–1865); they found that
soldiers in more ethnically cohesive units were more likely to reen-

list and less likely to mutiny and desert than soldiers from more mixed units. Cohesiveness seemed to have its rewards in military effectiveness (Costa and Kahn 2008).

Of course there are also arguments that could be made on the other side. The political scientist Stephen Rosen points out that the small-unit class structure of the Indian Army "will tend to produce an army that can be expected to be cohesive at the platoon and company level, less so at the battalion level, and even less at higher levels of organization. Such an army will tend to have difficulty carrying out military operations that require cooperation of units above the battalion level, such as a combined arms war involving rapidly moving battles and infantry, armor, signals and artillery units" (Rosen 1996, 115–116). And the US Army, among others, has also demonstrated that with sufficient attention to training and incentives, it is possible to move from an ethnically more cohesive to an ethnically diverse military and officer corps with no apparent loss in terms of efficiency and possibly some gains.

But in India, which is also much more diverse in terms of its ethnic heterogeneity than most countries where these debates have taken place, the army still believes in the advantages of class recruitment. In 1992 Indian Army headquarters apparently carried out a study on "Rationalisation of Class Composition," which apparently recommended that the "Vaidya" mixed battalions created in the aftermath of Operation Bluestar in the 1980s should be switched back to the old fixed-class or single-class system (Gautam 2009, 38). In 1998, General Ved Prakash Malik, who had spent his early career with a class regiment, the Sikh Light Infantry, passed an order to shift the Vaidya battalions back to their earlier class composition, the experiment having been deemed a failure. It is perhaps relevant to note that the Defence Minister at the time, Mulayam Singh Yadav, who had made his political career representing the interests of the backward castes, was perhaps more open to the idea of caste-based recruitment than some earlier Defence Ministers.[40] In August 1998, for instance, the Jat Regiment's mixed Twentieth Battalion received an order to reform as a 100 percent Jat class battalion, which it did by the end of 1999 (Bajwa and Rikhye 2001; Subramanian 2003). The Thirteenth Sikh and Ninth Dogra battalions went back to single-class

composition, sending their other classes back to their parent regiments. And in October 1998, the Twenty-First Rajputana Rifles,
which had been composed of Jats, Rajputs, Garhwalis, and South
Indians, was ordered back to the typical Rajputana Rifles regimental composition of Jats and Rajputs (Shrivastava 2000, 52). Military
academy case notes available on the web suggest that mechanized
infantry units, which had also apparently shifted to a mixed composition, were also moved back to single-class units around this time
(V. S. Verma n.d.). It should be noted, though, that officers and men
in these mixed battalions, where strong bonds had been built up as
a result of operational deployments and service together, felt that the
army was making a big mistake and that "their" units were performing just as well as the traditional class units. One retired officer said
that his mixed battalion had been working well after an initial set-
tling-in period of a few years, and that he saw no evidence of the advantages cited by the higher command in making the shift back, which
he thought was the result of prejudice rather than experience.[41]

A second, related reason for the "stickiness" of community patterns of representation in the army is that it is still logistically much
easier to create new battalions by forming them out of a core of existing servicemen and using existing regimental infrastructures to
train them than it is to start an entirely new unit and build these
fighting traditions from scratch. This is how the army expanded in
1914–1918, from 1939 to 1945, and after 1962, and the processes of
"milking" existing battalions for men and building new battalions
on top of existing class units and fighting traditions are deeply in-
grained. So these practices have also been adopted in recent years as
the army has added new Rashtriya Rifles (RR) battalions dedicated
to counterinsurgency and internal security. The idea of the RRs,
apparently, was to free up the line army units for their primary duties,
given what one MP, S. Jaipal Reddy, termed in parliament in 1995
the "grave concern . . . being voiced in many quarters about the ex-
cessive deployment of Army for dealing with civil disturbances
which is resulting in disorientation of Army."[42] The RR battalions
are trained by the army and under its operational control, but unlike
regular units they are trained specifically for counterinsurgency
roles and they are permanently based in their main areas of deployment. The first fifteen battalions of this new force were authorized

in 1990, and six of these were raised over the next few years. A further thirty battalions were authorized in 1994, when the conflict in Kashmir was reaching a peak, and several dozen battalions have been authorized since then.[43] By my estimate sixty-three of the seventy-two battalions added to the army from 1990 to 2012 were RR battalions, so the RR accounts for almost all the infantry expansion during this period.[44] These battalions freed up several army divisions for defense roles, and because the RR units are a separate line in the defense budget they also have eased the financial pressure of counterinsurgency duties on the army's overall budget (Rajagopalan 2010, 31–32).

To preserve the fighting cohesion of these units and enable the expansion to be done quickly with a reliable flow of good troops, it was decided to link each RR unit formally to a regiment in the army; troops from that regiment constitute most of the RR battalion and are seconded to it for a period of several years before returning to their "home" regiment. This cycling of men in and out created some initial problems. For one thing army units, not surprisingly, initially tried to send men to the RR units who were performing less well than those they felt they really needed. The other problem is that men who have served in the RR on counterinsurgency duties *do* return to their units, so some of the dangers of domestic deployments having an effect on the army can eventually come home to roost (Rajagopalan 2010, 33).

Despite these teething troubles and the fact the force does not completely insulate army troops from domestic counterinsurgency, the RR experiment has been seen as an overall success in two main ways: operationally in terms of counterinsurgency (although Rajagopalan notes the difficulties in assessing performance on this dimension), and in freeing up army units for their primary defense mission. One advantage of the RR model is that, as with the earlier Assam Rifles, permanent deployments in an area increase local familiarity and the opportunities to develop local community ties and intelligence links that help in operations (2010, 32–33).

The Sachar Controversy

Since independence India's Muslims have been underrepresented in government employment at both the national level and in the states for a variety of reasons including the relative economic and educational backwardness of the community, lack of political clout, and discrimination. In the army, where almost all Muslim units from India were transferred to or opted for Pakistan in 1947–1948, this underrepresentation has also been severe. In the summer of 2005 the whole question of Muslim representation in the military came to the fore in a very public way when the Sachar Committee, appointed by the Congress Party to examine the status of Muslims, asked all the defense and paramilitary services for details of their Muslim representation. The navy and air force and paramilitary forces did supply at least some data to the commission. Although these navy and air force data were not made public in the final report, they showed that in the navy 1.9 percent of the 2,260 A&B class *civilian* personnel and 3.2 percent of the 30,908 C&D class *civilian* personnel were Muslim in 2005.[45] That compares to 7.5 percent of A&B class employees and 7 percent of C&D employees, respectively, for India's 2-percent-strong Christian population in the navy. In the air force, the Muslim proportion was around 3.1 percent overall, with 0.9 percent of the senior officers and 1.9 percent of the junior and mid-ranking officers (up to wing commander). By comparison, the percentage of Sikh officers was 9.2 percent senior, 4.9 percent junior, and 2 percent overall, while Christians had 4 percent of senior officers, 4.4 percent of junior officers, and 2.8 percent overall. So unless there has been a big difference in recruitment patterns over time, Sikh officers both seem to stay in the air force longer and reach more senior ranks than their Muslim comrades.

The Sachar Committee's request for information created a particular problem for the army. First, because—as we have seen—one way it has protected its autonomy over recruitment since independence is by deliberately not responding to any requests for detailed breakdowns of its ethnic composition. Second, because the army understandably does not want to weaken its own cohesion by focusing too much on ethnic heterogeneity. The COAS of the army, General J. J. Singh, had been appointed as the country's first-ever Sikh COAS only six months before, on January 31, 2005. When he was appointed General Singh had been asked about the significance of his identity as a minority and had taken pains to stress that he was just as much a Maratha (his regiment) as a Sikh and that "I consider myself first and last to be an Indian" (Singh 2012, 197). As a Sikh, he must also have been especially conscious of the damage that Bluestar and the focus on religious divisions at that time had done to the army, and he was in no hurry to open that particular can of worms.

In an August 2005 letter responding to Sachar's original June 20 request for information, the Additional Director General Personnel Services in the Army, Major General K. P. D. Samanta, therefore emphasized to the committee that the army recruited primarily on the basis of each state's RMP, that "personnel from all castes, regions and religions are recruited as per their eligibility criteria," and that "data relating to various castes or religions is not maintained in the Army and it will also not be proper to collect or collate such data. This may convey the wrong message to the troops adversely affecting the well-established cohesion, regimental spirit and morale."[46]

This last point—the claim that the army does not even collect or collate data on caste and religion—must be inaccurate, for three reasons. First, we know that such information is collected from each soldier at the point of recruitment, and is necessary for a variety of purposes, including determining the proper rites and whether a soldier should be buried or cremated if killed in action (Navlakha 2006, 687). Second, we know that class regiments recruit men from their units' specified classes—Jats, Sikhs, Dogras, etc.—for most of their positions. Third, it is simply not possible to run such a class regiment and class company system without collecting information, each year, on how many of groups X or Y are in service now, what the expected wastage through retirement and other factors is going to be, and therefore how many of each group are required to be recruited during the following year to fill the vacancies for each class.[47] So information must be maintained in *some* form, which *could* be further aggregated without too much effort, even if the army might have been strictly correct in 2005 that these data were not aggregated for all units or the army as a whole as a matter of course. At times of special concern about particular groups the army also seems to know exactly what it needs to about levels of different groups' representation within its ranks. When asked by a journalist in 1986 about issues with Sikhs in the army in the aftermath of Operation Bluestar, COAS General

Krishnaswamy Sundarji answered immediately with a detailed count
of the number of Sikh battalions (fifty 100-percent-Sikh battalions
and a further fifty or so with "very large" Sikh representation), presumably the result of the army's own head count.[48] The Ministry of
Defence has also publicly released information on the breakdown of
particular units at times. In 2000, for instance, Defence Minister
George Fernandes, responding to a questioner who complained about
the Maratha Light Infantry's recruitment of other groups reducing
opportunities for Marathas, revealed that Marathas were still 86.13
percent of the unit's strength, and that Muslims, Mysorians, and
"Others" were only 4.16 percent, 4.16 percent, and 5.55 percent in the
unit, respectively.[49]

The Sachar Committee was not willing to let the matter rest with
Major General Samanta's initial August 2005 letter. In October
2005 the secretary of the committee, Abusaleh Shariff, spoke to
Defence Minister Pranab Mukherjee to let him know that the army
still had not provided the data, and to try to persuade him to make
them release it. According to one news report, the COAS then discussed the matter with the Defence Minister the next day, presumably to urge him not to press the army to release the data.[50] In any
event the conflict between the army and the Sachar Committee over
the release of data came to a head at a press conference in Visakhapat-
nam in February 2006, when General Singh was asked by some journalists why the army was not cooperating with the committee. He
replied that "We never look at things like where you come from, the
language you speak, or the religion you believe in. That has always
been our ethos and policy. We are an apolitical, secular and a professional force. Therefore we consider it important that all Indians
get a fair chance of joining the armed forces."[51] Whether the statement was, as General Singh portrays it, an off-the-cuff response to
a journalist's question, or a more tactical response to earlier news
reports, it had the effect of sparking off a storm of criticism of the
Sachar Committee. India's TV news channels all picked up on the
general's "rejection" of Sachar and the committee's alleged attempt
to communalize the armed forces. For the BJP in particular it was a
perfect issue, fitting in with the party's broader narrative that Congress was practicing the politics of pseudosecularism and minority

appeasement. The party forced a debate in parliament in which MPs including veteran BJP leader Jaswant Singh, an ex-cavalry officer himself, condemned the Congress Party's attempts to divide the army along communal lines. The Defence Minister at the time, Pranab Mukherjee—now India's president—defended the general purpose of the Sachar Committee while also emphasizing that the armed forces do not have reservations and "do not recruit on the basis of race, religion, caste or even region." Perhaps forgetting about the creation of the Naga Regiment in 1970, or the many Rashtriya Rifles units linked to existing class regiments, he also claimed that since 1950, "not a single regiment has been named after any region or after any race or after any group of people."[52] In the face of this storm in the media and parliament both the Prime Minister's office and Justice Sachar quickly backed away from the request, and the subsequent report contained no breakdown of minority representation in the army.

What is the level of Muslim representation in the army? We can come up with an initial (likely conservative) estimate if we take the proportion of battalions and companies that we know recruit from Muslims as the numerator, assume that Rashtriya Rifles units recruit Muslims in roughly the same proportion as the sister regiments from which they draw personnel, and assume no Muslim representation in any of the remaining units unless (as in the case of south Indian classes) we have specific evidence to confirm that Muslims are recruited. Then we can take the overall number of battalions in the infantry and armored corps as the denominator. This method may underestimate the proportion of Muslims by not including Muslim personnel in, for example, the Indian Army Service Corps or in infantry units with "all-India" composition. But given that we have no defensible method for applying a Muslim percentage to the many mixed units whose composition is unknown, this probably provides us with a reasonable initial estimate.

Using this method, and taking advantage of information on each battalion's composition from available sources such as Gautam (2009) and Sharma (2000) as well as the regimental histories, we can calculate the overall representation of Muslims in the army today as a little under 3 percent. The highest representation is probably in the armored corps (approximately 3 percent), largely because the corps inherited several units at partition that recruited Muslims from India, such as the Kaimkhani, or Muslim Rajputs. There is a squadron of Muslims in each of the Eighteenth, Sixty-First, and Seventy-Third Cavalry regiments as well as some Muslim representation in each of the Eighth, Sixteenth, and Forty-Fifth Cavalry. In the Infantry, the proportion of Muslims is smaller, and over two-thirds of these Muslim troops are concentrated in just a few regiments: the Grenadiers and the two Jammu and Kashmir regiments, the Jammu and Kashmir Rifles, and the Jammu and Kashmir Light Infantry. The Jammu and Kashmir Rifles and the Jammu and Kashmir Light Infantry recruit very large numbers of Muslims, 25 percent and 50 percent, respectively, reflecting, albeit not fully, the substantial Muslim population in that state. There are additional Muslim companies in the Maratha Light Infantry,[53] the Rajputana Rifles (Third, Sixth, and Eighth Battalions), the Rajput Regiment, the Mechanized Infantry Regiment, the Kumaon Regiment (Third and Eighth Battalions), and the Rashtriya Rifles, for a total of around 1.5 percent. With 1.5 percent in the Infantry, a somewhat higher percentage in the (smaller) armored corps, and maybe 3 percent or more Muslims in the noncombat branches, that leaves us with an overall estimate of around thirty battalions, or 2.5 percent Muslim representation for the army as a whole. That is not too far off from the apparently precise but unsourced estimate of roughly twenty-nine battalions and 29,093 (2.7 percent) Muslims in the 1.13-million-strong army provided by Defence Correspondent Shishir Gupta in an *India Today* article in February 2006 (Navlakha 2006, 687).

Assessing the level of Muslim minority representation in the officer corps presents some challenges, given that army lists are not available, but if we look at the proportion of Muslim names in the reported retirements of the most senior Major General and Lieutenant General positions in the 1990s and early 2000s it appears as if the proportion of very senior Muslim officers is around 1 percent. That is certainly low compared to the number of Sikhs and Christians in the army. But this in part reflects the socioeconomic backwardness of the Muslim community—now lower than SCs among the younger age groups—and we should point out that Muslim representation in India, like that of other minorities such as Sikhs and Christians, is also much higher than the level of minority represen- tation in the Pakistan army.

Conclusion

The Indian state still uses most of the same strategies to prevent a coup that were used in the 1950s, 1960s, and 1970s, with the excep- tion of hedging ethnicities at the very highest levels (COAS and lieu- tenant generals): it provides obstacles to military coordination against the state by having a diverse officer corps, ethnic balancing within the army, multiple recruitment streams, strong civilian oversight through multiple committees and a powerful Ministry of Defence, separate force hierarchies that prevent "jointness," balancing forces outside the army, and a watchful intelligence infrastructure (Horowitz 1985; Quinlivan 1999). Yet despite the state's success over the years at making sure the Indian Army is nonpolitical, politicians and the bu- reaucracy can still get nervous at times. Most recently, in the spring of 2012 several prominent journalists from the newspaper *Indian Ex- press* alleged that a few months earlier, on January 16–17, 2012, there had been unexplained large-scale troop movements in the direction of New Delhi that had made the civilian leadership and bureaucracy worry that a potential coup might be in progress.[54] The civilian leader- ship and intelligence services were especially nervous, it seems, be- cause the troop movements came in the midst of the very public fight between the COAS and Defence Minister A. K. Anthony over the proper seniority and retirement date of General Singh, a case which was due to be heard in the Supreme Court the next day. The reports of unexplained troop movements and the civilian reaction were im- mediately dismissed by the army, Defence Minister, and Prime Min- ister's office, and a coup attempt seems very unlikely, but there were still a few loose strands to the story, and in February 2014 retired Lieutenant General A. K. Choudhary, the former Director General of Military Operations under General V. K. Singh, seemed to con- firm many of the details of the original report in an interview with the *Indian Express*. Allegedly at 5:30 a.m. on the morning of January 16 the head of the Intelligence Bureau, Nehchal Sandhu, on hear- ing about the troop movements, phoned several former Defence

Secretaries to check on protocols that existed for troop movements in the National Capital Region. Not happy with the lack of clarity on the troop movements, Sandhu contacted the Defence Secretary, Shashi Kant Sharma, who phoned General Chaudhary just before midnight and asked him to account for the movements and order the troops back to base. Chaudhary was told that there was concern at "the highest level," and apparently the civilian and intelligence leadership was sufficiently worried to send a helicopter from Delhi the next morning with three intelligence officials on board (one from the Research and Analysis Wing), to check that the armored vehicles were indeed on their way back to Hisar (in Haryana) and driving away from New Delhi.[55] The troop movements were in apparent violation of what one well-informed interviewer—in a TV program after the report came out—said were established norms that there were to be no large-scale troop movements in the National Capital Region without prenotification and the permission of the Defence Ministry. The fact that these norms were in place was something tacitly admitted by Defence Minister of State Pallam Raju during an interview with TV journalist Karan Thapar, himself the son of a former COAS.[56] The controversy over the troop movements and whether they had or had not violated protocols that have surely been in place for the National Capital Region since at least the 1960s symbolized the continuing nervousness over potential threats from the army. Former COAS General V. P. Malik said in 2012 that "the harsh fact [is] that in civil and military relations, which have never been very cordial, the friction seems to have increased."[57] Lieutenant General Chaudhary, after his retirement in February 2014, referred to one reason for the civilian skittishness over the troop movements as due to distrust "between two individuals" and "immaturity" on both sides.[58] Chaudhury also reported that several months after the 2012 troop movements new rules were put in place to make sure the army informed the civilian leadership about all major army movements in the National Capital Region.

This friction and nervousness do seem to have increased over the past decade, as political party competition in India itself has become more fractured, and as the army becomes less a society apart and more influenced by the corruption, caste conflicts, and bureaucratic backbiting that characterizes other parts of the polity. That said, we should not go overboard; the army is still held in wide esteem as one of the best-functioning institutions in the country, and as the focus of national pride. It is also true that in the new cable news and Internet environment in India the mass media and press are ready to find controversy wherever they can, in the search for ratings and sales.

6

The Path Not Taken:
Pakistan 1947–1977

Introduction

WHY HAS MILITARY intervention in politics been more frequent in Pakistan than in India, despite the apparently similar legacies from colonial rule? The existing and ever-expanding literature on this question tends to highlight two factors. First, Pakistan was dealt a worse hand in 1947 in terms of its strategic challenges, its poorer economic endowments, its human capital, and its share of India's tax base, administrative, and military services. Second, the Muslim League in Pakistan was much weaker than the Congress Party in India, creating more instability, less opportunity to strengthen the country's political institutions, and greater opportunities for military intervention in Pakistan's first decade and a half than in India. Different authors place different emphases on these factors—for instance, Zinkin, Morris-Jones, and Jalal put more stress on bad legacies while Weiner, Oldenburg, and Tudor put more on weak parties—but there is a broad consensus that both of these factors are important (Zinkin 1959, 89–91; Morris-Jones 1967, 13–47; Weiner 1989; Jalal 1992, 1995, 9–28; Oldenburg 2010; Tudor 2013).[1] By 1958, when General Ayub Khan carried out a coup against President Iskander Mirza, many authors believe that it was already too late for Pakistan's government to take the steps that Patel, Nehru, Krishna Menon, and others had taken from 1947 to 1955 to control the army in India.

These arguments have been well made and documented by others, and I do not intend to simply repeat them here, or to provide a general history of Pakistan. But the existing accounts are also not a complete explanation for the divergence in civil-military outcomes between the two countries. So here I want to highlight the importance of several additional factors that I believe have received less attention than they deserve in explaining the outcomes over Pakistan's first three decades, a period in which much of the contemporary structure of civil-military relations seems to have been fixed.[2] First, I want to emphasize that the level of the ethnic imbalance in the army that Pakistan inherited at independence was much worse than that in the Indian Army. Pakistan's military was in fact so imbalanced that one province, West Punjab, had a quarter of the population but almost three-quarters of the infantry, while another major province, East Bengal, had virtually no representation despite having over half the population. West Punjab's dominance in the Pakistan Army gave the province more than twice the proportion that the most overrepresented province in India (East Punjab) had in the Indian Army, and the Punjabi proportion in India's military was also cross-cut by religious and caste identities that further reduced the political significance of Punjabi overrepresentation in India. These very high levels of ethnic imbalance have, comparatively, been associated with severe problems for democracy and an increased likelihood of civil war (Chandra and Wilkinson 2008). So Pakistan's military inheritance, despite being carved out from the same Indian Army in 1947, was much worse than India's.

The second factor I want to highlight is that Pakistan's inability to deal with civil-military control issues in its first decade, even when this might have been possible, was the product of a combination of the narrow and top-down nature of the Muslim League structure before independence—which limited the voices of those from underrepresented provinces such as Bengal—and the particular ideology of the new state and the particular nature of the Muslim League as a party that had represented a privileged minority in colonial India, a community that had been formally guaranteed a substantial share of the higher police, civil service, and military positions. In the 1930s and 1940s, Muhammad Ali Jinnah's and the League's insistence that Muslims were a single community and that a state for Muslims would solve all issues had deemphasized the importance within the party of thinking in detail about ethnic and linguistic issues and balancing the institutions of the new state, of which the military was obviously the most important. Lieutenant General Sir Ross McCay, a senior general in Pakistan throughout the first few years of independence, told Jinnah's biographer in the early 1950s that "Jinnah never spoke to me of the problems of the Army," a stance which McCay compared unfavorably with other national founders such as Garibaldi or Bismarck.[3] This lack of planning was to limit the kind of experimentation we saw in India in 1951–1955, when caste reservations and linguistic states were conceded that successfully defused and cross-cut larger identity conflicts.

This was especially problematic because of a third factor, the very deep regional grievances between Bengal on the one hand and Punjab and the North West Frontier Province (NWFP) on the other, which (and this is often overlooked in the literature on the Pakistan-India divergence) had long predated the foundation of Pakistan. As a result of colonial policies, Bengali politicians had complained for more than twenty years about the way in which their tax revenues had been used to support spending on an army recruited from the northwest, from which men from their own province were excluded. They had also complained about the very high levels of spending on Punjab compared to Bengal. So it is not exactly the case that, as Jalal puts it, "It had all started with Jinnah's pronouncement of Urdu [in 1947] as the national language" (Jalal 1992, 154).[4] The new state had in fact combined the most privileged province in British India with its most disgruntled and unhappy province, which felt that Pakistan ought to make amends for the many injustices that had been done to it. That proved a very combustible combination.

The combination of bad inheritances, a weak political party, and the three additional factors I have just mentioned left Pakistan unable to make the significant changes to the civil-military balance from 1947 to 1958 that might have coup proofed the new state. Politicians and the strength of political parties were weakened in part because the political leaders bypassed them in making the key decisions for the new state. Oldenburg cites Ahsan's description of how ""under Jinnah, Chaudhri Muhammad Ali set up a 'Planning Committee of the Cabinet' which became the alternate, indeed the real 'cabinet'" (Oldenburg 2010, 17). Thus bypassed by the bureaucracy and divested of decision-making powers, politicians began to look feeble. Nothing remotely like this happened in India" (Oldenburg 2010, 17). Exactly the same could be said of Jinnah, Liaquat Ali Khan, and Iskander Mirza's relationships with the military in these years, which were direct and close and in which major decisions—like the future federal structure of the whole country—were worked out by a few powerful civilian, military, and political leaders behind closed doors.[5]

There was, however, one further chance to change the balance fundamentally even after the missed opportunities in Pakistan's first decade. After the Pakistan Army's catastrophic defeat in the 1971 war with India, which led to the independence of Bangladesh, the military lost legitimacy in the country, blamed by junior officers within the army as well as the public at large for the loss of East Pakistan and military collapse. After 1971 the military was also balanced, unusually, by a democratically elected party with a solid majority in West Pakistan, the Pakistan People's Party, led by a charismatic and effective leader, Zulfikar Ali Bhutto, who had clear ideas on what needed to be done to balance the threat to his rule posed by the military from a decade of close interaction with the Pakistan military regime (including as Foreign Secretary) as well as deep study of other countries and historical civil-military tensions. Bhutto no longer had to worry about the East Pakistan–West Pakistan balance in the army and other state institutions that had dominated debates in the 1960s. Instead Bhutto forced the politically weakened army high command to accept a variety of control measures very similar to those that had already been adopted in India: control over the army's top appointments; the downgrading of the Commander-in-Chief position; and the hedging of the army with substantial new paramilitary forces drawn from different ethnic groups and loyal to the civilian leadership (Rizvi 2008; Nawaz 2008). If Bhutto had been more democratically inclined, these measures might have been successfully institutionalized in the 1970s. But this second opportunity was wasted in the event, because Bhutto's personal misuse of power undercut both civilian and military support for his regime, increased political instability, and paved the way for the 1977 coup. Since 1977, arguably, there has been no real attempt to alter the structure of the civil-military balance in Pakistan fundamentally.

Pakistan's Bad Inheritances

Pakistan inherited several enormous problems at independence. First, the boundary changes and enormous dislocations of partition were a much heavier burden on Pakistan than they were on India. Prior to independence the great commercial cities of Lahore and Karachi had run largely on Hindu capital and expertise, as had many of the other businesses and professions throughout the Muslim majority areas. For instance three-quarters of the property in urban areas by value had been held by non-Muslims, 80 percent of industries in West Punjab had been owned by non-Muslims, 80 percent of the property in Karachi had been controlled by non-Muslims, and the banking, insurance, and other financial sectors had also been run by Hindus (Vakil 1950, 133). The loss of almost all Hindus and Sikhs from West Pakistan had therefore imposed a much greater burden on the new Pakistani state—which lacked the diversified business base of India—than the loss of a similarly sized but less economically significant group of Muslims on India. For a time, in late 1947, major parts of the banking and insurance system simply ground to a halt in many places in West Pakistan because there was no Hindu staff left to process transactions.

Pakistan also faced enormous logistical problems in dealing with the demands of a large state with two wings separated by a thousand miles (three thousand miles by sea). Well before the creation of Pakistan several British generals had warned about the lack of "strategic depth" in the new state, its fragile north-south rail links, the fact it had only one good port in the west (Karachi), and all the practical and defense problems these issues might create. Pakistan also inherited the dangerous and hard-to-patrol border with Afghanistan, which had occupied the bulk of the colonial Indian Army and its military expenditure during peacetime. While this meant that the new state of Pakistan inherited many military bases and a disproportionate share of barracks, it did not inherit any of the big ordnance factories that had supplied this army or the all-India tax base that had paid for it.[6] The areas that made up the new state had supplied only around 17 percent of India's tax revenues before the war (Jalal 1992, 33). So right from the beginning, military expenditure on the

140,000 troops the new country inherited necessarily took a much larger share of the overall budget in Pakistan than in India, which of course crowded out virtually all development expenditure and forced the center to appropriate a much larger share of sales tax and excise revenues from the provinces than their leaders would have liked (Vakil 1950). In 1949–1950, India's budgeted military expenditures were INA 1.5737 billion, 48.7 percent of all Indian central government expenditure, while Pakistan was spending 65.4 percent of its total revenues on defense and an even higher proportion if we were to include capital expenditure.[7]

The regional imbalances within the new state as a result of the boundary changes were also much more severe than those in India. There were enormous imbalances in human capital, in party strength, in the military, and in the inherited fiscal structure of the new state, all of which, given the structure of provincial boundaries, tended to exacerbate conflict. There were very significant imbalances in the civil service, where Bengalis had been underrepresented by the British. Only one of the 95 Muslim Indian Civil Service officers who opted for Pakistan in 1947 was from Bengal, which meant that it would take years for new Bengali recruits to the senior service to rise to high positions (Rizvi 2000, 128). As we can see in Table 6.1, which shows the senior civil service cadres in 1955, these imbalances would have taken years to overcome, even with an aggressive program to promote Bengalis.

The most important of all these imbalances, by far, was the ethnic imbalance in the army. This imbalance was so severe because Pakistan had been carved out from the most overrepresented provinces (Punjab, NWFP) in the colonial Indian Army as well as from

Table 6.1. Provincial Composition of the Pakistani Civil Service, 1955

	From West Pakistan	From East Pakistan
Secretaries	19	0
Joint Secretaries	38	3
Deputy Secretaries	123	10
Undersecretaries	510	38

Source: Richard D. Lambert, "Factors in Bengali Regionalism in Pakistan," *Far Eastern Survey*, 28, no. 4 (April 1959), 49–58.

two of the provinces, Bengal and Sind, that had been among the most underrepresented.[8] In 1945–1946, when the Indian Army was still around 800,000 strong and in the middle of its postwar demobilization, there was a total of 19,000 Bengali troops in the military. But the overwhelming majority of these Bengalis were recent wartime recruits in noncombat and technical arms such as the Engineering Corps, the Ordnance Corps, the Medical Corps, and the Service Corps. Of the total of 123,153 Muslims in the 430,000-strong infantry, armored corps, and artillery at this time, only 95 men were from Bengal. By contrast, as we can see in Table 6.2, almost three-quarters (74 percent) of the Muslim troops in the combined infantry, armored corps, and artillery in 1945–1946 were from Punjab and a further 15 percent were Pashtuns. The remaining 11 percent of Muslim troops were mainly Hindustani Muslims and the so-called Ranghars, or Muslim Rajputs. The total number of Sindhis and Baluchis in all three of these main fighting arms at this time was even fewer than that from Bengal, with only 68 men.

So as the unfortunate result of the combination of British recruitment policies and the particular lines drawn by partition, two provinces of the new country, Punjab and NWFP, had almost all the trained soldiers, while Bengal, with more than half the population, and Sind, the next most important province, had virtually none at all.

Table 6.2. Percentage of Different Ethnic and Regional Groups among Muslim Troops in the Indian Army, 1945–1946

	Total Muslim Troops	Punjabi	Pathans	Baluchis	Sindhi	Bengali
Indian Armored Corps	8,136	54.2%	13.3%	0.0%	0.0%	0.0%
Infantry	96,821	71.1%	17.8%	0.0%	0.0%	0.0%
Artillery	18,196	97.6%	0.9%	0.3%	0.0%	0.3%
Total Army	**123,153**	**73.9%**	**15.0%**	**0.1%**	**0.0%**	**0.1%**

Source: Calculated from *Eighth Indian Manpower Review (1 August 1945–31 July 1946)*, Annexure "G": Estimated Distribution of Classes to Arms and Services—Combatants—Trained Men Indian Army Indian Office Records, British Library, London, L/WS/1/922 Manpower.

The demobilization of units in 1946–1947 and the transfer of units at partition altered the regional ratios of Muslim representation we see in Table 6.2 only a little. As we can see in Table 6.3, which shows the composition of the infantry units that constituted 58 percent of the 140,000-strong army that the new state inherited, the Pakistan infantry was now almost completely Punjabi and Pashtun, with 72 percent of the infantry from Punjab and a further 20 percent from NWFP and other Pashtun areas.[9] Most of the other Muslim troops were from Rajasthan, Central India, and a few areas of Uttar Pradesh. The only substantial number of Bengalis came from the two companies of the (noncombatant) Pioneer Corps, the only unit in the pre-1947 Indian Army that had recruited Bengalis in large numbers. These men, after retraining, would form the nucleus of the new East Bengal Regiment, whose first battalion was raised in February 1948 (Khan 1963, 52).[10]

Muslim recruitment to the pre-1947 armored corps had been somewhat less Punjab and NWFP-heavy than recruitment to the infantry. But according to my calculations on the basis of the Muslim units in the prepartition manpower reports, here too there were still very big imbalances. After partition the Pakistani armored corps had a

Table 6.3. Estimated Ethnic Composition of the Infantry Regiments Allotted to Pakistan in 1947 (includes Muslim Transfers from Regiments Allotted to India)

Punjabi Muslims	58,174	72.2%
Pathans	16,016	19.9%
Hindustani Muslims	801	1.0%
Mussalman Rajputs/Rajputana Mussalmans	5,328	6.6%
Ahmediyas	264	0.3%
Sindhis	—	0.0%
Baluchis	—	0.0%
Bengalis	—	0.0%
	80,583	100.0%

Source: Based on Column 10, "Total Assets," in *Tenth Indian Manpower Review (1 Jan. 1946–31 March 1947)*, Appendix I: Infantry Non-Tech Combatants—Summary by Regiments by Classes, Indian Office Records, British Library, London, L/WS/1/1613 Manpower. I assume transfers of all units of these ethnicities from the Indian to the Pakistan infantry regiments.

majority of its troops from Punjab (43 percent) and NWFP (14 percent) in West Pakistan, with Ranghars at 19 percent, Rajputana Muslims at 9 percent, and Hindustani Muslims at 14 percent making up the balance.[11] The armored corps that Pakistan inherited had no Muslims at all from Sind, Baluchistan, or Bengal, which accounted for close to 70 percent of the new state's total population. Around a third of the Ranghars were settled on government land in Sind after partition, despite the opposition of the premier. Khuhro, but that did not make them Sindhis.[12]

Partition and the transfer of army units had a positive effect in reducing the levels of ethnic imbalance in the Indian Army, as we saw in Chapter 3, with Punjab's overall share of the army in India dropping from over 60 percent of the Indian troops in 1939 (excluding Gorkhas) to 32 percent in 1948. And that 32 percent was cross-cut by religion (Sikh versus Hindu) and caste (Jat Sikh versus Mazhabi and Ramdasia Sikh). In Pakistan, by contrast, the partition made the levels of Punjabi imbalance even worse compared to the pre-war levels in India, with the Punjabi proportion in the army rising by more than 10 percent to 72 percent. And in Pakistan, unlike in India, this massive "Punjabi" representation was not cross-cut by any significant religious or intrareligious cleavages.

This regional inequality in the army was also evident in the officer corps, where Punjabis, Pashtuns, and Muhajirs from India were dominant at the senior levels, and Bengali and Sind Muslims were represented hardly at all. In Table 6.4, I show the share of the most senior officers in 1955, eight years after independence. Although all the West Pakistani provinces are lumped together, the share of Sindhis in this total is virtually zero. As we can see, the share of East Pakistani (that is, Bengali) representation was extremely low—only 10 percent in the air force and less than 1 percent in the army, only one of whom was among the 58 senior officers at the rank of Brigadier and above—despite the fact that East Pakistan accounted for more than half the population,.

There was also a significant undercurrent of preexisting antagonism, as we have seen, between the two wings of the country. Punjabis and Pashtuns in West Pakistan were already well represented in government and politics, and they had been joined by millions of

Table 6.4. Provincial Composition of the Pakistani Officer Corps, 1955

Rank	From West Pakistan	From East Pakistan (Bengal)
Lieutenant Generals	3	0
Major General	20	0
Brigadiers	34	1
Colonels	49	1
Lieutenant Colonels	198	2
Majors	590	10
Air Force Personnel	640	60
Naval Officers	593	7

Source: Richard D. Lambert, "Factors in Bengali Regionalism in Pakistan," *Far Eastern Survey* 28, no. 4 (April 1959), 49–58.

Muhajirs, refugees from India, who had disproportionately traveled to the major urban centers of Punjab and Sind rather than to East Bengal. The capital of Pakistan was Karachi, the major cultural center was the great city of Lahore, and army GHQ was in the cantonment town of Rawalpindi, surrounded by the three main recruiting districts for the infantry. So it was hardly surprising that West Pakistanis in general and inhabitants of Punjab in particular saw themselves at the center of the new state. East Pakistanis, on the other hand, saw themselves as having been milked for years before independence by the colonial government, which had taxed their jute exports and industry to pay for a national army from which they were excluded. While "loyal" Punjab had been showered with pensions and large-scale irrigation and infrastructure projects, Bengal, from their perspective, had been starved.[13] The dominant part of West Pakistan, Punjab, had been the recipient of enormous central spending and colonial government largesse before 1947. From 1919 to 1938 northeastern India, of which Bengal was the major province, had received 26 percent of all Indian gross public investment in infrastructure (railways, roads, power, and irrigation), despite having 55 percent of the overall Indian population. On the other hand northwestern India (the four provinces that constituted West Pakistan after August 1947) had received 23 percent of all public investment, more than double its 11 percent share of the population. Economic historians credit the extra government spending in Punjab, twice as much per capita as other provinces from 1919 to 1938 and even higher before World War I, for a good part of Punjab's better growth performance during the late colonial period (Kumar 2005, 914–915). This imbalance in government spending and growth also led to Punjab being able to afford the costs of provincial government much more easily than Bengal, which had a string of provincial deficits in the 1920s and 1930s despite raising taxes on its population several times. Even the British governor of Bengal, hardly a radical, had complained as far back as January 1929 that 45 percent of the central revenue came from his province "and at the same time she finds herself with hardly any money to run her own administration."[14] In the same year the governor, in a budget debate reply to A. K. Ghuznavi, a prominent Bengali Muslim politician, admitted that Bengal received only "5 annas in the rupee" (five-sixteenths) of the INR 750 million that it collected in revenue, which left little over for health, education, and "nation building activities."[15]

Pakistan also had a bad inheritance in one other important respect: the absence of serious thinking, within the higher reaches of the Muslim League, about whether the management of the army and its deep regional imbalances might be a problem. The focus of the Muslim League before partition had been advocating on behalf of Muslims, not on thinking deeply about the regional and ethnic imbalances or other issues that might divide them in a new state (Oldenburg 2010, 10). To the extent the Muslim League's senior leadership had thought about the army, they had seen it largely through the prism of the need to raise the Indian percentage in the officer corps (Jinnah had been on the committee appointed in February 1925 that eventually led to the creation of the Indian Military Academy) and the need to defend the overall Muslim percentage within the army as a whole—so as to make sure that Hindu interests could not dictate to Muslim interests in the new state and that a Muslim force was under Jinnah's sole control to defend the new state of Pakistan when it was created. The British, partly because of their own strategic objectives, tried to keep the Indian Army united and convince Jinnah that a common force would provide better protection and be more efficient. But when General Sir Arthur Smith tried to convince Jinnah of this in March 1946 he was told that Jinnah "had studied the subject, and was convinced that there must be entirely separate armies for both Pakistan and Hindustan."[16] The last viceroy, Louis Mountbatten, tried again in April 1947, once independence and a likely partition had become a reality, to persuade Jinnah to keep the army united. But Jinnah vetoed this once more. A separate Pakistani army, he said, was "the 'begin all and end all' of Pakistan . . . and nothing short of this could possibly satisfy them."[17]

So if we look through the Muslim League's various public statements and proceedings before independence, as well as the private correspondence and speeches of Jinnah and Liaquat Ali Khan, we do not see an equivalent of the many Congress pamphlets, op-eds, and letters worrying about the possible bad outcomes of the army's policy of ethnic "poise and counterpoise" after independence or of a structure that placed senior military officers in the cabinet.[18] The League pushed for further Indianization and more Muslim officers, and defended the significant contribution of majority Muslim provinces such as Punjab and NWFP to the defense of India.[19] Jinnah publicly defended the high Muslim percentage in the army, and also the high level of representation from the Punjab and NWFP.[20] In the contentious 1938 central assembly vote on the army bill (see Chapter 1) Jinnah and the Muslim League voted with the colonial government and against the Congress Party members who were critical of the "mercenary army."[21] Reflecting the League's elite background and its advocacy of a minority that was quite privileged in government service terms at least, we see little critical thinking about the problems of civil-military relations, provincial imbalances in the army, or the composition of the structure of the military as a whole. There is nothing from the League side similar to the 1930s Congress pamphlets, motions, and speeches on the need to reform the army, or the September 1946 memo from Nehru, which laid out a detailed plan for civil-military relations and redressing the regional imbalances in the new state's army. The only mention of civil-military control issues, out of the voluminous decades of Jinnah correspondence, is one reference Jinnah made during a June 1948 speech to the staff college that officers ought to remember that the civilian leadership was supreme, and to act in accordance with that (Cohen 1988, 118). Sir Frank Messervy, the first Commander in Chief of the Pakistan Army, reported in an interview he gave just a few years after Jinnah's death that "Jinnah was not really interested in the army; he had no ideas. He would say, 'I have had no military experience. I leave that entirely to you and Liaquat.'"[22] General Sir Douglas Gracey, Pakistan's second Commander in Chief, told Stephen Cohen the same thing, saying that Jinnah and the other senior politicians "were completely abysmally ignorant of what was going on in the military."[23]

The Failure to Hedge 1947–1958

Pakistan had a brief opportunity after independence to address its civil-military relationship, coup proof the regime, and broaden the ethnic composition of the military. It was unable to make these changes for several reasons: first, the relative weakness and unpreparedness of the Pakistani military compared to India's, which made any restructuring of the army seem very risky; second, the fundamental mistrust of Bengalis and their fighting abilities on the part of the Punjabis, Pashtuns, and Muhajirs who led the army; third, the weakness of Pakistan's political parties and institutions, which left the military much more autonomous and powerful than in India, and provided the cause for intervention.

Even if the Muslim League's leadership had been deeply concerned with the military threat and the problem of ethnic imbalance, Pakistan inherited very weak political structures for dealing with these inequalities and difficult legacies. The Muslim League had, it is true, won an overwhelming majority of the Muslim seats in the elections for the Central Legislature in 1945–1946. But this victory was not built on the basis of decades of party organization in the provinces, as was the Congress Party's victory. For most of its existence the Muslim League had been a deliberately elitist party, with membership dues and organizational forms that excluded all but the Muslim landed elites and professional classes. Before the 1940s the League was far from being an all-India party (Weiner 1989; Oldenburg 2010; Tudor 2013). It won less than a quarter of the Muslim seats in the 1936–1937 elections—109 out of 482. The League was strongest in the United Provinces (now Uttar Pradesh), Bombay, the Central Provinces, and to a lesser extent Madras, but was extremely weak in all the Muslim-majority areas that were later to become part of Pakistan: Punjab, NWFP, Baluchistan, Sind, and East Bengal. The League lost every single one of these provinces in the 1936–1937 elections, winning no seats at all in NWFP, 1 percent of the seats in Punjab, 0 percent in Sind, and only 31 percent of Muslim seats in Bengal. By contrast the League had won 51 percent of Muslim seats in Bombay and 43 percent in U.P. in the last substantial elections before World War II (Jalal 1994).

In the late 1930s and 1940s, as war broke out and politics moved away from the provincial legislatures and toward national-level negotiations, powerful provincial party leaders cut opportunistic deals with the Muslim League; they would throw their support behind the League as a national party for the Muslims, as long as the League left their local party structures, alliances, and patterns of dominance untouched. So the massive majorities that the League won in the Muslim seats in Bengal, Sind, and Punjab in 1945–1946 did not reflect a huge change in the League's power as a party on the ground. In fact, even as late as July 1944, the League party leaders in Punjab were reporting that "most district Leagues had existence only upon paper" and that "the most urgent task was to set up the preliminary scaffolding of the organization in the district(s)."[24]

The problem this lack of party organization created after independence when combined with the League's oligarchical form of organization was that it provided no good way of resolving political tensions within the party, in the way that tensions over language, federalism, and caste could be resolved within the Congress Party in India (Oldenburg 2010, 10). In the absence of these conflict-moderating mechanisms, League leaders were tempted to use their government executive powers rather than party negotiations and compromises to resolve disputes. The prominent Baluchi leader, Sherbaz Khan Mazari, who lived through this period, perceptively describes the dynamic: "The true tragedy lay in the fact that the leadership of the original Muslim League had no political base in what became Pakistan. They were Urdu speakers and had come to the new country as refugees. Mr. Jinnah's death had to a large extent politically isolated them. Even powerful individuals such as Liaquat Ali Khan had no political support on the ground, nor did they have constituencies from which they could get themselves re-elected. Faced with hostile provinces they chose to exercise power through the Executive. . . . This remedy was resorted to even where elections or inter-play of party politics to resolve a crisis would have been the proper course in the democratic tradition" (Mazari 2000, 53).

So after Jinnah's death, Liaquat Ali Khan and other League leaders used their executive powers under the colonial Government of India Act 1935, which was still in force, to impose central rule on recalcitrant provinces and leaders rather than negotiate and compromise. In January 1949 the central government imposed emergency rule to dismiss the elected Mamdot ministry in Punjab, the Khuhro ministry in Sind in April 1948 and December 1951, and the newly elected United Front ministry in East Bengal in May 1954 (Callard 1957, 160–161). The dismissal of the United Front ministry was especially disastrous, because the party had just convincingly beaten the League government in provincial elections on a mandate that called for a more equal federal relationship. Callard points out that this was a missed opportunity to show that "democracy in Pakistan was strong enough to allow different parties to control central and provincial governments without disrupting the state" (1957, 161).

The military's view was that it was only drawn into politics gradually, and that it was ultimately forced to act, against its wishes, to prevent the country from descending into political chaos. General Ayub Khan's autobiography is at pains to point to his lack of personal political ambition. General Khan emphasizes that he was asked to intervene militarily in 1954 but refused, and also that people were begging the army to save the country from chaos and the politicians. The general opinion, he said, was that the army was "the only disciplined organization that could give the country the necessary covering fire, in order to enable it to steady itself and extricate itself from the evils that had surrounded it. Things did not look like improving. But I hoped that someone might rise to the occasion. I would have been the first person to welcome him and to give him all support. I kept hoping and praying" (Khan 1967, 58–59).

Hasan-Askari Rizvi and Tudor largely agree with this story, and Tudor says that "when Pakistan's Commander-in-Chief did announce the military coup of 1958, he claimed that he had been encouraged on numerous occasions to seize power and chose not to do so. These facts are more consistent with Pakistan's dominant political party failing to provide for stable governance than with a military waiting in the wings to seize power at the earliest possible opportunity" (Tudor 2013, 30). However, Ayub Khan was perhaps not telling the whole truth. Penderel Moon points out that in some ways he anticipated military rule with a detailed 1954 memo laying out the one-unit scheme and other constitutional plans, four years before the coup (1967, 812). And even earlier, at the end of 1950, Major General Sher Ali Khan Pataudi reports a conversation in which Ayub Khan, as head of the army, told Pataudi to accelerate some advanced staff courses he was doing "because I won't be able to spare you after that. This Army has a much greater and wider role to play than people realize. The C.-in-C., in fact, is a more important man than the P.M. in our country as the situation stands today" (Pataudi 1978, 132).

In a very good 1965 article Wilcox also points out that a number of detailed planning documents had been prepared in the months and years before the 1958 coup, which occurred just a few months before Ayub's term as Commander in Chief ended, making it what he sees as a "then or never" moment for Ayub (148). He also demonstrates that as early as 1952 the army had been pursuing a substantially independent course in foreign policy, which included exploring an alliance with the United States without seeking the approval of the civilian leadership (146). Stephen Cohen's assessment seems accurate; military intervention in Pakistan was due to a combination of political weakness *and* military ambition (1988, 107–117).

The League was also hampered because the ideology of Muslim unity, which had been so effective in winning Pakistan, was much less effective as a way of dealing with the many ethnic and regional cleavages in the new state. Unlike the Congress Party, which had supported linguistic states, the League had never been committed to ethnofederalism or the idea that a Muslim state ought to acknowledge caste, regional, and linguistic cleavages. When Jinnah went to Dacca in March 1948 and was confronted by very respectfully phrased demands that Bengali be made a joint official language with Urdu, he responded not with compromise but with absolute certainty that the acceptance of ethnofederalism would weaken the Muslim unity for which he had fought so hard: "Let me make it very clear to you that the State Language of Pakistan is going to be Urdu and no other language. Anyone who tries to mislead you is really the enemy of Pakistan. Without one State language, no nation can remain tied up solidly together and function."[25] Both Liaquat Ali Khan and Jinnah responded to demands for more genuine federalism and measures to reduce ethnic inequalities not by directly addressing the demands, but instead by urging their citizens to focus on their common Muslim identities and forget their provincial allegiances. In an Urdu speech to naval ratings in April 1948, Liaquat said that "I feel that only one thing can harm Pakistan and that is the spirit of provincialism. One must not think in terms of being a Sindhee or a Pathan, or a Baluch, or a Panjabee, or a Bengalee. If the spirit of provincialism prevails and if we think in provincial terms, then Pakistan will be a weak state. I desire that the Pakistan Navy, Army and Air Force should set an example and by that example prove that we all are only Pakistanis. We should forget provincialism."[26]

But the immediate postindependence period showed that, as in India, the ethnic and linguistic cleavages among Pakistanis were very real, and that many people were not prepared to put their provincial grievances aside. There were complaints from Sindhis who felt swamped by the tide of Muhajir and Punjabi refugees; from Muhajirs who felt that they were being discriminated against; from Baluchis who felt that their traditional tribal rights were being trampled on; and from Pushtuns, who had voted against the Muslim League in 1945–1946 and resented the imprisonment of their leader Khan Sahib and the League's domination of the province. There were also many complaints from Hindus, Christians, and lower castes about their poor treatment in the new state.[27] And above all there were complaints from Bengal. Bengalis wanted equal treatment in terms of their language and culture and an end to the patronizing attitude of some West Pakistani politicians and leaders. They also wanted a reduction in taxation, which fell more heavily on Bengal than the west, and a much more equitable share of central government spending in a whole host of areas where, as Table 6.5 shows, they were receiving much less than their proportional allocation.[28]

In India the Congress Party, after initially opposing states reorganization and genuine federalism, was forced to accept them because of strong support for the measures in the south as well as the party's own previous commitments and its democratic organizational

Table 6.5. Central Government Spending in Pakistan Provinces, 1947–1955

	West Pakistan PKR (millions)	East Pakistan PKR (millions)	Percentage in West Pakistan	Percentage in East Pakistan
Financial Assistance	10,000	1,260	88.8	11.2
Capital Expenditure	2,100	620	77.2	22.8
Grants-in-Aid	540	180	75.0	25.0
Educational Grants	1,530	240	86.4	13.6
Foreign Aid Allotted	730	150	83.0	17.0
Defense Expenditure	4,650	100	97.9	2.1
Foreign Trade (Exports)	4,830	4,940	49.4	50.6
Foreign Trade (Imports)	6,220	2,580	70.7	29.3

Source: Richard D. Lambert, "Factors in Bengali Regionalism in Pakistan," *Far Eastern Survey* 28, no. 4 (April 1959), 49–58.

structure. But in Pakistan the leaders found it more difficult to de-emphasize the most damaging cleavages (such as religion) and think creatively about federal solutions for a number of reasons. First, as a result of the campaign for Pakistan the Muslim League was ideologically committed to the unity of Muslims and to the special place of Urdu as a central symbol of Muslim unity. Second, the League was committed to separate religious electorates, even though these were strongly opposed by many of the religious minorities they were allegedly supposed to benefit. Third, Pakistan's leaders did not contemplate serious states reorganization that might, as in India, have brought out some important crosscutting cleavages within the Bengali or Punjabi communities. This was largely because there was a clear tactical need to balance the demographic power of an increasingly unhappy Bengal with a single large province in the west. General Ayub Khan, as Commander in Chief in the early 1950s, seems to have come up with the idea of two units as a solution to the problem of Bengali regionalism, and then encouraged the higher leaders to adopt it (1967, 187–188). In the event, the two-unit policy ended up pleasing neither Bengal, which saw it as a deliberate attempt to blunt its demographic majority, nor the non-Punjabi provinces in the west that saw their separate needs artificially subsumed within a single structure.

Given the weakness of the Muslim League as a party, and the strength of a Punjabi- and Pashtun-dominated military in an increasingly bureaucratic and authoritarian government, there was neither the push nor the capacity for changing the civil-military balance or hedging against the power of the army as was done by Nehru, Patel, Krishna Menon, and others in India from 1947–1960. Politicians made sincere promises about the major role to be played by Bengalis in the army and administration. For instance, Jinnah visited East Pakistan in March 1948 and made a special point of visiting Bengali soldiers and praising their contribution. And later the same year Liaquat told a crowd in Dacca that he was "glad to find the Bengali regiment smartly turned out, which belies the old assumption prevailing during the British regime that Bengalis are cowards and can never be fighters. The Bengalis have, in the old order of things, been kept out of the Army but it is the policy of the Pakistan Government that the Army should fully represent all sections of the nation."[29]

Despite these political promises, however, the army was unwilling to make substantial changes. There were a couple of early sops to Bengali public opinion, such as the raising of the new East Bengal regiment in 1948 with a lot of fanfare but not many soldiers. As one Pakistani Brigadier later admitted: "The First East Bengal regiment (Senior Tigers)—though a predominantly Bengali outfit was officered by the West Pakistanis with a hard core of JCOs and NCOs taken from various West Pakistan regiments. The raising of the E.B. Regiment was, in practical terms, little more than a sop to the Bengalis clamouring for their share in the army. The fact remained that the first E.B. Regiment was only one of eight infantry regiments not to speak of the overwhelming preponderance of the Punjabis and the Pathans in the other arms and services of the Pakistan Army" (Siddiqi 1986, 7–8).

So the progress of ethnic rebalancing in the army was very slow. In 1952 there was a committee appointed by the Constituent Assembly to look into Bengali representation in the army. This committee, though, was privately opposed by most of the senior officers in GHQ from the start. The Commander in Chief, Ayub Khan, reportedly called in the army's representative on the committee, Major General Muhammad Sher Ali Khan Pataudi, and gave him a verbal brief urging him to go slow on expanding Bengali recruitment, on the grounds that the most urgent task was to build the armed forces up to serve where they would be most needed, in the west (Pataudi 1978, 135–138). Of course demand was only one side of the issue: with no tradition of military recruitment the supply of prospective recruits from the east was also relatively small. In 1950 Governor General Khwaja Nazimuddin bemoaned the fact that the Service Selection Board had received applications from only 125 East Pakistanis compared to 2,000 from West Pakistan.[30] However, the fact that new regiments could be quickly raised in the late 1960s from Bengal showed that these supply problems could be solved if the military wanted to address them.

In the mid-1950s Lieutenant General Nasir Ali Khan apparently issued a special army order laying out the recruiting percentages for the army, which fell far short of Bengali aspirations or a serious attempt to rectify the massive ethnic imbalances in the forces. The quota laid out in this order was 2 percent for Bengal, 2 percent for Sind, 5 percent for Baluchistan, and 1 percent for Pakistan's small Hindu, Buddhist, and Christian minorities.[31] Not surprisingly the order was not publicized by the army at the time, and its existence only came out during a parliamentary debate in 1964 when the member who tried to discuss it was quickly ruled out of order for giving publicity to secret defense information. The reality, though, was that the number of soldiers from East Bengal was only a small percentage of the overall Pakistan Army, as we can see in Table 6.6. And the "risk" of even these few Bengalis was hedged in several ways;

Table 6.6. Ethnic Composition of the Pakistan Army, 1965

	Infantry	Artillery	Engineers	Signals
Punjab Muslim	57%	90%	87%	84%
Pathan Muslim	18%	5%	6%	4%
Baluchistan and Sind	20%	—	2%	3%
East Pakistan	5%	5%	3%	7%
Minorities	—	—	2%	2%

Source: Calculated from information provided by Mizanur Rahman Chowdhury in *Assembly Debates: National Assembly of Pakistan Debates, Official Report Sat 26th June 1965* (Manager of Publications, Karachi 1965).

non-Bengali officers, NCOs and junior commissioned officers, and the deployment of 40 percent of the Bengali troops in West Pakistan, near regiments of Punjabis and Pashtuns who could keep an eye on them.[32] From the West Pakistani perspective, this policy was only prudent; in March 1971, as Pakistani repression in Bengal increased, several units of the East Bengal Regiment and East Pakistan Rifles mutinied and sided with the rebels, and the East Bengal Regiment overwhelmed the few companies of regular Pakistan troops in Chittagong. In Dacca, superior Pakistan Army forces attacked and overwhelmed the East Pakistan Rifles barracks.[33]

The level of imbalance was reduced a little in the 1960s, especially in the navy and air force, though East Pakistanis still felt, correctly, that they were not fully trusted. No ordnance factory was set up in the east, despite frequent angry demands. The services were all headquartered in the west. The artillery was staffed by Punjabis and Pashtuns. And even the new East Pakistan Rifles, which the center held out as a sign that it was meeting Bengali concerns, was effectively neutralized as a potential security risk by being deployed alongside Rangers, Scouts, and other West Pakistani units. The East Pakistanis tried to enlist the underrepresented Western Pakistani provinces on their side, with one prominent East Pakistani politician arguing in 1964 that "Sir, I say this is not only a problem of East Pakistan but it is a problem of the whole of Pakistan against Punjab."[34] Another member, Syed Abdul Sultan, complained about the constitutional provision that the Defence Minister be a senior officer, which as he noted meant that "there is not going to be any Defence Minister from East Pakistan or from any other part of the Pakistan except a particular part [Punjab] from where people are in overwhelming majority in the army."[35] But Sindhis and Baluchis, their identity shaped by the "one unit" policy that welded them with other Pakistanis into "West Pakistan" against the east, voted consistently with Punjab and the NWFP in the National Assembly debates on the military.

For Bengalis, as is well known, this discrimination in the military was only the most visible sign of a long list of grievances about how they were treated by the Pakistani state: the use of Bengali foreign exchange earnings to fund federal Pakistan expenditures that went to the west; the far greater investments in the west;[36] the imposition of President's rule (emergency central government administration) on the east in the mid-1950s; and the fact that senior civil servants were still, ten or fifteen years after independence, drawn overwhelmingly from the west. In 1962 none of 16 secretaries and only 1 of 36 joint secretaries, 21 of 117 deputy secretaries, and 91 of 743 other senior civil servants were from the east.[37] Perhaps most of all, Bengalis resented the fact that the west saw itself as the center of the state and Bengal as the less civilized periphery. The prominent Pashtun politician Mohammad Aslam Khan Khattak describes a dinner he had with a senior Punjabi senior civil servant in East Pakistan, well before independence, at which the officer told him of the need to civilize "these Bengalis" and make decent human beings out of the local populace (Khattak 2005, 152–153). General Ayub Khan, writing while he was president of Pakistan, describes Bengalis as belonging to the "very original Indian races" and having "all the inhibitions of down-trodden races and have not yet found it possible to adjust psychologically to the requirements of the new-born freedom. Their popular complexes, exclusiveness, suspicion and a sort of defensive aggressiveness probably emerge from this historical background" (1967, 187).

The extreme imbalance in military strength was matched by an extreme fiscal imbalance—much more imbalanced than in India because the new state of Pakistan included East Bengal, which contributed enormous amounts to Pakistan's central budget and earned most of the country's foreign exchange through jute exports, but had no representation in the army. This imbalance was then exacerbated, as East Pakistani politicians pointed out, by spending on the army's supplies, infrastructure, and army hospitals and schools, which again were almost all in the west.

The Last Attempt at Serious Command and Control

The disastrous 1971 war with India and the secession and independence of Bangladesh created a second major opportunity to change the civil-military balance in Pakistan. The army's prestige was very low after its defeat and the country had a popular and powerful civilian

leader with a significant popular mandate, Zulfikar Ali Bhutto. Unlike earlier leaders, President Bhutto seems to have had a clear plan
to diminish the power of the military, which he put into action soon
after taking power when the military stepped down in 1971. His
biographer tells us that Bhutto, a voracious reader, had already studied at length the various methods through which Hitler and Mus-
solini had controlled their top generals, and a long apprenticeship
under General Ayub Khan had also given him plenty of opportunity to assess the personalities, strengths, and weaknesses of many of
the top generals as well as the structural problems with Pakistan's
existing civil-military structures (Wolpert 1993, 184).

Two months after taking office, on March 3, 1972, Bhutto invited
the head of the army, General Gul Hasan, and the head of the air
force, Air Marshal Rahim, to the President's house, where each was
given a letter of resignation to sign, then escorted away by an armed
associate of Bhutto. In order to prevent the rest of the military coordinating against this action, the Chief of General Staff, Director
of Military Operations, and head of Military Intelligence were all
summoned for a meeting elsewhere at the same time (Mazari 2000,
231). Bhutto then took a series of steps which were almost exact rep-
licas of the measures that Nehru, Patel, and their Defence Secretaries had taken in India from 1947 to 1955: he abolished the position
of Commander in Chief and he downgraded the titles and perks of
the new chiefs. Most important of all, Bhutto established the same
kind of control over top appointments in the Pakistan Army that
Nehru, Patel, and H. M. Patel had established, with a three-man committee of Bhutto, his newly appointed Army Chief, Tikka Khan,
and his own military secretary, Major General Imtiaz Ali Ahmed,
taking all the decisions over top promotions and vetoing those that
appeared to pose any threat to civilian leadership (Mazari 2000,
231). Twenty-seven army officers at the rank of Brigadier or higher
were forced to retire, as well as seven senior navy officers and seven
senior Air Force officers. As in India in the 1950s, Bhutto also created a civilian intelligence agency, the new Federal Investigation
Agency, to counterbalance the power of the Directorate for Inter-
Services Intelligence, the powerful services intelligence agency set
up in 1948. For good measure, article 6 of the new 1973 constitution

made it clear to army officers that plotting a coup was now high treason, punishable by death, and officers also had to take an oath not to take part "in any political activities whatsoever" (Richter 1978, 407).

The second major element was the attempt to hedge the power of the Punjabi-dominated military by creating a new force drawn from Bhutto's own ethnic support base.[38] In 1973, Bhutto started to create a paramilitary Federal Security Force (FSF), well armed and well paid, and largely recruited from his home province of Sind. This force, which expanded from 14,000 in 1974 to close to 20,000 by 1977, was intended to be both a praetorian guard, personally loyal to him, and a civilian hedge against the power of the army. Bhutto's initial caution about a confrontation with the army was shown by the fact that there was never a "Federal Security Act." The force was created by simple executive order. In January 1975, as part of a move to indoctrinate the force ideologically, there was even a proposal— ultimately disallowed—that FSF men take a personal oath of loyalty to Bhutto (Mazari 2000, 330; Richter 1978).

The Bhutto strategy failed, though, for two reasons. First, and most importantly, Bhutto lost popular support because of his increasingly authoritarian rule and the use of the FSF as a praetorian guard and (allegedly) a hit squad against his political opponents, either with or without his knowledge. FSF Director Masood Mahmood turned state witness against Bhutto after the 1977 coup, and implicated the FSF and Bhutto in the murder of several political opponents (Wolpert 1993, 308–309). As President Bhutto encountered more and more opposition domestically, he also started to rely more and more on the army and sought advice and cooperation from the corps commanders, which some observers argue only encouraged the generals to think of removing him (Mazari 2000, 477).

Second, the strategy of improving command and control and ethnically hedging against the power of the regular military failed because it ran into significant opposition from the army high command. As Horowitz says, "the growing power of ethnically differentiated paramilitary units or the changing ethnic composition of regular forces at the instance of politicians is resisted because it portends, at best, misfortune and, at worst, disaster for soldiers and civilians belonging to the ethnic group whose strength is being diluted"

(1985, 469). Cohen interviewed a lieutenant general who had been asked by Bhutto to head the FSF and refused, warning him that "too many of our rulers have tried to rule with a stick" and that "if you [Bhutto] use a stick too often, the stick will take over—this has always been the history of the stick" (Cohen 2006, 51). Shortly after its coup against Bhutto, the military regime disbanded the FSF in November 1977.

Conclusion

Since 1977, there has been no sustained attempt to change the existing civil-military structure in Pakistan or the prerogatives of the army over important aspects of the defense budget, intelligence, and foreign and defense policies. In many respects, the army is now more deeply entrenched than ever in Pakistani society because, as Ayesha Siddiqua has shown, its land and business interests are so extensive that it now has substantial domestic interests to defend (Siddiqa 2007). And unlike in China, where the Communist Party has acted over the past decade to downgrade the influence of the People's Liberation Army in society, there is no strong party in Pakistan to play this counterbalancing role. The history of Pakistan since 1947 demonstrates, then, the importance of timing. Early moves in India prevented the military from building up the kind of influence and critical mass that now prevents structural change in Pakistan.

Conclusion

ARMY AND NATION

IN APRIL 1938, V. V. Kalikar moved a resolution in the Council of State in which he proposed to replace the existing army with "a national army recruited from all classes and provinces." There were two main dangers to India's existing army structure, he said. First, the composition of the army posed a major threat to democracy and civil power, and raised the threat of one region of the country, Punjab and the northwest, dominating all the others. The second big problem was the fiscal inequity of a system in which taxpayers from regions like his own Central Provinces, which was underrepresented, had to pay most of the expenses for an army from which they were excluded. This would lead to either an increase in regional conflicts or an underfunded army that would leave India unprotected, neither of which would be a good outcome. "You cannot have a national army," he said, "unless its doors are thrown open to all areas and all classes."[1]

The general literature on conflict and democracy suggests that Kalikar was, broadly speaking, correct. John Stuart Mill argued that armies composed of "different nationalities" had been the "executioners of liberty throughout the whole duration of modern history." In states in which the army is from a different group than the population, Mill argued, "the grand and only effectual security in the last resort against the despotism of the government is in that case wanting: the sympathy of the army with the people" (1861, 231). In many postcolonial states, ethnically imbalanced armies have served the interests of very narrow political parties and their leaders, or else taken over the state themselves (Horowitz 1985). High ethnic imbalances in the army, we have seen elsewhere, have also been associated with a higher likelihood of civil war (Chandra and Wilkinson 2008; Harkness 2013).

India inherited just the sort of imbalanced army that Mill identified as a problem for democratic government, one that had been carefully constructed to allow the British to conquer, divide, and rule. However, India has managed to overcome the disadvantages of its colonial military legacy. India has had uninterrupted civilian rule since independence, and only one relatively brief brush with authoritarianism, immediately before and during the 1975–1977 emergency. To Indian politicians, nearly seven decades after independence, the army no longer appears a threatening and authoritarian force, but instead the focus of national pride. In public opinion polls, 55 percent of Indians say they place a "great deal" of trust in the army, compared to 38 percent in Pakistan, with 74 percent of Indians having a generally positive opinion of the military, either "somewhat" or "greatly" trusting the army.[2] The Indian Army has consistently been held in the highest esteem of just about any Indian institution since organized opinion polls first started in the 1960s.

One interesting aspect of this success story, as I have shown, is that it has been achieved despite the fact that much of the army is still drawn heavily from the same groups, and structured in the same way, as the "martial class" army that was the object of so much concern to Indian nationalists before independence. Though promises were made in 1949 to radically reshape the army's recruitment patterns, a combination of the conservatism of the military as an institution, a belief in the effectiveness of class units, and the need after 1962 to expand quickly to deal with external threats from China and Pakistan have all greatly delayed the progress toward an "all-India" military.

As I have explored, the reasons for India's success in civil-military relations despite the absence of massive ethnic restructuring were, first, the federal and broad-based character of the Congress Party and a series of crucial decisions the party took from 1947 to 1953 to abolish religious electorates and religious reservations, allow linguistic reorganization of India's states, and enable caste reservations. Second, it has to be acknowledged that India faced fewer inherited challenges than Pakistan, especially in terms of ethnic imbalances in the armed forces. And third, the Indian state took a number of specific steps in its first decade to control its military that the Pakistani state did not: a diversification of recruitment of the officer corps in general, diversification in the appointments of the most senior Generals and Lieutenant Generals, ethnic balancing within the army, reducing the military's prestige by reducing pay and perquisites, adding a new Ministry of Defence bureaucracy with substantial oversight over the army, and downgrading the Commander-in-Chief position so that the army head was now one of three nominally equal chiefs (Rudolph and Rudolph 1964).

There have been several major challenges over the years to the success of these strategies. After the disaster of defeat by China in 1962 it seemed for a time as if pressure to reestablish the C-in-C position—to be renamed Chief of the Defence Staff—might reverse some of the command and control measures introduced by Patel and Nehru. In the 1970s the army was pressured by Defence Minister Jagjivan Ram to introduce Scheduled Caste reservations into the army, as in other areas of government employment. In the 1980s and 1990s, the army was threatened by the Sikh militancy, which endangered its class recruitment structure and also the peace and stability of a major recruiting area, moreover one on the border with Pakistan. More recently, there have been the continuing challenge posed by long-term anti-insurgency deployments in Kashmir and the northeast, on the one hand, and the increasing encroachments of caste and regional politics and societal corruption, on the other. General J. N. Chaudhuri, interviewed by the Rudolphs in 1963, pointed out to them that "a conservative army attached to its traditions is likely to be a non-political army."[3] But the recent scale of social, economic, and political changes in India is now challenging the army's traditional structure and its military hierarchies as never before.

Several other developments, however, have worked to reduce conflict over the military during the same period. First, the military itself has become less attractive as an avenue of employment than it was in the patronage-driven days of the 1930s, when high officer salaries, land grants, tax remissions, and various other incentives made military recruitment a major focal point for group competition. Gujaratis, Bengalis, and Tamils are not as upset about their low representation in the army as they were in the 1930s, because there are now many more opportunities to be had in the wider economy than there were then. In fact, ever since the immediate postindependence 40 percent pay cuts for commissioned personnel the army has had significant problems recruiting and retaining officers, even though recent pay commissions have improved their conditions. This is in sharp contrast to the situation in Pakistan, where there is intense competition for the scarce positions at the Pakistan Military Academy in Kakul, and where the monetary rewards for senior officers (which include big land grants at retirement for the top generals) are much higher than in India. The problem of attracting recruits also seems to be growing for the ordinary enlisted soldier, something that prompted the army to introduce a system of open recruiting rallies in 1998, in which the recruiters travel to the districts, rather than the old system of Branch Recruiting Offices to which the recruit had to travel, sometimes quite long distances, in order to enlist. The facts that military recruitment is less competitive than in the past and that those who are denied employment in the military have many more options surely lower the political stakes in debates over the composition of the army. The composition of the army is still the focus of political debate, but it no longer has the central political and economic importance that it did in the immediate pre- and postindependence period.[4]

Another reason that conflict seems to have been reduced is that the ethnic imbalances in the Indian Army, unlike in the pre-1947 period, are no longer large enough to threaten the security of the country. In India the states of Punjab, Himachal Pradesh, Haryana, and Chandigarh (the prepartition Indian Punjab) have around 6 percent of India's population but less than 20 percent of the current army recruits. The important point politically is that their degree of overrepresentation is not anywhere near a Punjabi majority in the army, as it was before World War II, and it is certainly not enough to allow one state to dictate to the others or to endanger the overall stability of the country. Moreover the Punjabi soldiers are themselves cross-cut by religious affiliation, between Sikhs and Hindus. The

Sikhs are also divided, politically and militarily, between Jat Sikhs on the one hand and Mazhabi and Ramdasia Sikhs on the other. When Jat Sikhs mutinied in a few units in 1984, officers expressed confidence to journalists that their Mazhabi and Ramdasia Sikh brethren in the Sikh Light Infantry would not follow because of these differences, and they were right.

In the early years of independence the regimental and class recruiting structure of the Indian Army was threatened by a secular desire to remove caste and religion as legitimate organizing principles for government administration. Nehru and Krishna Menon initially wanted what we might think of as a modern and "color-blind" India, in which caste and community would play no role in government recruitment. Nehru saw caste reservations for the Scheduled Castes as a necessary evil, given the extent of prejudice and discrimination against them. But his general view was that caste reservations were bad because they entrenched caste and community, and his ultimate goal, as he wrote to a fellow member of the Congress Party in 1954, was to end the caste system, which he saw as "the biggest weakening factor in our society" (Gopal 1983, 324–325).

The principle of government recruitment by caste for any purpose, which was under severe threat because of this impulse in the immediate postindependence years, is now widely entrenched within Indian political life. The 1951 constitutional amendment allowing "backward class" reservations, combined with the necessities of electoral competition, has meant that the number of groups and the proportion of the population eligible for reservations has steadily increased since the 1950s, to the point where over half the government jobs and educational spots in some states are now allocated on the basis of caste. Politicians win and keep office by promising caste reservations in general and more benefits to particular castes and regions. In this new political environment, which is a long way from the anticaste rhetoric of the immediate postindependence years, it is obviously less likely that politicians will take a public stance in favor of a completely caste- and region-blind military once they are in government.

The fact that allocation by caste is now an accepted principle in public life, however, poses a different challenge for the army. As we have seen, the army still recruits heavily from traditional military regions and castes, and in fact continues to inculcate soldiers into particular religious and community traditions as part of their training and regimental life, as it did in the 1920s. In the Sikh Regiment, for instance, a regimental history written in 2010 describes the life of new recruits at the regimental center at Ramgarh:

> The first week at the Centre is to familiarize the young recruits with the army environment, the change from a civilian to a military mindset. Greenhorns are lectured on the routine ahead, personal hygiene, turnout, wearing of various uniforms, and footwear, and social graces. The evenings are spent at the Regimental Gurdwara Sahib, where the Religious Teacher or *Babaji* imbibes in him the values of the Khalsa warrior, building upon the history and the great traditions of their forefathers. The raw recruits, many of whom may not always have maintained articles of their faith, are very quickly so ordained and there is no compromising on these values. Attendance every Sunday morning at the Gurdwara parade is obligatory.
>
> The recruits spend much time in the Motivation Hall, the "Nalwa Training Hall and Library," named after the legendary warrior Hari Singh Nalwa. There they are exposed to traditions of the Khalsa warriors, the great battles of the Anglo-Sikh wars in 1845–1949, which are co-related with battles of yore over the next century and a half, to both inspire and motivate them. (Sikh Regimental Officer's Association 2010, 222–223)[5]

The Sikh Regiment may be more cohesive than the average regiment, as a single-class unit with a specific religious identity, but every class regiment has some type of assimilative and identity-building process during and after training. Building unit cohesion in this way is central, army leaders believe, to operational effectiveness. The obvious problem for the army, though, is that if it publicizes that it recruits so heavily on the basis of caste and religion, and emphasizes these identities so much in training and regimental life, it will be much harder to resist calls from every other caste, religious, and regional group in India to get "their" own regiment as well (MPs have asked for Ahir, Yadav, Muslim, Kalinga, Kannada, Manipur, and Bodo regiments, among many others). The last thing the army wants is for its own internal structure to be micromanaged by politicians with reservations at every level of recruitment, promotion, and perhaps even deployment. So to prevent that from happening, the army maintains that it is a completely secular institution in which community, caste, and religion are completely irrelevant. In its response to the December 2012 public interest suit on caste recruitment, for instance, the force filed an affidavit with the Supreme Court claiming that "all citizens are eligible for enrolment in regular Army, and no discrimination has been made on the grounds of religion, race, caste, sex, descent, place of birth, residence or any of them."[6] To do otherwise would open up the whole question of which group gets what, at every level, which would—the officers are convinced, and they are probably right—harm the army's operational effectiveness.

What are the lessons of the Indian story that can be applied to other cases? Perhaps the biggest one is that the many excellent studies that look at democratic breakdowns tend to look at them either from the perspective of the military and its organization or from the perspective of parties and democratic institutions, but tend not to bring these approaches together. The Indian and Pakistani cases show, however, that it is hard to understand why progress is made in controlling the military's role in politics without paying attention to both the detailed aspects of force organization and command and control, *and* those factors that create the necessary stability in the polity at large and sufficient legitimacy for the government to carry out these measures. When Prime Minister Nehru and Defence Minister Y. B. Chavan were interviewed by the Rudolphs in February 1963 to explain why the military played less of a role in India than in Pakistan, their answers tellingly mentioned a *combination* of party political factors such as Congress's democratic structure and long history and India's federal structure (which made it harder to capture power and control the country) with military ones such as the downgrading of the Commander in Chief and the new command and control structures.[7]

The Indian case confirms the general sense in the literature, that what Horowitz terms "compositional strategies" can be highly effective in reducing the risk from the postindependence army, just as they were effective in reducing the risk from the pre-1947 military. Diversifying the officer corps, especially at the higher ranks, reduced the risk of coordination among the corps commanders (Horowitz 1985). The army as a whole is also now regionally much more diverse than at independence, in contrast to Pakistan, despite the fact that it does not recruit equally from all segments of the country. No state in India had more than 13 percent of the total army recruits from 1998 to 2009 (the state that came closest was Uttar Pradesh, which was somewhat underrepresented compared to its 16 percent of the national population). And unlike in Pakistan, where Punjabis are a majority of the army, no individual "class" in the Indian Army now makes up more than 10 percent of the force's strength. In the infantry and armored corps taken together, the largest categories in the 2010s, according to my estimates, are Gorkhas, Dogras, Jats, Sikhs (excluding Mazhabi and Ramdasia Sikhs), and Rajputs, respectively, each of which has between 6 percent and 9.2 percent of the total strength.

India has also been aggressive in trying to "balance outside the army," with a huge increase in its paramilitary forces since the 1962 war with China (Horowitz 1985; De Bruin 2014). These forces are now more than 850,000 strong, larger than the infantry and armored corps. They perform an important dual role, both as a direct hedge against the military, and much more importantly as an indirect hedge in keeping the military insulated from the sort of frequent interventions into politics and society (such as Ayub Khan's imposition of martial law in Lahore in Pakistan in the early 1950s) that have paved the way for military coups in other states. By performing a variety of policing roles, for instance, in putting down communal riots and in anti-Naxal operations, they help keep the army insulated from important societal and political cleavages. These paramilitary forces are also, unlike the army, broadly reflective of India's overall population.

India has been able to balance the power of the military because it inherited a strong, broad-based party that had—unusually among nationalist parties—thought deeply about issues of civil-military control before independence, and had quite clear ideas about what needed to be done. In his first week in office, in September 1946, Nehru was already thinking of the measures that he needed to carry out to reduce the influence of the military in politics, all of which were implemented over the next decade. Because the Congress Party was a large democratic party that had won an overwhelming victory in the 1952 elections, Nehru also had the unquestioned legitimacy and authority to make these changes, unlike the Pakistan government. Because the "Congress System" allowed for many difficult conflicts to be worked out within the Congress Party, political rivals and disappointed factions were also less likely to try to influence officers to try to intervene in politics on their behalf.

To some extent, as we explored in Chapter 5, civil-military relations have had their problems over the past decade (Mukherjee 2011; Raghavan 2010b). The Defence Minister from 2006–2014, A. K. Anthony, was generally regarded as weak and indecisive, reflecting perhaps an indecisive coalition government that was reluctant to carry out its own 2011–2012 Naresh Chandra committee's recommendation to appoint a Permanent Chairman Chiefs of Staff, a measure that would have gone some way to meeting the army's demand for a Chief of Defence Staff (Mukherjee 2014, 43–44). The army's leadership has either openly challenged or privately briefed and leaked against the political leadership over its stance on demilitarizing the Siachen Glacier (scuppering negotiations with the Pakistanis in 2007) and by successfully blocking the partial reform of the Armed Forces Special Powers Act (Cohen and Dasgupta 2010; Raghavan 2010b).[8] Many Indians, and not just those most affected by the act in Jammu and Kashmir and in the northeast, see the act as a blot on Indian democracy. And the recent public controversy over General V. K. Singh's retirement date and whether there were or were not unauthorized troop movements when General Singh was fighting his case in the courts and with the political leadership have shown neither the Defence Ministry nor the military leadership in the best light.[9] The new BJP government elected in May 2014, however, seems to want to calm the waters, and it acted quickly in June 2014 to prevent an effort by General Singh (now a BJP MP and Minister of State in the new government) to publicly criticize the incoming COAS General Dalbir Singh.[10]

Despite these recent problems, I would argue that it is still hard to disagree that India and its leaders made a lot of good decisions in the first decade after independence, decisions that explain why India handled its military much better than most countries. It is important, of course, not to credit Nehru with too much in the way of flawless judgment and foresight. As we have seen, the civilian control measures he and others implemented before 1962 were if anything too strong, and they substantially weakened the military's ability to defend the country from China. As Cohen and Dasgupta put it "the price of extraordinary civilian control of the military in India is military and strategic inefficiency (2010, 161)." It is also a fact that two of the specific measures that have helped India the most to moderate macroconflicts over region and religion over the years—the introduction of caste reservations and the creation of linguistic states in the early 1950s—were strongly opposed by both Nehru and Sardar Vallabhai Patel in the late 1940s. Nehru was ultimately forced to accept both of these measures in 1951–1952 because of widespread protests in the south, and it is always possible, if Patel had still been alive (he died in December 1950), that the decisions on reservations and linguistic states might have come out differently.

It is possible, but unlikely. That is because the Congress Party in India was a much better institutionalized party than the Muslim League in Pakistan (Oldenburg 2010, 10). The party's structure, history, democratic norms, and (most importantly) its diverse ethnic, religious, and regional character let party members and regional leaders challenge Congress leaders when they were wrong or opposed by significant segments of the population. The legitimacy that the "Congress system" created, combined with its ability to moderate wider ethnic and religious conflicts and the party's long experience thinking about the problems of civil-military interaction, help to explain independent India's much happier experience with army and nation.

APPENDIX

NOTES

REFERENCES

ACKNOWLEDGMENTS

INDEX

Appendix

DATA ON THE CHANGING
COMPOSITION OF THE INDIAN
MILITARY SINCE 1930

Prior to World War II data on the Indian military's composition are widely available at an aggregate level, often in response to questions asked in the Indian Council of State and Central Legislative Assembly. The Indian Statutory Commission (1930) provides a detailed provincial-level breakdown of recruitment. A large number of secondary works also provide systematic data on recruitment (e.g., Mazumder 2003; Omissi 1994; Yong 2005). More detailed unit-level data are available in the annual Indian Army Lists, which frequently list units' class compositions, as well as in the *Confidential Annual Return Showing the Class Composition of the Indian Army*, a series which is available in the India Office collections of the British Library for the years before 1942 (L/MIL/14/236).

During World War II, as I have explored in this book, the colonial government made a great effort to limit the amount of information on the provincial and class composition of the army. The most widely available comprehensive source on patterns of recruitment during the war is Bisheshwar Prasad's *Expansion of the Armed Forces and Defence Organisation 1939–1945*, Volume 5 of Official History of the Indian Armed Forces in the Second World War 1939–45 (Calcutta: Combined Inter-Services Historical Section, 1956). But much more detailed information is available in two other sources: Bisheshwar Prasad, ed., *Monographs, Adjutant General's Branch* (Combined Inter-Services Historical Section, 1950); and the pre-1947 annual Manpower Reports, which list the composition of each unit in the army, its expected wastage, and its anticipated manpower needs for the next year. These Manpower Reports are available in the British Library India Office Records, e.g., Eighth Indian Manpower Review (1 August 1945–31 July 1946): Annexure "G" Estimated Distribution of Classes to Arms and Services—Combatants—Trained Men Indian Army (L/WS/1/922 Manpower).

There are few good published sources for district-level recruitment patterns before 1947. Three provincial district-level breakdowns at least seem to have survived, for Madras, NWFP, and Punjab. They are available in 1) Appendix C Recruiting 1939–1945, in Lt. Col. E. G. Phythian-Adams, *The Madras Soldier 1746–1946* (Madras, Government Press, 1948), 2) J. G. Acheson, ICS *Post-War Employment on the North-West Frontier, Marked 'Confidential'* (Peshawar: NWFP Government Press, 1944), and 3) Subhashish Ray "The Sikhs of Punjab and the Tragedy of 1947," unpublished ms., data from Punjab State Archives, Chandigarh, File 14446/175/259.

The best district estimates for recruitment in World War II are available in Jha and Wilkinson (2012), which uses Commonwealth War Graves casualty data to estimate the district composition of each army unit, and then applies these ratios to all Indian districts using known unit recruitment data. These correlate quite highly with the independently generated district data in the sources above.

Post-1947, as this book has explored, the state, district, and class composition of the military has generally been treated as confidential by the defense establishment. This book therefore gathers data from several main sources:

1. *Unit-level data on each battalion.* The available Indian Army Lists, the many detailed regimental histories (e.g., Longer 1980; Sethna and Valmiki 1983; Shrivastava 2000) and a general reference works on the army's battalions and regiments (Gautam 2009; Sharma 2000) contain a wealth of information on each battalion's raising, composition, and (where applicable)

reorganization. Taken together these sources contain information on virtually every battalion in the Infantry and Armored corps. If we know the raising date of each unit, its company or squadron composition, and its reorganization or end date, we can therefore calculate, over time, the shifting composition of the army as a whole. This is the method used to compile, e.g., Figures 4.2 and 4.3.

2. *District-level data on army recruitment.* There are wide differences in district-level patterns of recruitment to the armed forces. The Ministry of Defence releases very little data on district patterns of recruitment, though occasionally district breakdowns of recruitment for a year or two for one state are given in response to questions in parliament. However systematic data on district recruitment patterns are available for ex-soldiers, because the ex-servicemen's board publishes detailed statistics showing where ex-soldiers live, e.g., *Kendriya Sainik Board Annual Report 2009*, table 1(a), "Zila-Wise Population of Ex-Servicemen in the Country." Of course not all ex-servicemen live in their home district, but given the fact that many units recruit from rural districts a lot more servicemen return to their home districts than we might think, so these data, while a lagging indicator, still provide a good general guide to recruitment patterns several decades ago. These data were used to generate Figure 5.2.

3. *State-level recruitment data from Lok Sabha and Rajya Sabha answers and debates.* These answers typically give out no more than a year or two's data at one time, but are easily available through the Lok Sabha and Rajya Sabha proceedings (data are provided for an FY basis in the Army and a calendar year in the Navy and Air Force). The tables and graphs in the book that cover recent state-level recruitment draw on the following sources: "Army Recruitment in 1995–1996 to 1999–2000, Northeast States" from Shri Kagen Das, *Rajya Sabha* question 1187, March 7, 2001, 74–75; "Army and Navy Recruitment in 1999–2002," Shri Ramdas Athawale, *Lok Sabha Debates*, unstarred question No. 601, November 21, 2002, "Recruitment in Defense Forces"; "Army, Navy, and Air Force Recruitment

1998–1999" from Srimati Bhavana Pundikrao Gawali, *Lok Sabha Debates*, unstarred question No. 818, November 23, 2000, "Recruitment in Armed Forces"; "Army, Navy, and Air Force Recruitment 1991–1992 to 1996–1997 for eastern states" from Ashok Mitra and Dipankar Mukherjee, *Rajya Sabha*, starred question No. 113, June 3, 1998, "Recruitment in Armed Forces"; "Percentage of Army Recruitment 1971–1972 to 1973–1974 (April–December 1973 only) from Sanat Kumar Raha, *Rajya Sabha*, question 285, 59; "Army, Navy, and Air Force Recruitment 2003–2004 to 2005–2006"; *Lok Sabha Debates*, unstarred question No. 2436, August 17, 2006; "Army and Navy Recruitment for 2002–2003" from statement referred

to in reply to *Lok Sabha Debates*, unstarred question No. 1421, Part A, December 11, 2003, "Number of Defense personnel recruited during 2002 and 2003 State-Wise"; "Army, Navy and Air Force Recruitment from 2005–2006 to 2006–2007 for Army and 2006 and 2007 for Navy and Air Force" from "List of Recruitment of PBOR in Army, Navy and Air Force, Annexure B," referred to in the reply to *Lok Sabha Debates*, unstarred question No. 485; "2006–2009 Army, Air Force, and Navy Recruitment" from Appendix II given in the statement in parts (a) to (f) of *Lok Sabha Debates*, unstarred question No. 3666, August 16, 2010.

Notes

Introduction: Army and Nation

1. Jawaharlal Nehru to Sir Claude Auchinleck and Mr. Philip Mason, September 12, 1946. Auchinleck Papers, Manchester University, Rylands Library. The first Indian Defence Member, Sardar Baldev Singh, only took office on September 19, 1946. "League Likely to Join Interim Cabinet," *Times of India*, Sep. 20, 1946.

2. Composition of senior officers in 1946 calculated from *Indian Army List October 1946* Part I (Government of India Press, 1947), OIR 355.33, 50–159.

3. "Resolution re recruitment of all classes to the Indian Army, March 13, 1935, moved by P.N. Sapru, *Council of State Debates, March 13 1935* (Simla: Government of India Press, 1935), 541–568. See also "Council of State: Plea to throw open army ranks to all classes," *Times of India*, March 14, 1935.

4. See especially Horowitz 1980; Horowitz 1985, 446–454; on Iraq, see Tarbush 1982; on Ghana, see Gutteridge 1962, 42–45; on Burma see Callahan 2003, 34–36; on Indonesia, see Chauvel 1990, 145–146.

5. Field Marshal Sir Claude Auchinleck, draft response to Nehru's letter of September 12, 1946. Auchinleck Papers, Manchester University, Rylands Library.

6. "Young soldiers warned against politics; Army must be worthy of people's trust," *Times of India*, March 9, 1949. See also "Encroachment on Few Privileges," *Times of India* September 4, 1950, and "Maintenance of Internal Peace: Gen. Cariappa against Use of Army," *Times of India*, December 5, 1950.

7. These two points are also recognized by Aqil Shah in his recent fine analysis of reasons behind the Pakistani military's interventions into politics (Shah 2014, 5–6).

8. "Nation Needs President's Rule, Feels Cariappa," *Times of India*, March 11, 1970, 13. This statement prompted the Union Home Minister to criticize his remarks as "irresponsible and utterly uncalled for." Earlier, in an article in

the *Indian Express* in mid-1965, Cariappa had suggested that a two-year period of President's Rule might be needed to restore order and proper standards of administration. "General Cariappa and Editor of Daily 'Exonerated,'" *Times of India*, August 13, 1965, 7. In 1964 Cariappa argued that "adult franchise, when the majority of our people are illiterate and whose votes have been and are being 'bought' by many unscrupulous persons blessed with money, has been the main cause for many of our avoidable political and social ailments" (Cariappa, 1964, 15). K. M. Cariappa, *Let Us Wake Up* (Madras: City Printers, 1964).

9. "Ex-Officers Back General Cariappa," *Times of India*, February 21, 1971, 11.

10. Points also made by Rudolph and Rudolph (1964) and Oldenburg (2010, 49). See also the interviews between the Rudolphs and General J.N. Chaudhuri cited in Chapter 4 in which he explains Ayub Khan's coup in Pakistan as an effort to "put things right."

11. Baldev Singh, *Constituent Assembly of India (Legislative) Debates* vol. I no. 9, February 9, 1948, 33, vol. II, March 7, 1949, 1220–1221.

12. "Recruitment to Indian Army: Class Differences to Be Abolished," *Times of India*, February 2, 1949. See also Khandhuri 2006, 216–217.

13. "The post-Independence policy of the Government is not to raise any new regiment on the basis of a particular class, creed, community, religion or region, but to have an Army in which all Indians have representation." Defence Minister A.K. Anthony, *Rajya Sabha*, March 5, 2008. See also Response of Minister of Defence George Fernandes to unstarred question 764, *Rajya Sabha Debates*, November 30, 2005; Response of Minister of Defence A.K. Anthony to unstarred question 4233 *Lok Sabha Debates*, August 3, 2009, "Recruitment in Army."

14. See, for example, Statement of Defence Minister A.K. Anthony, March 18, 2013, in response to *Lok Sabha* unstarred Question No. 3395 on "Recruitment in Army."

15. Tudor acknowledges that "an astonishing number of recruits into the British colonial army were drawn from a few districts in Punjab, all of which became part of Pakistani Punjab upon independence (2013, 29)." But she does not regard this factor or the economic imbalances created by partition as critical.

16. Party institutionalization, as defined here, is different from the "political institutionalization" highlighted in Staniland's explanation for the India-Pakistan divergence, which draws on Huntington's influential account (Staniland 2008, 336).

17. Ambedkar was not of course in Congress when he wrote *Thoughts on Pakistan* in 1941, but he later joined the first postindependence Congress government in 1947.

18. Tudor (2013, 30–34). See, for instance, the many complaints of Bengalis, Baluchis, Sindhis, Muhajirs, and others to Jinnah in 1947 and 1948 reproduced in Jinnah's collected correspondence, which are full of complaints about ethnic discrimination and favoritism (Zaidi 2001, 16–24, 99–106, 253–255, 277–279; Zaidi 2002, 144–145, 354–359).

19. "Make no mistake about it. There can only be one State language, if the component parts of this State are to march forward in unison. And that language, in my opinion, can only be Urdu" (Zaidi 2002, 272–275).

20. See also Shankar 1971, 86.

21. The proportion of Indian-recruited "single-class units" drawing completely or almost completely from Sikhs, Dogras, Kumaonis, and similar groups was around a quarter of the infantry battalions in 1947, according to my data. This calculation excludes the Gorkha units recruited from Nepal, which constituted around 23 percent of the total infantry strength by the end of 1948. India did not disband these "single class" regiments, despite the potential dangers they posed (Horowitz 1985, 536–537), but their proportion of the overall army has been reduced in every decade since independence. Source, Wilkinson Indian Army dataset.

22. Nehru to premiers, August 16, 1948, in Nehru 1985, 175–187.

23. Guha 2007 provides a good discussion of the Cariappa appointment. Chaudhuri's memoirs describe how the High Commissionership was sprung on him by Defence Minister Chavan shortly before Chaudhuri stepped down as COAS (1978, 195).

24. For instance, General K.V. Krishna Rao (2001, 228), COAS from 1981 to 1983, reports that in 1983 "As calls for deployment of the Army for internal security in Delhi mounted, I had ordered for an infantry brigade to be moved from Meerut, and permanently located in Delhi so as to be readily available. On this, strangely, we were questioned by the ministry, who were told that I had been moving a whole corps or more of troops and needed no permission. Perhaps the usual fear of a 'coup' was rekindled in the minds of the political leaders!" More recently, in January 2012 the director general of military operations of the army was urgently called in and questioned after intelligence reports of unauthorized movements of armored brigades toward Delhi were passed up to the political leadership and top bureaucrats (see Chapter 5). See also Maxwell 1970, 439–441, who discusses the fear of politicians when troops were brought into Delhi by COAS General Chaudhuri to keep order during Nehru's funeral.

25. Comments from Paul Staniland and Erica De Bruin have greatly helped me to understand this point.

26. See Baruah (2005), chapter 3. General J. J. Singh became governor of Arunachal Pradesh after retirement in 2007; he was succeeded in 2013 by Lieutenant General Nirbhay Sharma. In Assam Lieutenant Generals S.K. Sinha and Ajai Singh were governors, successively, from 1997 to 2003 and 2003 to 2008. In Nagaland General K.V. Krishna Rao was governor from 1984 to 1989; and Lieutenant General V. K. Nayyar held the office in 1993–1994. In Tripura Krishna Mohan Seth governed from 2000 to 2003; in Jammu and Kashmir General K.V. Krishna Rao did so in 1989 and 1990 and from 1993 to 1998; Lieutenant General S.K. Sinha governed from 2003 to 2008.

27. See also Cohen and Dasgupta (2010, 64). See also the cable report, released by Wikileaks, of separate meetings by Deputy National Security Advisor Leela Ponappa and Joint Secretary T.C.A. Raghavan, in meetings with visiting Ambassador Anne Patterson on August 27, 2008, https://wikileaks.org/plusd/cables/08NEWDELHI2401_a.html.

28. For details of the fourteen "technical" unit mutinies between 1886 and 1930, see table 4.2 in Omissi (1994, 136) and his thorough discussion, 134–141.

29. Satish Nambiar, "Officer Man Relationship in the Indian Army," *Trishul* 20, no. 1, 14–20. Figures on fratricide from *Lok Sabha Standing Committee on Defence (2009–10) Action Taken by the Government on the Recommendations Contained in the Thirty-First Report of the Committee (Fourteenth Lok Sabha) on "Stress Management in Armed Forces,"* 4, 12. The committee also reports 635 suicides in this period. See also "Fratricide in Armed Forces," *Rajya Sabha* starred question 205, December 6, 2006, 28–32.

30. See, for example, "Soldiers and Officers of an Army Unit Clash, Three Injured," *Indian Express,* October 11, 2013, which also contains details of several more serious incidents, including one in Leh in May 2012 that involved 168 personnel from an artillery unit, the 226th Field Regiment.

31. The budget data are from "Rs. 157.37 Crores Defence Estimates Passed," *The Statesman,* March 12, 1949.

1 *Divide and Rule*

1. This policy was justified, when it became a political issue after the 1920s, on the false pretext that the King of Nepal had insisted in the nineteenth century that his subjects only serve in British-officered units. As Major General A. A. "Jicks" Rudra later pointed out, "This was patently a made-up story, because *before 1920 there were no Indian King's commissioned officers.*" See Palit (1997, 296–297).

2. "Record of Lord Kitchener's Administration of the Army in India 1902–1909," Minto Papers, National Library of Scotland, 118–119 (hereafter cited as Kitchener's Administration).

3. "Pug" was Hastings Ismay, later Lord Ismay, Churchill's main military advisor during World War II; "Mo" was Sir Mosley Mayne, Military Secretary of the India Office from 1945 to 1947. Both were former Indian cavalry officers.

4. "Policy in Regard to the Proportion of British to Native Troops in India," Minto Papers, National Library of Scotland; Kitchener's Administration. Gorkhas were counted as Indian in calculating this ratio, which provided an additional safety buffer from the British perspective. The army ratio still stood at 1 to 2.8 in 1938, even with the threat of a major European war on the horizon (Willcox Committee 1945).

5. Kitchener's Administration, 285–286.

6. S. K. Sinha, interview, New Delhi, June 2012.

7. The current preferred term is "Pashtun," though virtually all the literature I cite here uses the older British-preferred term "Pathan." In cases where I reproduce tables, regimental names, or quotes I leave the original terminology intact. These Fortieth Pathan Regimental orders also insisted that no new men could be recruited at Regimental HQ who did not have existing members of the regiment willing to stand for their good character, because of worries over the risks posed by those without clear ties and community obligations.

8. Omissi (1994, 6–46) is excellent on this debate.

9. In 1885 Roberts said that "'I have no hesitation myself in stating that except Gurkhas, Dogras, Sikhs, the pick of Punjabi Muhammadans, Hindustanis of the Jat and Ranghur casts [and] certain classes of Pathans, there are

no Native soldiers in our service whom we could venture with safety to place in the field against the Russians" (Marston 2014, 10).

10. The remaining eleven Madras battalions all met a similar fate between 1922 and 1928.

11. Chaudhuri quotes Lord Roberts, who in 1887 argued "In India the least warlike races possess the highest intellectual capacities. The Gurkhas, the Pathans, and to a less extent the Sikhs, are notoriously as averse to mental exertion as they are fond of manly sports—as apt to fight as they are slow to learn. Once make education the chief criterion of fitness to command, and you place the desirable candidates at a disadvantage, possible overwhelming."

12. J. M. Wilkeley, *Handbooks for the Indian Army: Punjabi Musalmans* (Calcutta, 1915).

13. See the February 1934 debate in the Bengal legislature in which several members spoke out in favor of the Bengal units' performance in World War I. *Council Proceedings of the Bengal Legislative Council, Forty-Third Session, February 19–March 10,1934* (Alipore: Government Press, 1934). February 26, 1934, 284–295.

14. Indian Statutory Commission, Report, 1929–1930 [Cmd. 3568], volume 1, survey chapter 10, 98.

15. For discontent over jute duties see *Council Proceedings of the Bengal Legislative Council, Forty-Fifth Session, 1935—February 11–28* (Alipore: Government Press, 1935), 416–423. For Bengali complaints about recruitment in the central assemblies, see starred question 1162 of Brajendra Narayan Chaudhury, *Legislative Assembly Debates*, September 2, 1938, 2754–2755 (Simla: GI Press, 1938), and question No. 1060 of Amarendra Nath Chattopadhyaya on September 15, 1938.

16. See *Indian Legislative Council Proceedings*, February 11, 1920, 669; *Legislative Assembly Debates*, September 9, 1931, 83–84; *Indian Legislative Assembly Proceedings*, December 11, 1933, 2948.

17. K. C. Banerji, *Council Proceedings of the Bengal Legislative Council, Forty-Third Session, February 19–March 10, 1934* (Alipore: Government Press, 1934), 286–287.

18. "The Simon Report on India, VIII: The Army," *Manchester Guardian*, June 19, 1930, 6. See also "An Indian National Army: The 'Martial Races' Theory," *Manchester Guardian*, July 23, 1931, 3.

19. *Council of State Debates*, March 1, 1935, 541–552, See also Sapru's points in the 1938 debate, *Council of State Proceedings*, September 13, 1938.

20. *Council of State Proceedings*, September 13, 1938, motion by David Devadoss (Madras), 43. Earlier, in 1935, Sapru had asked "Why should Assam or why should Bengal contribute to the defence expenditure of this country when Bengalis and Assamese cannot get admission to the rank and file of the army?" *Council of State Proceedings*, March 13, 1935.

21. "Plea for Advisory Committee on Defence Rejected," *Times of India*, March 12, 1936, 4.

22. "Recruitment of Madrasis for New Indian Artillery, *Times of India*, February 9, 1933.

23. See, e.g., "Martial Races" Protest Deputation to C.-in-C," *Times of India*, August 25, 1927, 10; "Punjab Premier Defends Army Recruitment," *Times of India*, September 6, 1938, 15.

24. The correct communal proportions in 1939 are reported in Question 881. Strength of the Indian Army (VCOs and Other Ranks) by Community, p. 1762, *Legislative Assembly Debates* 12 March 1947, 1762–1763.

25. For a recent instance, see Rajput MP Jitender Singh's March 9, 2012, question in the Lok Sabha about whether recent moves to equalize states' share of recruitment has badly affected "candidates from other States [like, presumably, Rajasthan] who are more suitable for recruitment in the Army?" *Lok Sabha Questions*, unstarred question 317, March 9, 2012. Singh's constituency, Alwar, where he is from the former ruling family, is one of the most heavily recruited districts in the country, with more retired veterans in 2008 than any other district in Rajasthan except Jhunjhunu.

26. *Council of State Debates*, March 13, 1935, 565. The charge was fiercely denied by Sapru.

27. *Council of State Debates*, March 13, 1935, 568.

28. "Army Recruitment Bill Passed," *Hindustan Times*, September 9, 1938.

29. "Punjab Premier Defends Army Recruitment," *Times of India*, September 6, 1938.

30. *Legislative Assembly Debates*, September 20, 1938, 2754–2755.

31. *Hindustan Times*, September 5, 1938.

32. The influence of these pre-1939 debates on Bengali underrepresentation and the use of Bengali taxes to finance a Punjabi army, and on the post-1947 debates in Pakistan between East and West over the East's share in the army is important, particularly as some of the same individuals were involved. But it has not yet been given the attention it deserves.

33. "Papers Relating to the Fourth Earl of Minto's Refusal to Sign the Punjab Colonization Bill 1906–1907," Minto Papers, National Library of Scotland.

34. Fox (1985, 91–93), citing NAI Home Poll Files A, 459, II, & K.W. 1922.

35. See, e.g., the "Minutes of Weekly Home Dept.—War Dept.—IB—MI Meeting Held on 21st June 1946," National Archives of India, at which the policy of bringing political pressure to bear on the princely states was discussed by officials from the Intelligence Bureau, Military Intelligence, War Department, and Home. For the actual policy see "Minutes of Weekly Home Dept.—War Dept.—IB.—MI Meeting Held on 17th Sep 1946," "Question of the Employment of the Ex-Member of the "Indian National Army" in the Indian States Forces and Other Government Services," National Archives of India, Home Poll (I) 21/20/46.

36. Intelligence Bureau Note in file, "Secret Service Grant—Decision that with Effect from 1939–40, the Yearly Grant Made to the General Staff Branch from the IB's—For Work of the Nature of Counter-Propaganda in the Army and Recruiting Areas Should be Discontinued and Other Arrangements Made to Finance These Activities," National Archives of India, Home (Poll) 39/10/38.

37. Ibid.

2 *War and Partition*

1. The best recent work on the Indian Army during the war and transition to independence, which covers a much wider range of issues than are covered here,

for instance wartime performance and the Indian Army's involvement in contro-versial postwar operations in Southeast Asia is Daniel P. Marston's *The Indian Army and the End of the Raj* (Cambridge: Cambridge University Press, 2014).

2. Memorandum by the Secretary of State for India, Mr. Leo Amery, Amery Papers, Churchill Archives, Cambridge.

3. "Indian army morale and possible reduction 1943–45," India Office Records, British Library, London, IOR L/WS/1/707 (all India Office records indicated hereafter by IOR number).

4. "The Theory of martial and non-martial classes was completely ex-ploded during the war" (Venkateshwaran 1967). This official history was writ-ten at the instance of P. V. R. Rao (Defence Secretary 1962–1966) and with full cooperation from the Ministry of Defence.

5. The only author I am aware of who has fully appreciated this is Daniel Marston.

6. Extract from letter, "New Units raised in India since the outbreak of war 1939–1943," July 4, 1940, IOR L/WS/1/394.

7. The Gorkhas are included in this table, which deflates the Punjab and NWFP percentages.

8. Handing over Note as SDO, Kasur, January 19, 1942–January 15, 1944, Arthur Papers, Cambridge South Asia Archive, File 3, p. 53 (hereafter referred to as SDO Note).

9. W. M. G. Baker, Note from Adjutant General's Branch on Indian Man-power, 2nd November 1942, IOR L/WS/1/1680, Recruitment in India.

10. Major General G. N. Molesworth to Mr. Jenkins, September 1943 in response to note of 17 July 1943, IOR L/WS/1/1680, Recruitment in India.

11. Calculated from Prasad (1956) appendix 16, Indian Armed Forces—Recruit Intake by Provinces and States, 3 September 1939 to 31 August 1945.

12. Handing Over Notes, Attock, October 4, 1946; SDO Note, p. 53, Ar-thur Papers (AJV Arthur, ICS), Cambridge South Asia Archive, File 3, File 4.

13. For the success of recruitment among poor Punjabi Christians, see SDO Note, p. 53.

14. "Widening Bases of Recruitment: C-in-C's Promise," *Times of India*, March 7, 1941. The Mazhabi and Ramdasia Sikhs had earlier been recruited to the Sikh Pioneers, but all the pioneer units were disbanded as an economy measure in 1933 (Marston 2014, 17). Of course the army's caste biases ex-plained a lot about which units were felt to be expendable when economies needed to be made.

15. *Eighth Indian Manpower Review,* Annexure 'G', IOR L/WS/1/922, Manpower.

16. Auchinleck, who was much broader minded on the issue than most In-dian Army officers, had recommended to the Secretary of State in 1940 that raising new units from unrepresented regions and groups "will greatly help in meeting the political demand for the wider representation in the army." In Connell (1959) he is quoted in 1943 correspondence to London on the military value of the previously nonrecruited groups. The relatively liberal nature of Auchinleck's views compared to his peers also comes through in Stephen P. Cohen's December 17, 1963, interview with him. Stephen P. Cohen Interview

Transcripts 1963–1964. I am grateful to Professor Cohen for making this and subsequent interview notes used here available to me.

17. See the India Office correspondence in response to the Legislative Assembly motion by P. L. Talib, MLA, on November 19, 1943, urging that recruitment be thrown open to all scheduled castes and not the monopoly of a few privileged classes. IOR L/WS/1/1680 Recruitment in India (hereafter referred to as Recruitment in India).

18. "Comment by the C-in-C on Note by the Hon. Member for External Affairs," September 1946, Auchinleck Papers.

19. IOR L/WS/1/707 *Indian Army Morale and Possible Reduction 1943–1945*; Connell (1959, 757).

20. The committee was chaired by Lieutenant General H. B. D. Willcox, with Brigadier W. G. S. Thompson, Brigadier K. M. Cariappa, Brigadier Enoch Powell, and Air Commodore J. E. Powell, with Lieutenant Colonel J. D. Butler as secretary.

21. This abolition of subclass distinctions was put into practice soon after, in March 1946, in Indian Army Order 33–45/1946, which specified that "under no circumstances in future in any units in the Indian Army will any subclass be segregated in any sub-unit." Indian Army Orders (Special) 1946, 159.

22. IAO 80\S\46 "Enrolment of Pathans in Indian Infantry," IOR/L/MIL/17/5/296; Indian Army Orders (Special) 1946, 326. See also IAO 33\S\46, "Nomenclature of classes for recruiting purposes," 157–168.

23. "The result of this experience [of recruiting new groups in World War II] is to show that it would be unsound to count upon recruiting any class which has not demonstrated in war its suitability for the type of service which it would be required to perform" (Willcox Committee, 1945, section 157, 2–3).

24. "Note on Sikhs," Appendix A, IOR L/WS/2/44.

25. "Question of the Employment of the Ex-Members of the 'Indian National Army' in the Indian States Forces and Other Government Services," Home Poll (I) 21/20/46, National Archives of India, New Delhi.

26. For instance the Muslim Rajputs of Skinners Horse, a regiment that was assigned to India, opted for Pakistan. Several other Muslim units apparently changed their minds after making an initial decision to opt for India. The Hindustani Muslims of PAVO Cavalry (Eleventh Frontier Force), for example, a regiment assigned to Pakistan, originally opted for India, then decided for Pakistan, where they rejoined their regiment in November 1947 (Effendi 2007, 140–141).

27. Calculations on the religious proportions of the regiments made by me, on the basis of information on the division of the army, probably from a senior army officer, in *The Statesman*, July 18 and 19, 1947, as well as the *Ninth Indian Army Manpower Review*, which provides the last known prepartition group composition of each unit. *Ninth Indian Manpower Review*, IOR L/WS/1/1613.

28. After the partition, the creation of new linguistic states out of Madras, and the renaming of Madras state as Tamil Nadu, these groups are now termed "South Indian Classes."

29. "Note for the Joint Defence Council by the Supreme Commander [Auchinleck] on the Future of the Punjab Boundary Force (Top Secret)," *Deci-*

sions on Military Items of the Partition Council and Proceedings of the Provisional Joint Defence Council and the Joint Defence Council, No. 15, 28 August 1947, Partition Proceedings 1947–1950, Volume 5, NEG 3659, 272.

30. For details on the deployment of Fifth Gurkhas and Fourth Madras in September 1947, see "150 Dead in New Delhi Communal Outbreak," *Daily Telegraph*, September 9, 1947, 1.

31. Douglas Brown, "100,000 Feared Dead in Punjab Civil War," *Daily Telegraph*, September 1, 1947; "1,200 Moslems Die in New Punjab Massacre," *Daily Telegraph*, September 25, 1947, 6.

32. Colonel Sherkhan [?], Report on East Punjab Situation Adv[o] HQ Military Evacuation Organisation, Amritsar, Pakistan, 24 September 1947 (Secret). MSS. Eur. F. 164/16.

33. "150 Dead in New Delhi Communal Outbreak," *Daily Telegraph*, September 9, 1947, 1.

3 *Protecting the New Democracy*

1. "Sardar Baldev Singh on Task of Nationalization in Army," *Times of India*, December 23, 1947, 9.

2. Calculated from Table IV, "Muslims and Non-Muslims in the Higher Commissioned Ranks of the Indian Army in 1947," in Rizvi (1988, 31).

3. For the prewar promotion standards, see "Recommendations of the Armed Forces Nationalisation Committee 1947," Nehru Memorial Museum and Archives, Private Papers, 3–4.

4. Thimayya, in his evidence to the 1947 committee, pointed out that no Indian had been posted as GSO 1 to a division during the war (Marston 2014, 253).

5. The British officers, in their conservatism and wish to retain control frequently exaggerated the risks of Indianization and the insufficient preparation of Indian officers for the highest posts, as we can see from their evidence to the 1947 Nationalization committee report (ibid.). But Indian military histories and biographies have on the other hand probably underestimated the problems that the lack of senior officers and the rapid 'pushing up' of Indian officers caused to the military's overall effectiveness in the 1950s and early 1960s.

6. *Indian Legislative Assembly Debates*, March 12, 1947, 174–180.

7. Marston (2014, 268) cites a few cases where Muslim officers were encouraged to leave the Indian Army against their will in 1947.

8. Calculated from data in *Half Yearly Army List, September 1951, corrected as of 15th September 1951* (Calcutta: Government Press, 1952) (hereafter referred to as Half Yearly Army List). See also Baldev's statement to parliament in March 1949, which arrives at a similar total. *Constituent Assembly of India (Legislative) Debates*, March 7, 1949, 1220–1221.

9. The most famous Muslim officer who stayed in India, Brigadier Mohammad Usman, was killed in battle in July 1948, while fighting Pakistani forces in Kashmir. For obvious symbolic reasons, his brave service—as a Muslim who remained loyal and died fighting for India against Pakistan—is celebrated by the army to this day, with wreath-laying ceremonies attended in recent years by both the COAS and defense minister.

10. *Ninth Indian Manpower Review, 1945–1946* IOR L/WS/1/1613.

11. Sixteenth Light Cavalry, a prestigious unit founded in 1784, had just switched its composition to South Indian Classes from Jats, Rajputs, and Kaimkhanis the year before, in 1946 (Sharma 2000, 20–21).

12. These tables are based on column 10, "Total Assets," in *Tenth Indian Manpower Review (1 Jan 1946–31 March 1947)*, Appendix I, Infantry Non-Tech Combatants—Summary by Regiments by Classes. IOR L/WS/1/1613 Manpower.

13. Rizvi cites official figures as saying that there were 155 Bengalis in the Pakistan Army in 1947, in a force of over 100,000. Some of these men were probably Urdu speakers from Bengal, not Bengalis, and others were in support units, making the representation overall even smaller than this 0.1 percent.

14. Table 8 in Sinha and Chanda (1992).

15. Half Yearly Army List. Percentages do not add up exactly to 100 because of rounding.

16. My own estimates on proportions here are broadly similar to (Venkatasubbiah 1958, 16, note 1). Venkatasubbiah, who used the army list from 1953, two years after the one I use here, put Sikhs and Punjabi Hindus together at 53 percent, a little higher than my figures, with Marathas at 5 percent and Rajputs at 4 percent.

17. These units were the Seventh and Sixteenth Light Cavalry and six infantry battalions (2/1 Punjab, 4/19 Hyderabad, 5/5 Mahrattas, 1/14 Punjab, 1/7 Rajputs, 2 Madras Pioneers).

18. Another Indian Major General originally commissioned in First/Fourteenth Punjab had retired on medical grounds the year before. "General Dhillon Retires: Loss to Indian Army," *The Statesman*, September 16, 1950, 6.

19. See the debate on R. R. Diwakar's resolution, "Abolition of Castes and Religion, Etc. from Government Registers, Forms and Records," *Constituent Assembly of India (Legislative) Debates*, 17th February 1948, 836.

20. *Constituent Assembly of India (Legislative) Debates*, March 13, 1948, 2082.

21. See, e.g., starred question of V. C. Kesava Rao, *Constituent Assembly of India (Legislative) Debates*, February 18, 1948, 657.

22. B. Das, *Constituent Assembly of India Proceedings*, August 5, 1949 http://164.100.47.132/LssNew/constituent/vol9p6.html.

23. "Nehru on India's Security: Army Reduction Policy Explained," *The Statesman*, December 23, 1950, 1.

24. Quoted in Munshi (1950, 175–181). See also Shankar's earlier warning that "at present it would be virtually impossible to start any process of disbandment of the Armed Forces" (Shankar 1971, 86).

25. For Cariappa's tendency to speak up publicly where he disagreed with policy, see the Adjutant General's warning letter to him after a press interview he gave in April 1947. Adjutant General Reginald Savory to Cariappa, April 8, 1947, Cariappa Papers.

26. Cariappa also differed, sharply, with the committee on the pace of Indianization, writing "Not agreed to" in the margin next to the fifteen-year timetable, and also disagreeing with the proposed British-Indian proportions in the army as a whole.

27. Nehru to Auchinleck, letter and statement, September 12 , 1946, Auchinleck Papers. This letter has been surprisingly little cited by scholars. The only other place I have seen it cited are as an appendix to S. L. Menezes's history of the Indian Army, presumably from a separate copy in the Ministry of Defence Historical Section's archives (Menezes 1999), and in the new book by Daniel Marston (2014, 245) who uses the copy in the Auchinleck papers cited here.

28. See also Sapru's points in the 1938 debate, *Council of State Proceedings*, September 13, 1938. Thimayya and other officers had several long conversations in the late 1920s with Motilal Nehru and other nationalist politicians while stationed in Allahabad (Evans 1960, 116–125).

29. Nehru to Sir Rob Lockhart, Commander in Chief designate, August 13, 1947, enclosure to Nehru's letter to Cariappa. Cariappa Papers, NAI, Group XXI Part 1 S(2). See also Guha (2007, 748–750).

30. Jawaharlal Nehru to K. M. Cariappa, August 13, 1947, Cariappa Papers.

31. "Our attention has been drawn from time to time to senior officers in the Army receiving public addresses and sometimes delivering speeches. We should like to discourage this. It is not usual for army officers to deliver public speeches and there is no reason why we should encourage this practice in India." Cariappa to chief ministers, New Delhi, October 2, 1949 (Parthasarathi 1985, 477–478).

32. See the Adjutant General's stern letter to then Brigadier Cariappa, April 8, 1947, regarding Cariappa's reported views in an interview with the *Hindustan Times* on April 3, 1947. NAI, Cariappa Papers Group XXII S. Nos 1–161, Part 1. The British officers in charge of the army's April 1947, No. 1 Selection Board decided that "the majority opinion was in favour of Brigadier Rajendrashinhji as it held it to be doubtful whether Brigadier Cariappa possesses that degree of stability essential to the officer who was to hold the appointment as Head of the Army" (Greenwood 1981, 269).

33. "No Job after Retirement: C-in-C's Reply to Query," *Times of India*, December 11, 1952, 1.

34. "New Envoy to Australia," *Times of India*, April 30, 1953, 3.

35. Mark Pizey to Louis Mountbatten, February 1, 1955, MB/I225 folder 2, cited in Mukherjee (2014, 38). Pizey then goes on to say that he is sure the Prime Minister does not think this, but as Mukherjee rightly says this seems to have been an attempt not to offend Mountbatten, with whom Nehru was close.

36. Jawaharlal Nehru, interview with Lloyd I. Rudolph and Susanne H. Rudolph, February 13, 1963, Rudolph 1962–1963 Interviews. I am grateful to Professors Lloyd I. Rudolph and Susanne H. Rudolph for their generosity in making these notes available to me.

37. Cariappa's intense frustration at his early retirement and the country's unwillingness to employ retired officers in general and himself in particular in more public roles is evident in his 1956 conversation with President Rajendra Prasad (Choudhary 1992, 246–248). See also the Cariappa papers in the National Archives of India, which contain many letters to and from Cariappa in which he is trying (usually unsuccessfully) to insert himself in public debates and policy discussions.

38. This policy has been partly reversed by his successors, as we discuss elsewhere, and a very high proportion of governors in Jammu and Kashmir and the northeast in the past few decades have been retired senior military officers. Outside of these "militarized" areas on the periphery, though, there are not many appointments of generals as governors.

39. Krishnaswamy Subrahmanyam reports that external intelligence was transferred over to an "unwilling" Intelligence Bureau after the "disastrous failure" of one operation in 1952 (Subrahmanyam 1970, 282).

40. J. N. Chaudhuri, interview with B. R. Nanda, New Delhi, March 23, 1973, quoted in Roy (2010, 71).

41. The first Punjabi officer to serve a full term as COAS, General O. P. Malhotra, was appointed by the newly elected Janata government in March 1978, took up his position in June 1978, and served until 1981.

42. Sardar Surjit Singh Majithia, interview with Stephen P. Cohen, New Delhi, October 1964. Cohen Interviews 1963–1964. I am grateful to Professor Cohen for sharing this transcript with me.

43. See, e.g., the letter from Serbjeet Singh complaining about four Sikh generals who had been "bypassed on one pretext or another" over the past thirty years. *Times of India*, July 30, 1983, 8.

44. "Discrimination in Armed Services, Sikhs Charge," *Times of India*, January 28, 1953. Of the twenty-two Major Generals in 1951 who might have later been in line for the top job, eight were Sikhs.

45. "Maj-Gen Anis Ahmed Khan, the First Indian Muslim to be Appointed a Major General in the Indian Army," *The Statesman*, September 10, 1949, 6.

46. For General Cariappa's views before and after his 1949–1953 term as Commander in Chief, see Chapter 2; for General Thimayya (1957–1961), see Khanduri (2006, 216–217); for General Chaudhuri, see Chaudhuri (1966, 33). Field Marshal Manekshaw (1969–1973) made his views very clear in his foreword to his friend Jogindar Singh's book (1993, xvii), where he said "I have heard rumours for the proposed re-organisation of the Indian Army into mixed units on the basis of State population, under the garb of recruitment imbalance. Should this happen, God forbid, it would transform the battlefield scenes completely: the old battle slogans and rallying of units during moments of crisis will have no substitute, more so, when there is no national integration and India as yet has not become a 'Nation State': 'Olive Green' will not be able to keep the ethnic and political virus in isolation, which breeds indiscipline. If this imprudent proposed political decision is accepted by sycophantic generals, I forecast doom and calamity." See also the Stephen P. Cohen interview with General B. M. Kaul, December 25, 1964, for the views of another senior general.

47. An August 1950 *Times of India* Independence Day feature that had a segment on the army, obviously done with significant assistance from the army public relations officers, says that "To make the Army representative of all sections of the people, irrespective of caste or creed, the system of class composition based on fixed percentages and the distinction between the so-called martial and non-martial classes have been abolished. Recruitment is now open to all, and is governed strictly by competitive merit and physical fitness alone." "Large Scale Expenditure on Defence Forces," *Times of India*, August 15, 1950, V.

48. "No Non-Martial Provinces: C.-in-C.'s Statement," *Times of India*, March 9, 1949, 7; "No Provincialism in Indian Army: General Cariappa's Appeal," *Times of India*, April 4, 1949, 7. "No Communalism in Indian Army: General Cariappa's Call," *Times of India*, March 21, 1949, 6.

49. "No Discrimination in Indian Army: General Cariappa's Assurance," *Times of India*, April 16, 1949, 5.

50. "Indian Territorial Army: Bengal's Contribution," *Times of India*, October 22, 1949, 5.

51. The Guards was initially created from four existing elite "martial class" units, but henceforth these units were to be recruited on a mixed-class basis. "Guards Brigade for Indian Army: Government Plan," *Times of India*, April 27, 1949, 7.

52. "Notes, India Office to PM 1943–1944 (File 1) and 1940–1943 (File 2)," Churchill Archives, Cambridge, AMEL 1/6/21.

53. The letter and file are in the Ministry of Defense Historical Section and are still unavailable to academic researchers. Khanduri quotes from it extensively in Khanduri (2006), though without giving a date or file number.

54. "Refusal to Furnish Defence Details," *Times of India*, February 24, 1940, 11.

55. "Class Composition of the Army in India 1909–1942," Defence Department, Government of India to Secretary of State for India, February 25, 1942, IOR L/WS/1/456.

56. See e.g. Deputy Minister of Defence Sardar S. S. Majithia's April 26, 1956, response in the *Rajya Sabha* to Maulana M. Faruqui's question on under-recruited communities and steps to remedy underrepresentation.

57. P. S. Deshmukh asked for the policy on recruitment of different groups as well as the percentages of Marathas, Rajputs, Sikhs, Scheduled Castes, and Muslims in the Constituent Assembly in February 1948. *Constituent Assembly of India (Legislative) Debates*, February 9, 1948, 432–433.

58. K. M. Cariappa, Commander in Chief, January 1949 (cited from original Ministry of Defence records in Khanduri 2010, 216–217, 240) (emphasis added); Baldev Singh's statements in *Constituent Assembly of India (Legislative) Debates*, Vol. I, No. 9, February 9, 1948, 33; Vol. II, March 7, 1949, 1220–1221.

59. However, Pataudi was a rival of Ayub Khan, so the story should be regarded with some suspicion.

60. Constituent Assembly of India, *Report of the Linguistic Provinces Commission 1948* (New Delhi: Government of India Press, 1948), 81.

61. Y. B. Chavan, interview with Lloyd I. Rudolph and Susanne H. Rudolph, February 13, 1963, 1962–1963 Interviews.

62. Frank Anthony, interview with Stephen P. Cohen, New Delhi, January 20, 1963, 1963–1964 Interviews. I am grateful to Professor Cohen for making the transcripts of these interviews available to me.

63. Lieutenant General S. D. Verma interview with Stephen P. Cohen, November 28, 1963, Midhurst, Sussex. Aruna Asaf Ali, interview with Stephen P. Cohen, New Delhi, January 20, 1965, 1963–1964 Interviews.

64. Confidential Reports on Indian Officer Cadets at Sandhurst[o], 1923–1928, Indian Office Records, British Library, London. These reports emphasize the

importance of sport, mess life, and adopting the social and habits of English officers to officer cadets' success at Sandhurst.

65. See, e.g., Cariappa (1964, 15); "Nation Needs President's Rule, Feels Cariappa," *Times of India*, March 11, 1970, 13; "Cariappa's Plea to Defer General Election," *Times of India*, September 17, 1970, 3.

66. "General Cariappa and Editor of Daily 'Exonerated,'" *Times of India*, August 13, 1965, 7.

67. "Ex-officers Back Gen. Cariappa," *Times of India*, February 21, 1971, 11.

4 *From 1962 to Bluestar*

1. J. N. Chaudhuri, interview with Lloyd I. Rudolph and Susanne H. Rudolph, February 11, 1963. Rudolph 1962–1963 Interviews. I am grateful to Professor Lloyd I. Rudolph and Susanne H. Rudolph for their generosity in making these notes available to me.

2. For other instances of such balancing outside the army in an effort to reduce the risks of military intervention, see Horowitz 1985, 544–549; Quinlivan 1999; Nordlinger 1977, 75–78.

3. Total strength estimated from *Ministry of Home Affairs Report 1979–80*, Tables "Growth of Police Personnel in CRPF," 74; "Growth of CISF personnel," 77. Assam Rifles strength listed as twenty-one battalions in *Ministry of Home Affairs Report 1972–73*, 4.

4. The history of the 1962 India-China war has been very well covered elsewhere and it is not necessary to go into it at any great length here. For an introduction, see, e.g., Dalvi (1969), Neville (1970), and Srinath Raghavan's excellent *War and Peace in Modern India* (2010a).

5. There is an important revisionist view on this, recently put forward by Srinath Raghavan in (2010a) and (2010b) that emphasizes the deeper reasons behind the Thimayya resignation in 1959—the result of military intrusion into policy rather than civilian interference in professional matters, as Raghavan sees it—and the fact that the army in Raghavan's view has had more autonomy and clout than traditional accounts offered by Dalvi, Maxwell, and a generation of analysts have suggested. This deeper account of the Thimayya resignation as well as the military's own lack of a policy to deal with the Chinese in 1960–1962 is fascinating. And Raghavan is completely right, I think, to point to the army's substantial operational autonomy, as I discuss in Chapter 5. As its domestic operations have increased in recent years due to the prolonged insurgencies, it has necessarily taken a larger role in some domestic decision making. My own view is that the weight of the evidence on civil-military relations since the 1950s still seems to favor the more traditional view of a dominant bureaucracy and a weaker military leadership than the revisionist version. Otherwise it is difficult to make sense of the persistent and strong military complaints over the years about the many problems of the command and control systems.

6. V. K. Krishna Menon, interview with Lloyd I. Rudolph and Susanne H. Rudolph, March 16, 1963. Rudolph 1962–1963 Interviews.

7. Of course, this might just be dismissed as Patel's desire to highlight his own administrative talents compared to his successors and his own lack of

responsibility for the China disaster. After all, Patel's own ethnic hedging when he was Defence Secretary had led to the premature retirement of Lieutenant General Sant Singh in 1953, after he was passed over for promotion to COAS on the retirement of Cariappa.

8. Maxwell (1970, 232) reports the army's many critical shortages of equipment just before the war.

9. This was around 30,000 short of the army's sanctioned strength at the time.

10. *India's Defence Plan and Requirements, 1964–69* (Ministry of Defence, Government of India, March 1964). Enclosure in Public Record Office DO 133–186, "Indian Defence Plan 1964," 1.

11. *India's Defence Plan and Requirements, 1964–69* (Ministry of Defence, Government of India, March 1964). Enclosure in Public Record Office DO 133–186, "Indian Defence Plan 1964."

12. "Menon Quits Cabinet: Nehru Bows to Party Pressure," *The Statesman*, November 8, 1962, 1.

13. See, e.g., the views of General S.M. Shrinagesh (COAS 1955–1957), Lieutenant General S.K. Sinha (former Chief of Western Command) in Sinha's "Foreward" to Issar (2009, 18–19); see also J. J. Singh (2012, 232). For political support for the CDS, see "Government Accused of Complacency in Defence," *Times of India*, March 22, 1964, 8.

14. One point to note about this graph is that it probably overestimates the number of "single class" units relative to "fixed" because I categorize the twenty-seven battalions of the Madras Regiment in 1972 as "single class." Arguably the regiment should be categorized as "fixed class" because it is composed of specified and diverse "Southern Indian Classes" that are already quite heterogeneous within a unit, and therefore hedge risk.

15. The 8th Raj Rif, raised in 1963, was an exception, with a 50 percent Rajput, 25 percent Jat, and 25 percent "Hindustani Muslim" composition, as was the 9th Raj Rif, raised in 1964, which had 50 percent Jats, 25 percent Rajputs, and 25 percent Gujaratis (Sethna and Valmiki 1983, 133–134).

16. Chavan told the House that "the proposal is under consideration, but it should be pointed out that the general policy of Government is to broad-base recruitment as much as possible without affecting the efficiency of the Army and that calling a regiment by a new sectional name would be inconsistent with this policy." This prompted Shri Noreen Ghosh to say "In view of the fact that in our Army there are Tamil regiments, Dogra regiments, Gorkha regiments, etc.—something like linguistic groups—what is there to object to having a Bengali regiment as well?" *Rajya Sabah*, answer to starred question 112 by A. D. Mani, February 27, 1963.

17. *Ministry of Defence Report 1963–64*, 23.

18. Answer to question by G. Lakshman, MP, *Rajya Sabha*, March 7, 1975, 86.

19. Y. B. Chavan, interview with Lloyd I. Rudolph and Susanne H. Rudolph, February 13, 1963. Rudolph 1962–1963 Interviews.

20. In a 1964 interview with Stephen P. Cohen, Ram made it clear that he had opposed caste units in the army in cabinet and tried to get more mixed units created. Jagjivan Ram, interview December 9, 1964. Cohen 1963-64 Interviews.

21. *Lok Sabha Debates*, March 14, 1974.

22. S. K. Sinha interview, June 18, 2012, New Delhi.

23. J. N. Chaudhuri, "Introduction," *Chanakya Defence Annual 1973–74*, cited by Inder Malhotra, "Guns, Ghee and Olive Green," *Times of India*, September 15, 1974, 6.

24. "Manekshaw Next Army Chief," *Times of India*, May 21, 1969, 1.

25. "Rumour has it that Defence Minister Jagjivan Ram and some senior bureaucrats had convinced Mrs. Gandhi that Prem was too well regarded in the Army and would not be a politicians' General. It was even said that perhaps Prem was too popular with his men. It is perhaps relevant to mention that Indira Gandhi declared Emergency a year later in 1975—a decision that Prem, had he been Army Chief, would have vehemently opposed." See also Ashali Verma (Bhagat's daughter), interview, November 21, 2012, http://www.youtube.com/watch?v=-yOVZGyPNSw (hereafter cited as Verma [2012]).

26. Verma (2012).

27. EFG (Frank) Maynard, "Reports on Armed Forces of India" (1972), November 2, 1970.

28. Sam Manekshaw, interview with Karan Thapar, "Face to Face," July 28, 1999, http://www.youtube.com/watch?v=L-tgRl_VK_Q.

29. For the difficulties of integrating demobilized Naga militants into the army and efforts to direct them into other corps, see "Rehabilitation of Captured Underground Nagas—The Question of Nagaland Regiment—Papers re. GI MEA Naga Unit Section," National Archives of India, New Delhi.

30. This is not to imply that the army has not had its own human-rights issues with long-term deployments. See, e.g., Haksar and Hongray (2011).

31. "B. K. Nehru, Governor Assam to Minister of Home Affairs (Chavan), Jan 6th 1970," 9/75/69; "MHA Ministry of Home Affairs B.2.II Minutes of HM's morning meeting No. 170 dt 8.12.69 regarding substitution of Assam Rifles in place of CRP in NEFA." National Archives of India, New Delhi.

32. Neville Maxwell, "Must the Military Intervene in India?" *The Times*, February 28, 1968.

33. Hoon has an account of the attack and aftermath from the perspective of an army insider, albeit one who only visited Amritsar after the attack.

34. Details of the main mutinies at the Sikh Regimental Centre, Ramgarh, 18th Sikh, 9th Sikh, 14th Punjab (a 75 percent Sikh and 25 percent Dogra unit) and 171st Field Regiments are given in Bhuller (1987, 11–39).

35. "Punjab Militants' Bid to Rope in Ex-Servicemen," *Times of India*, September 28, 1990, 7.

36. There is a historical precedent here, of course, as the Akali movement mentioned in Chapter 1 also drew much of its strength from districts with high levels of army recruitment and many retired veterans. Fox (1985, 91–93), citing NAI Home-Poll Files A, 459, II, & K.W. 1922.

37. These new "Vaidya" units are reported in various sources as 20th Jat, 13th Sikh, 21st Rajputana Rifles, 20th Rajput, 18th Garhwal, 12th Assam, 14th Assam, 16th Bihar, and 19th Dogra. There may have been others.

5 *Army and Nation Today*

1. Mukherjee (2014) provides a fine account of these reform proposals and their lack of success, beginning with the 1990 Arun Singh committee and ending in 2011.

2. All quotes from Standing Committee on Defence (2009–2010), *Action Taken Report on the Recommendations/Observations of the Committee Contained in the Thirty-Sixth Report (Fourteenth Lok Sabha) on 'Status of Implementation of Unified Command for Armed Forces,'* Lok Sabha Secretariat, December 2009 (hereafter referred to as Standing Committee).

3. "Task Force to Review Kargil Panel Proposals," *Deccan Herald*, June 24, 2013, http://www.deccanherald.com/content/171116/task-force-review -kargil-panel.html.

4. Standing Committee, 5–6.

5. Karan Singh Yadav, "Need to Raise an Ahirwal Regiment in the Indian Army," *Lok Sabha Debates*, Matters under Rule 377, August 24, 2005.

6. See "Answer to Sukhendu Sekhar Roy's Demand for a Bengal Regiment," *Rajya Sabha Proceedings*, May 16, 2012.

7. "Raising of New Military Regiments," Written Answers to Starred Questions, starred question 541, *Lok Sabha Debates*, May 14, 1997.

8. Written answer 317 to question from Jitender Singh, September 3, 2012, *Lok Sabha Proceedings*. For another question in this vein, see Harish Rawat MP's query as to "Whether Government are aware of declining ratio of re-cruitment in traditional recruitment areas of Army (particularly Utta-ranchal)?" Q. 794, *Rajya Sabha Proceedings*, July 12, 2004.

9. For example, Satbir Singh remarked on the problems caused by the shortage of officers in the army, which leads to a shortage of officers at the bat-talion level, which in turn leads to frequent turnover and fewer officers at the companies and platoons, where managing relations with the men is most im-portant. NDTV, May 15, 2012.

10. "Now Army Probes Bribe Charge against ASC Major General in Jammu and Kashmir," *India Today*, June 25, 2012.

11. "Politicians, Babus, Army Bent Rules to Grab Adarsh land: CAG," *Indian Express*, August 9, 2011, http://www.indianexpress.com/news/politicians -babus-army-bent-rules-to-grab-adarsh-land-cag/829404/o; "No Parallel to Adarsh Scam, Says CAG," *Times of India*, October 27, 2011, http://articles.time sofindia.indiatimes.com/2011-10-27/india/30327763_1_cag-report-adarsh-scam -adarsh-cooperative-housing-society.

12. For World War II literacy data see Report of Infantry Committee, Appendix "A," "Comparison of Educated Personnel in Various Arms of the Service." Indian Office Archives, British Library, London. In 1943 no infantry-men at all had matriculated or studied up to ninth or tenth standard.

13. "Wake Up Call for the Army," *The Hindu*, March 26, 2013, http://www .thehindu.com/opinion/editorial/wakeup-call-for-the-army/article4548120.ece.

14. "Soldiers and Officers of an Army Unit Clash, Three Injured," *Indian Express*, October 11, 2013; "Army Officers, Jawan Injured in Scuffle during Boxing Match," *The Hindu*, October 11, 2013, http://www.thehindu.com/news

/national/other-states/army-officers-jawan-injured-in-scuffle-during-boxing
-match/article5224933.ece.

15. "Scuffle between Officers and Jawans," answer to Lok Sabha unstarred question No. 3671, delivered September 3, 2012. Gautam (2009, 46) provides the composition of the cavalry units, and the composition of the 22nd Field Regiment is provided in R. K. N. Singh, "Nyoma Incident: Have Maoists Infiltrated the Indian Army?" *Canary Trap*, May 24, 2012, http://www.canarytrap.in/2012/05/22/nyoma-incident-have-maoists-infiltrated-the-indian-army/.

16. *Left, Right, and Centre*, NDTV, May 15, 2102, http://www.youtube.com/watch?v=BjMRacJvGCY; "Ladakh Troop Revolt Underlines Army Class Tensions," *The Hindu*, May 12, 2012, http://www.thehindu.com/news/national/ladakh-troop-revolt-underlines-army-class-tensions/article3412907.ece.

17. "Ladakh Troop Revolt Underlines Army Class Tensions."

18. For instance, officers at the rank of lieutenant general retire two years later than officers at the rank of major general. So if a major general is not promoted to a vacant position at the rank of lieutenant general before his retirement date, even if he has been approved for promotion, he has to leave the service. As might be imagined, this system offers lots of scope for senior officers and bureaucrats to try to block particular officers and advance others by manipulating vacancies, seniority levels, and promotions to make sure that positions are open or closed at the "right" time. In the past two decades candidates who have lost out in these battles have been increasingly willing to take their cases to court, where the armed forces tribunals have sometimes overturned the army's promotion decisions. On the general issue of recruitment controversies in the courts see Anand (2012) and for the specifics of the General V. K. Singh controversy see V. K. Singh (2013, 265–266).

19. For instance Lieutenant General Sant Singh (Eastern Command) quickly and quietly resigned from the service when superseded by General Thimayya, who became COAS in 1957 (Thorat 1986, 173). Lieutenant Generals S. D. Verma and S. P. P. Thorat did the same in 1961 when superseded by General Thapar (Verma 1988, 122–123).

20. "Govt. Wary of Caste Angle," *Hindustan Times*, January 18, 2012, http://www.hindustantimes.com/india-news/newdelhi/govt-wary-of-caste-angle/article1-798767.aspx.

21. "Dalbir Singh Suhag to head Eastern Army Command," *Times of India*, June 15, 2012, http://timesofindia.indiatimes.com/india/Dalbir-Singh-Suhag-to-head-Eastern-Army-Command/articleshow/14153578.cms.

22. By the way, these statements are not strictly accurate as at least one new class regiment has been raised. The Naga Regiment, raised in 1970 at Ranikhet, is 50 percent Naga; the balance of recruits are Kumaonis, Garhwalis, and Gorkhas. This raising was less a change in general policy, however, than an ad hoc step, taken as part of a 1960 peace deal with Naga rebels, who insisted on some of their cadre being absorbed into the army and paramilitary forces (Praval 1976, 302–303). It might also be argued that the Rashtriya Rifles is a new class regiment, given that it draws heavily from existing class units, with which its battalions are linked. Several post-1950 raisings of armored

regiments with a fixed-class composition, such as Sixty-Second Cavalry, raised in 1956 with Dogra, Jat, and Sikh squadrons, also appear to breach the promises made in 1949.

23. WA 299 to question by Santosh Bagrodia, *Rajya Sabha Proceedings*, February 25, 1998.

24. *Kendriya Sainik Board Annual Report 2009*, Table 1(a), "Zila-Wise Population of Ex-Servicemen in the Country," 2–13.

25. Not all ex-servicemen, of course, return to their home districts after service. Some settle near cantonments or the areas in which they have served; others move to be near new jobs or family members. But the facts that the infantry and the armored corps have displayed a preference for rural recruits and that the same districts that are full of retirees now are often the same ones with very heavy recruitment in the past, make the ex-serviceman criterion a good general guide to past recruitment.

26. For example, battalion and company composition data can be found in Gautam (2009), Sharma (1990), and the various individual regimental histories such as Longer (1981), *The Gallant Dogras* (2005), *Garhwali Paltan ka Sankshipta Paricaya* (1996), and Praval (1975).

27. Where the specific dates of battalion formation are not known, they can often be inferred from the unit numbers and the known raising dates of other battalions in the regiment.

28. Sources for data used in these maps: state recruitment data provided in Rajya Sabha and Lok Sabha's written answers, and listed in Appendix A, normalized by 1981 Population Data from Ashish Bose, *Demographic Diversity of India* (Delhi: D. K. Publishers, 1991); Table 6, 52; 2011 Population Data" from *Census of India* website, http://www.censusindia.gov.in/2011census/population_enumeration.aspx; "1971 Population" estimated by subtracting 1971–1981 growth data from 1981 population totals, Table 9, "Decadal Growth of Population," in *Demographic Diversity of India*, 56.

29. Gujaratis have not volunteered in large numbers over the years even when units have been specifically created for them. After the integration of the princely states, several units of state forces from Gujarat were reformed as the Seventh Grenadiers and were originally assigned a composition of troops from Saurashtra and Kutch, but this had to be abandoned because Gujaratis from these regions apparently did not come forward in large enough numbers (Sharma 1990, 81–82).

30. *I. S. Yadav v. Union of India*, Writ Petition (Civil) NO(s). 524 of 2012, Supreme Court of India. For coverage of the case see "How Can Caste, Region-Based Recruitment Continue in Army Regiments," *The Hindu*, December 11, 2012, http://www.thehindu.com/news/national/how-can-caste-regionbased-recruitment-continue-in-army-regiments/article4185517.ece; "Recruitment Not Based on Caste, Region or Religion, Army Tells Court," *The Statesman*, October 29, 2013.

31. "Army Denies Racism in PBG Picks," *The Pioneer*, October 3, 2013.

32. For details of the case's dismissal, see *Times of India*, April 21 2014, http://timesofindia.indiatimes.com/india/SC-refuses-to-relook-its-verdict-on-Army-recruitment-policy/articleshow/34058842.cms.

33. "Scottish Recruitment Crisis Means One in 10 Soldiers in Scots Regiments Are Foreign-Born," *Daily Record*, 6 March 2011, downloaded 22 November 2013 from http://www.dailyrecord.co.uk/news/scottish-news/recruitment-crisis-means-one-in-10-1096793.

34. Data on Indian Army recruitment from 1971–1972 to 1973–1974 from the written answer to Sanat Kumar Raha, *Rajya Sabha*, question no. 285, 59.

35. "Recruitment in Army on Fake Documents," *Lok Sabha*, unstarred question No. 5017, April 28, 2005; "Document Racket for Army Jobs Busted," *The Hindu*, April 14, 2004.

36. "Army Battles Fake Domicile Certificate Menace in Gujarat," *Indian Express*, January 31, 2009, http://www.indianexpress.com/news/army-battles-fake-domicile-certificate-menace-in-gujarat/417425/.

37. See *Kumar v. Union of India*, Armed Forces Tribunal, regional bench, Jaipur, July 19, 2010, in which the appellant was dismissed from the army after two years of service, in March 2005, for providing false documentation that he was a resident of Delhi when in reality he was from Alwar in Rajasthan. In another case heard by the same court, a second man from Rajasthan, Narsingh Sharan Sharma, enrolled in II Mahar, and was discharged after six years, in 1999, on the grounds that he was from Rajasthan, not from Himachal Pradesh as his documents claimed, and therefore was not eligible to join his unit as a Dogra. *Sharma v. Union of India*, Armed Forces Tribunal, regional bench, Jaipur December 12, 2011.

38. The only exception is the Mazhabi and Ramdasia Sikhs, which according to my estimates had an equivalent battalion strength of 2.4 percent in the 1940s, 3.9 percent in the 1980s, and have 3.7 percent now. The more heavily recruited Jat Sikhs have gone down over the same period from 11.2 percent to 7.2 percent, probably a reflection of the booming agricultural economy in Punjab over the past decades, and perhaps also the demand side in the aftermath of the Punjab militancy.

39. In fact the new BJP government and its Defence Minister Arun Jaitley worked hard to lower the temperature over the appointment of Lieutenant General Dalbir Singh Suhag, which the BJP had originally objected to as premature, coming as it did from a "lame duck" government immediately before the 2014 Lok Sabha elections. Jaitley confirmed Suhag's appointment as settled in a statement in the Rajya Sabha, signaling to the army (and his own Minister of State General V. K. Singh, who had allegedly tried to block Suhag's promotion to the top area command when he was COAS), that the issue was closed. "Jaitley isn't V. K. Singh's defence minister; backs Dalbir Singh's appointment as the next army chief," *Indian Express*, June 12, 2014, http://indianexpress.com/article/india/politics/jaitley-isnt-vk-singhs-defence-minister-backs-dalbir-singhs-appointment-as-the-next-army-chief/.

40. In fairness to Yadav it should be pointed out that those earlier politicians who spoke of a caste-blind society were usually upper castes—who were free to proclaim the virtues of a casteless society, one might argue, precisely because caste had already advantaged them in so many ways.

41. Retired officer from one of the 'Vaidya' units, interview, June 2012.

42. "Strength of Rashtriya Rifles," answer to starred question No. 423, *Rajya Sabha Debates*, May 4, 1995, 27–34.

43. Ibid.

44. Rajagopalan (2010, 32) refers to sixty-six Rashtriya Rifles units being authorized, but I could find raising information for only sixty-three battalions as of 2012.

45. K. P. D. Samanta to Shri Abusaleh Shariff, [exact date unclear] August 2005, Sachar Committee Proceedings, NMML.

46. Ibid.

47. For examples, see the pre-1947 Indian Army yearly manpower reports. India Office Records, British Library, London.

48. "The Thinking Man's General," *India Today*, February 18, 1986, 78–79.

49. "Recruitment of Non-Marathis in Maratha Light Infantry," answer to unstarred question No. 187, *Lok Sabha Proceedings*, February 24, 2002.

50. Shishir Gupta, "How Many Muslims Do You Have, Gov't Asks Armed Forces," *Indian Express*, February 11, 2006.

51. (V. K. Singh, 2005, 290–291).

52. *Rajya Sabha* debates, 21 February 2006, 317.

53. Reply of Defense Minister George Fernandes to unstarred question No. 187, *Lok Sabha questions*, February 24, 2000.

54. Shekhar Gupta, Ritu Sarin, and Pranab Dhal Samanta, "The Night Raisina Hill Was Spooked," *Indian Express*, April 4, 2012, http://m.indianexpress .com/news/the-january-night-raisina-hill-was-spooked-two-key-army-units -moved-towards-delhi-without-notifying-govt/932328/. General J. J. Singh completely denies the story in his autobiography (Singh 2012, 335–336).

55. "Morning after DGMO Meet Government Chopper Flew to Check If Troops Were on Way Back," *Indian Express*, February 22, 2014, http://indian express.com/article/india/india-others/morning-after-dgmo-meet-govt -chopper-flew-to-check-if-troops-were-on-way-back/99/.

56. Pallam Raju, interview with Karan Thapar, *Devil's Advocate*, IBN Live, April 8, 2012, http://www.youtube.com/watch?v=z9k4w3tMvJg.

57. V. P. Malik, "Army Should Not Look Like It's Losing Its Values," *Tehelka Magazine* 9, no. 14, April 7, 2012, http://archive.tehelka.com/story_main52 .asp?filename=Op070412Olive.asp.

58. "Top General Speaks: Def Secy Summoned Me Late Night, Said Highest Seat of Power Was Worried, Troops Must Go Back Quickly," *Indian Express*, February 21, 2014, http://indianexpress.com/article/india/india-others/top -general-speaks-def-secy-summoned-me-late-night-said-highest-seat-of -power-was-worried-troops-must-go-back-quickly/.

6 *The Path Not Taken: Pakistan 1947–1977*

1. Tudor (2013) offers a revisionist account that puts much more emphasis on weak parties and class coalitions than on bad socio-economic and ethnic imbalances or on coup-proofing legacies.

2. Though these points are made in fine analyses by Stephen P. Cohen (1988, 139) and Philip Oldenburg (2010, 49–50). Another good analysis is in Wilcox 1965.

3. Sir Ross McCay, interview with Hector Bolitho, Bolitho diaries November 1951–May 1953, 104. Transcript by Stephen P. Cohen. I am grateful to Professor Cohen for making this transcript available.

4. Jalal's book is the best in looking at the twin effects of bad inheritances and the need for foreign financial and military support in determining Pakistan's trajectory in its first decade.

5. See the revealing accounts of the private meetings at which important policy decisions got made in Ayub Khan's *Friends Not Masters* (1967).

6. Arthur Smith to Sir Mosley Mayne, April 3, 1946, "Defence Implications of a Partition of India into Pakistan and Hindustan," copy No. 34, enclosure (hereafter referred to as Implications). See also Wainwright 1994, 73–74.

7. "Rs. 157.37 Crores Defence Estimates Passed," *The Statesman*, March 12, 1949, 6. See also Vakil (1950, 55–56), who points out that as a result of the very heavy defense expenditure Pakistan could spend only PKR 10 million on development grants to its provinces in 1950–1951, compared to the Indian government's INR 250–300 million.

8. Although there was a Baluch Regiment, it in fact had no Baluchis at all before 1947. It was composed of 50 percent Punjabis, 25 percent Pathans, and 25 percent Dogra Brahmins. *Ninth Indian Manpower Review (1 Jan 1946–31 March 1947)*, Appendix I, "Infantry Non-Tech Combatants—Summary by Regiments by Classes," L/WS/1/1613 Manpower.

9. Estimate of total army size from F. M. Khan (1963, 42).

10. A second battalion followed in December 1948.

11. Estimated from the squadron breakdown given in Elliot (1965, Appendix B, 359–363).

12. "Notes on Action Taken by Pakistan Army to Assist Ranghars and Kaimkhannis [*sic*] by General Gracey," 23rd August 23, 1948, Ismay Papers, Liddell Hart Archives, King's College London.

13. For a sample of these Bengali complaints see "Glaring Financial Injustice in Bengal," *Modern Review*, March 1929, 395–396; the 1935 budget debates in *Council Proceedings of the Bengal Legislative Council, Forty-Fifth Session 1935—11th–28th February 1935* (Alipore: Government Press, 1935); and the debates over the provincial imbalance in the army in *Legislative Assembly Debates 20th Sept 1938*, 2754–2755.

14. "Injustice to Bengal" *Modern Review*, 1929, 5572, p. 29.

15. "Bengal's Case for a Revision of the Meston Settlement," *Times of India*, January 22, 1929, 13.

16. Implications.

17. Quoted in Wainwright (1994, 67).

18. This statement reflects a reading of the following sources: Pirzada (1984, 1986a, 1986b); Afazal (1967); Jinnah (1999); Muhammad Reza Kazimi, ed., *Jinnah-Liaquat Correspondence* (Karachi: Pakistan Study Centre, 2003). I have also searched the secondary literature as well as the *Times of India* for the preindependence period.

19. See, e.g., Pirzada (1970, 51 [presidential address of Abdur Rahim, December 1925], 164–166 [presidential address of Muhammad Iqbal 1930]).

20. Jinnah also consistently overestimated the Muslim percentage in the army in his public statements. "Mr. Jinnah Defines Pakistan," *Times of India*, November 9, 1945.

21. "Government Victory on the Army Bill—Congress Defeat in Assembly—Mr. Jinnah's Strong Support," *Times of India*, August 24, 1938, 13.

22. Sir Frank Messervy, interview with Hector Bolitho, Hector Bolitho diaries 1951–1953, 181. Transcript by Stephen P. Cohen. The Bolitho diary also records an interview with Lieutenant General Sir Ross McCay, chief military advisor to the Pakistan Army at the time, who told Bolitho that "Jinnah never spoke to me of the problems of the Army." These extracts were kindly made available to me by Professor Stephen P. Cohen.

23. Douglas Gracey, interview with Stephen P. Cohen, London, November 25, 1963. Stephen P. Cohen Interviews 1963–1964.

24. Punjab Provincial Muslim League, report of work for June and July 1944 submitted to the All India Committee of Action, Lahore, July 28, 1944.

25. Zaidi (2002, 227–235).

26. Afazal (1967, 139).

27. Zaidi (2002). On the frustrations for Hindu and Dalit politicians in the new state, see Sen (2012). For the difficulties of the Ahmadiyya minority, see Sir Zafrulla Khan, interview, New York, November 17, 1963, http://www.alis-lam.org/library/books/Sir-Zafrulla-Khan-Interviews.pdf.

28. See, e.g., Statement of Nur Islam in *Constituent Assembly of Pakistan Debates, Monday, 27th March, 1950*, volume 7, No. 1 (Karachi: Manager of Publications, 1950); Muhammad Toaha and others to M. A. Jinnah, Dacca, 22 March 1948; Memorandum by Joint State Language Committee of Action, Dacca, 24 March 1948, in Zaidi (2002), 253–255, 277–279.

29. Afazal (1967, 190–191).

30. "Problems of East Bengal," *Leader*, December 8, 1950; *The Statesman Weekly*, December 16, 1950, 3.

31. Mizanur Rahman Choudhury, *National Assembly of Pakistan Debates*, June 24, 1964 (Karachi: Government of Pakistan Press, 1964), 1691–1695.

32. Muhammad Afsaruddin (East Pakistan) *National Assembly of Pakistan Debates*, June 20, 1962 (Karachi: Government of Pakistan Press, 1962), 201.

33. Mr. Pumphrey, High Commissioner, Islamabad to Foreign Secretary Sir Alec Douglas-Home, 21 May 1971, National Archives, London, FCO 37/870 Political Situation in Pakistan (1971) Part 1.

34. Debate on defense expenditure, *National Assembly of Pakistan Debates*, June 24, 1964 (Karachi: Government of Pakistan Press, 1964), 1691–1695. This information appears to overstate the Sindhi and Baluchi percentages in the infantry, probably because it counts Punjabis who enrolled from these provinces.

35. Ibid., 1675.

36. On these capital and current spending imbalances see, A. K. M. Fazlul Kabir Chowdhury, *Assembly Proceedings East Pakistan Provincial Assembly: Second Session 1963 25 June–3rd July 1963* (Dacca: East Pakistan Government Press, 1964), 427–431. Chowdhury pointed out that "You know, Sir, that 80 per cent of our Budget is spent after Defence, and in the matter of purchase of commodities, purchase of foodstuff and of equipment for the Army, East Pakistan market is ignored and all purchases are done from West Pakistan. So, Sir, money from the Army to all intents and purposes is spent, distributed and

circulated in West Pakistan market and money is never in circulation in East Pakistan in proportion to its needs and requirements."

37. *National Assembly of Pakistan Debates*, June 20, 1962 (Karachi: Government of Pakistan Press, 1962), 194.

38. What Horowitz (1985) would term "balance outside the army."

Conclusion: Army and Nation

1. "Resolution *re* formation of a national army recruited from all classes and provinces," *Council of State Debates*, April 4, 1938, 594–607.

2. SDSA Team 2008, Table 4.7, Level of Trust in the Army by Gender, Locality and Social Strata.

3. J.N. Chaudhuri, interview with Lloyd I. Rudolph and Susanne H. Rudolph, New Delhi, February 11, 1963. Rudolph 1962–1963 Interviews.

4. "Question re Caste Based Regiments in the Army," *Rajya Sabha Debates*, vol. 160 (August 26, 1991–September 18, 1991); "Question re caste based regts. in army," September 12, 1991, 177.

5. Today's practices are not so different from those before World War II, when the Sikh regiments insisted that "men will observe the customs of their faith" and had punishments for those who did not. *Standing Orders for the Fourth Batallion Eleventh Sikh Regiment* (Landikotal, March 1939), section 35, part 11.

6. The affidavit also said that "The assessment of the petitioner with regards to single castes based regiments is incorrect since Dogra, Garhwal Rifles, Madras Regiment are not defined by caste but by region. These regiments are drawn from specified social and linguistic groups without reference to caste being the source of recruitment." "Recruitment not based on caste, region & religion: Army tells SC," *The Statesman*, October 8, 2013, http://www .thestatesman.net/news/17471-recruitment-not-based-on-caste-region-religion -army-tells-sc.html.

7. Jawaharlal Nehru and Y.B. Chavan, interview with Lloyd I. Rudolph and Susanne H. Rudolph, New Delhi, February 13, 1963. Rudolph 1962–1963 Interviews.

8. Cohen and Dasgupta (2010, 64). See also the cable report, released by Wikileaks, of separate meetings by Deputy National Security Advisor Leela Ponappa and Joint Secretary T.C.A. Raghavan, in meetings with visiting Ambassador Anne Patterson on August 27, 2008, https://wikileaks.org/plusd/cables /08NEWDELHI2401_a.html.

9. Shekhar Gupta, Ritu Sarin, and Pranab Dhal Samanta, "The Night Raisina Hill Was Spooked," *Indian Express*, April 4, 2012, http://m.indianexpress .com/news/the-january-night-raisina-hill-was-spooked-two-key-army-units -moved-towards-delhi-without-notifying-govt/932328/. General V.K. Singh's successor as COAS, General J.J. Singh, completely denies the story in his autobiography (Singh 2012, 335–336), but it was apparently confirmed by General V.K. Singh's retired director of military operations, who had firsthand information of the events in January 2012, in a new interview in February 2014. "Lt.-Gen. A.K. Choudhary: 'Troop Movements should've been avoided if they knew General V.K. Singh's court date,'" *Indian Express*, February 21, 2014,

http://indianexpress.com/article/india/india-others/troop-movement-shouldve
-been-avoided-if-they-knew-v-k-singhs-court-date/Feb 22 2014.

10. "V. K. Singh, now minister, slams next Army Chief; accuses Dalbir Singh
of protecting unit that 'kills innocents'," *Indian Express*, June 12, 2014, 6/12/2014,
from http://indianexpress.com/article/india/politics/v-k-singh-now-minister
-slams-next-army-chief/; "Jaitley on V. K. Singh row: Army chief Lt General
Dalbir Singh Suhag's appointment is final," *India Today*, June 11, 2014, http:
//indiatoday.intoday.in/story/lok-sabha-congres-demands-resignation-of-v-k
-singh/1/366307.html, June 12, 2014.

References

Primary Sources

National Archives of India, New Delhi
CARIAPPA PAPERS

to K. M. Cariappa, 8 April 1947. Group XXII S. Nos 1–161 Part 1.

Jawaharlal Nehru to K. M. Cariappa, 13 August 1947.

Jawaharlal Nehru to Sir Rob Lockhart, Commander in Chief–designate. August 13, 1947, enclosure to Nehru's letter to K. M. Cariappa. Group XXI Part 1 S(2).

Reorganization of the Army and Air Forces in India: Report of a Committee Set Up by His Excellency the Commander-in-Chief in India. 1945. Volume 1—Text (Secret, Copy No. 67), Group XXII S. Nos 1–161 Part 1 [Willcox Committee].

HOME (POLITICAL) PAPERS

Intelligence Bureau Note, Home Poll 39/10/38.

"Minutes of Weekly Home Dept.-War Dept.-IB-MI Meeting Held on 21st June 1946," Home Poll (I) 21/20/46.

"Minutes of Weekly Home Dept-War Dept-IB-MI Meeting Held on 17th Sep 1946," "Question of the Employment of the Ex-Member of the 'Indian National Army' in the Indian States Forces and Other Government Services," Home Poll (I) 21/20/46.

"B. K. Nehru, Governor Assam to Minister of Home Affairs (Chavan) Jan 6th 1970." 9/75/69 Ministry of Home Affairs B.2.II "Minutes of HM's morning meeting No. 170 dt 8.12.69 regarding substitution of Assam Rifles in place of CRP in NEFA."

"Question of the Employment of the Ex-Members of the 'Indian National Army' in the Indian States Forces and Other Government Services," Home Poll (I) 21/20/46.

"Rehabilitation of Captured Underground Nagas—The Question of Nagaland Regiment—Papers re. GI MEA Naga Unit Section."

National Archives, London
FOREIGN AND COMMONWEALTH OFFICE

EFG (Frank) Maynard. Report to Foreign and Commonwealth Office on visit to Seventh Light Cavalry, 2 November 1970. Enclosure in FCO file 37–634 "Reports on Armed Forces of India" (1972).

India's Defence Plan and Requirements, 1964–69 (Ministry of Defense, Government of India, March 1964). Enclosure in Public Record Office DO 133–186 "Indian Defence Plan 1964."

National Library of Scotland, Edinburgh
MINTO PAPERS

"Papers Relating to the 4th Earl of Minto's Refusal to Sign the Punjab Colonization Bill 1906–1907." MS. 12633.

"Policy in Regard to the Proportion of British to Native Troops in India." Record of Lord Kitchener's Administration of the Army in India 1902–1909, MS. 12601.

"Record of Lord Kitchener's Administration of the Army in India 1902–1909." MS. 12601, 118–119.

NEHRU MEMORIAL MUSEUM AND LIBRARY, NEW DELHI

"Recommendations of the Armed Forces Nationalisation Committee 1947." Private Papers.

Rylands Library, Manchester University
AUCHINLECK PAPERS

"Comment by the C-in-C on Note by the Hon. Member for External Affairs," September 1946, GB 133 AUC/1193.

Jawaharlal Nehru to Defense Secretary. Letter and Statement, 12 September 1946 GB 133 AUC/1193.

India Office Records, British Library, London

Arthur Smith to Sir Mosley Mayne, "Defence Implications of a Partition of India into Pakistan and Hindustan, enclosure, 3 April 1946. Copy No. 34. L/WS/1029.

Baker, W. M. G. Note from Adjutant General's Branch on Indian Manpower, 2 November 1942. L/WS/1/1680 Recruitment in India.

Class Composition of the Army in India 1909–1942. L/WS/1/456.

"Comparison of Educated Personnel in Various Arms of the Service," L/WS /1/1371 Report of Infantry Committee.

Confidential Reports on Indian Officer Cadets at Sandhurst, 1923–1928. L/MIL /9/319.

"Defence Implications of a Partition of India into Pakistan and Hindustan," L/WS/1029.

Eighth Indian Manpower Review (1 August 1945–31 July 1946): Annexure "G" Estimated Distribution of Classes to Arms and Services.—Combatants.— Trained Men Indian Army. L/WS/1/922 Manpower.

Extract from Letter No. B/61666/II/AGS Army HQ India, Adjutant General's Branch, Simla, 4 July 1940, L/WS/1/394 "New Units Raised in India since the Outbreak of War 1939–1943."

Indian Army Morale and Possible Reduction 1943–1945, L/WS/1/707.

Indian Army Orders. 1946. Special Orders. /L/MIL/17/5/296.

Major General G. N. Molesworth to Jenkins, September 1943, L/WS/1/1680 Recruitment in India.

Ninth Indian Manpower Review. L/WS/1/1613.

"Note for the Joint Defence Council by the Supreme Commander [Auchinleck] on the Future of the Punjab Boundary Force (Top Secret)." Decisions on Military Items of the Partition Council and Proceedings of the Provisional Joint Defence Council and the Joint Defence Council, No. 15, 28 August 1947. Partition Proceedings 1947–1950, Volume 5, NEG 3659.

"Note on Sikhs," Appendix A, L/WS/2/44.

Tenth Indian Manpower Review (1 Jan 1946–31 March 1947): Appendix I Infantry Non-Tech Combatants—Summary by Regiments by Classes. L/WS/1 /1613 Manpower.

Wilkeley, J. M. 1915. *Handbooks for the Indian Army: Punjabi Musalmans*. Calcutta. L/MIL/17/5/2166.

MUDIE COLLECTION

Colonel Sherkhan [?], Report on East Punjab Situation Adv HQ Military Evacuation Organisation, Amritsar, Pakistan, 24 September 1947 (Secret). MSS. Eur. F. 164/16.

Churchill Archives, Cambridge

AMERY PAPERS

Memorandum by the Secretary of State for India, Covering a Note by Major-General R. M. M. Lockhart, Secret W.P. (42) 107 2 March 1942 War Cabinet—India Policy, AMEL 1/6/9 File 1 of 2.

Notes, India Office to PM 1943–1944 (File 1) and 1940–1943 (File 2), AMEL 1/6/21."

Cambridge South Asia Archive
ARTHUR PAPERS (A. J. V. ARTHUR, INDIAN CIVIL SERVICE)

Cambridge South Asia Archive, File 3. File 4. Handing-Over Notes, Attock, 10-4-1946; Handing-Over Note as Sub-Divisional Officer, Kasur 19/1/42 to 15/1/44.

Liddell Hart Archive, King's College London
ISMAY PAPERS

Notes on Action Taken by Pakistan Army to Assist Ranghars and Kaimkhannis [*sic*] by General Gracey 23 August 1948, 3/7/38/2.

National Army Museum, London
SAVORY PAPERS

Letters and Other Papers of February 1947–July 1948 Relating to Its Partition and Its Immediate Aftermath. 7603-93-83 43.

Interview Transcripts

Lloyd I. Rudolph and Susanne H. Rudolph, 1962–1963 interviews.
Stephen P. Cohen, 1963–1969 interviews.

Official Publications

Appendices to the Report of the Special Commission to Enquire into the Organization and Expenditure of the Army in India. Volume 1. Simla: Government Press, 1879 [Eden Commission].
Assembly Debates: National Assembly of Pakistan Debates, Official Report Sat. 26th June 1965. (Manager of Publications, Karachi 1965).
Constituent Assembly of India (Legislative) Debates 1946–1949.
Constituent Assembly of India, Report of the Linguistic Provinces Commission 1948.
Council Proceedings of the Bengal Legislative Council.
Expansion of the Armed Forces and Defence Organisation 1939–1945. Volume 5 of Official History of the Indian Armed Forces in the Second World War 1939–45. 1956. Edited by Bisheshwar Prasad. Calcutta: Combined Inter-Services Historical Section.
Half-Yearly Indian Army Lists.
India Council of State Proceedings 1935–1945.
India Legislative Council Proceedings 1920–1933.
Indian Statutory Commission 1930.
Lok Sabha Debates.

Ministry of Defense Annual Reports.

Ministry of Home Affairs Annual Reports.

Monographs, Adjutant General's Branch. 1951. Edited by Bisheshwar Prasad. Calcutta: Combined Inter-Services Historical Section.

Proceedings of the Committee on the Obligations Devolving on the Army in India, Its Strength and Cost, Appointed by His Excellence the Governor-General in Council Volume 1. Majority Report. Simla: Government Central Branch Press, 1913 [Army in India Committee, 1913]. Also known as the Nicholson Committee.

Rajya Sabha Debates.

Report of the Commissioners Appointed to Inquire into the Organisation of the Indian Army; Together with the Minutes of Evidence and Appendix, 1859 (Cmd. 2515) [Peel Commission].

Newspapers and Journals

Daily Telegraph (London)

The Guardian (Manchester)

The Modern Review (Calcutta)

The Statesman (Calcutta)

The Times of India

The Times (London)

Dissertations

Chima, Jugdep Singh. 2002. "Sikh Political Leadership and the Trajectory of the Sikh Separatist Movement in Punjab-India (1978–1997)." PhD diss., University of Missouri-Columbia.

De Bruin, Erica. 2014. "War and Coup-Prevention in Developing States." PhD diss., Yale University.

Des Chene, Mary. 1991. "Relics of Empire: A Cultural History of the Gurkhas, 1815–1987." PhD diss., Stanford University.

Harkness, Kristen. 2013. "The Origins of African Civil-Military Relations: Ethnic Armies and the Development of Coup Traps." PhD diss., Princeton University.

Mukherjee, Anit. 2012. "The Absent Dialogue: Civil-Military Relations and Military Effectiveness in India." PhD diss., SAIS, Johns Hopkins University.

Sen, Dwaipayan. 2012. "The Emergence and Decline of Dalit Politics in Bengal: Jogendranath Mandal, the Scheduled Castes Federation, and Partition, 1932–1968." PhD diss., University of Chicago.

Books and Articles

Afazal, M. Rafique, ed. 1967. *Speeches and Statements of Quaid-i-Millat Liaquat Ali Khan (1941–51).* Lahore: Research Society of Pakistan/University of the Punjab.

All-India Congress Committee. 1934. Being the Resolutions Passed by Congress, the All-India Congress Committee and the Congress Working Committee during the Period between January 1930 and September 1934. Allahabad: All-India Congress Committee.

Ambedkar, B. R. 1941. *Thoughts on Pakistan.* Bombay: Thacker and Company.

Anand R. K. 2012. *Assault on Merit: The Untold Story of Civil-Military Relations.* New Delhi: Har-Anand.

Bajwa, Mandeep S., and Ravi Rikhye. 2001. "The Jat Regiment." *Bharat Rakshak Monitor* 3, no. 4 (January–February 2001). http://www.bharat-rakshak.com/MONITOR/ISSUE3-4/bajwa.html.

Banerjee, Abhijit, and Lakshmi Iyer. 2005. "History, Institutions and Economic Performance: The Legacy of Colonial Land Tenure Systems in India?" *American Economic Review* 95, no. 4, 1190–1213.

Barany, Zoltan. 2012. *The Solider and the Changing State.* Princeton, NJ: Princeton University Press.

Barrier, N. Gerald. 1967. "The Punjab Disturbances of 1907: The Response of the British Government in India to Agrarian Unrest." *Modern Asian Studies* 1, no. 4, 353–383.

Baruah, Sanjib. 2005. *Durable Disorder: Understanding the Politics of Northeast India.* New Delhi: Oxford University Press.

Bayly, Christopher, and Tim Harper. 2010. *Forgotten Wars: The End of Britain's Asian Empire.* London: Penguin.

Bedlington, Stanley S. 1980. "Ethnicity and the Armed Forces in Singapore." In *Ethnicity and the Military in Asia*, Dewitt C. Ellinwood and Cynthia C. Enloe, eds. State University of New York at Buffalo Special Studies Series No. 118, 127–139.

Bhagat, P. S. 1965. *Forging the Shield: A Study of the Defence of India and South-East Asia.* Calcutta: The Statesman.

Bhullar, Pritam. 1987. *The Sikh Mutiny.* New Delhi: Siddharth Publications.

Bose, Ashish. 1991. *Demographic Diversity of India.* Delhi: D. K. Publishers.

Brown, Douglass. 1947. "100,000 Feared Dead in Punjab Civil War." *Daily Telegraph*, September 1.

Callahan, Mary P. 2003. *Making Enemies: War and State Building in Burma.* Ithaca, NY: Cornell University Press.

Callard, Keith. 1957. *Pakistan: A Political Study.* New York: Macmillan.

Cariappa, K. M. 1964. *Let us Wake Up.* Madras: City Printers.

Chandra, Kanchan, and Steven Wilkinson. 2008. "Measuring the Effect of 'Ethnicity.'" *Comparative Political Studies* 41, 515–563.

Chari, P. R. 1977. "Civil Military Relations in India." *Armed Forces and Society* 4, no. 3, 3–28.

———. 2012. "Defence Reforms after 1962: Much Ado about Nothing?" *Journal of Defence Studies and Analyses* 6, no. 4, 171–188.

Chaudhuri, J. N. 1966. *Arms, Aims and Aspects.* Bombay: P. C. Manaktala & Sons.

———. 1978. *Gen. J. N. Chaudhuri: An Autobiography as Narrated to B. K. Narayan.* New Delhi: Vikas.

Chaudhuri, Nirad C. 1930a. "The Martial Races of India, Part I." *The Modern Review* (Calcutta). July, 41–51.

———. 1930b. "The Martial Races of India, Part II." *The Modern Review* (Calcutta). September, 295–307.

———. 1931a. "The Martial Races of India, Part III." *The Modern Review* (Calcutta). January, 67–79.

———. 1931b. "The Martial Races of India, Part IV." *The Modern Review* (Calcutta). February, 215–228.

———. 1931c. "The Indian Military College Committee, 1931." *The Modern Review.* October, 460–467.

———. 1935 [N. Chaudhry]. *Defence of India or Nationalisation of Indian Army.* Allahabad: Congress Golden Jubilee Brochure no. 8.

Chauvel, Richard. 1990. *Nationalists and Separatists: The Ambonese Islands from Colonialism to Revolt 1880–1950.* Leiden: KITLV Press.

Choudhary, Valmiki, ed. 1992. *Dr. Rajendra Prasad: Correspondence and Select Documents; Volume 18 Presidency Period January 1956 to December 1957.* Bombay: Allied Publishers.

Chowdhury, S. P. Roy. 1948. "Are the Bengalis a Non-Martial Race?" *The Modern Review.* May, 373–380.

Cohen, Stephen P. 1969. "The Untouchable Soldier: Caste, Politics and the Indian Army." *Journal of Asian Studies,* 453–468.

———. 1988. *The Pakistan Army.* Oxford: Oxford University Press.

———. 1990a. *The Indian Army: Its Contribution to the Development of the Nation,* 2nd ed. New Delhi: Oxford University Press.

———. 1990b. "The Military and Indian Democracy." In *India's Democracy: An Analysis of Changing State-Society Relations,* edited by Atul Kohli, 98–143. Princeton, NJ: Princeton University Press.

———. 2006. *The Pakistan Army* (1998 edition). Karachi: Oxford University Press.

———.2010. "The Militaries of South Asia." In *Routledge Handbook of South Asian Politics: India, Pakistan, Bangladesh, Sri Lanka and Nepal,* edited by Paul R. Brass, 348–363. New York: Routledge.

———., and Sunil Dasgupta. 2010. *Arming without Aiming: India's Military Modernization.* Washington, DC: Brookings Institution Press.

Connell, John. 1959. *Auchinleck: A Biography of Field-Marshal Sir Claude Auchinleck.* London: Cassell.

Constable, Philip. 2001. "The Marginalization of a Dalit Martial Race in Late Nineteenth- and Early Twentieth-Century Western India." *Journal of Asian Studies* 60, no. 2, 439–478.

Coser, Lewis. 1956. *The Functions of Social Conflict.* New York: The Free Press.

Costa, Dora L., and Matthew E. Kahn. 2008. *Heroes and Cowards: The Social Face of War.* Princeton, NJ: Princeton University Press.

Dalvi, J. P. 1969. *Himalayan Blunder: The Curtain-Raiser to the Sino-Indian War of 1962.* Bombay: Thacker.

Decalo, Samuel. 1990. *Coups and Army Rule in Africa: Motivations and Constraints*. New Haven, CT: Yale University Press.

Deshmukh, B. G. 2004. *From Poona to the Prime Minister's Office: A Cabinet Secretary Looks Back*. New Delhi: HarperCollins India.

Deshpande, Anirudh. 1996. "Hopes and Disillusionment: Recruitment, Demobilisation and Emergence of Discontent in the Indian Armed Forces after the Second World War." *Indian Economic and Social History Review* 33, 175–207.

Effendi, M. Y. 2007. *Punjab Cavalry: Evolution, Role, Organisation and Tactical Doctrine 11 Cavalry (Frontier Force) 1849–1971*. Karachi: Oxford University Press.

Elliott, J. G. 1965. *A Roll of Honour: The Story of the Indian Army 1939–1945*. London: Cassell.

Enloe, Cynthia. 1980. *Ethnic Soldiers: State Security in Divided Societies*. Athens: University of Georgia Press.

Evans, Humphrey. 1960. *Thimayya of India: A Soldier's Life*. New York: Harcourt Brace.

Finer, S. E. 1962. *The Man on Horseback: The Role of the Military in Politics*. New York: Praeger.

———. 1988. *The Man on Horseback: The Role of the Military in Politics*, 2nd ed. Boulder, CO: Westview Press.

Fox, Richard F. 1985. *Lions of the Punjab: Culture in the Making*. Berkeley: University of California Press.

The Gallant Dogras: An Illustrated History of the Dogra Regiment. 2005. New Delhi: Lancers/Dogra Regimental Center.

Garhwali Paltan ka Sankshipta Paricaya. 1996. Lansdowne, Uttarakhand: Garhwal Regiment.

Gautam, P. K. 2009. *Composition and Regimental System of the Indian Army*. New Delhi: Institiute for Defense Studies and Analyses.

Ghosh, S. K. 1994. "Army's Contribution to Peace-Keeping." In *Encyclopedia of Police in India, Volume 2—Section B: Police at Work*, edited by S. K. Ghosh, 1133–1136. New Delhi: Ashish Publishing House.

Gopal, Sarvepalli. 1983. *Jawaharlal Nehru: An Anthology*. Delhi: Oxford University Press.

Greenwood, Alexander. 1981. *Field Marshal Auchinleck*. Durham: The Pentland Press.

Guha, Ramachandra. 2007. *India after Gandhi: The History of the World's Largest Democracy*. London: Macmillan.

Gutteridge, William. 1962. *Armed Forces in New States*. London: Institute on Race Relations/Oxford University Press.

———. 1969. *The Military in African Politics*. London: Methuen & Co.

Habibullah, Enayat. 1981. *The Sinews of Indian Defence*. New Delhi: Lancers.

Haksar, Nandita, and Sebastian M. Hongray. 2011. *The Judgement that Never Came: Army Rule in North East India*. New Delhi: Chicken Neck.

Hoon, P. N. 2000. *Unmasking Secrets of Turbulence: Midnight Freedom to a Nuclear Dawn*. New Delhi: Manas.

Horowitz, Donald L. 1980. *Coup Theories and Officers' Motives*. Princeton, NJ: Princeton University Press.

————. 1985. *Ethnic Groups in Conflict.* Berkeley: University of California Press.

Human Rights Data Analysis Group. 2009. *Violent Deaths and Enforced Disappearances During the Counterinsurgency in Punjab, India.* January 2009, https://hrdag.org/content/india/Punjab_cvr_2009-01.pdf.

Huntington, Samuel P. 1957. *The Soldier and the State: The Theory and Politics of Civil-Military Relations.* Cambridge, MA: The Belknap Press of Harvard University Press.

Issar, Satish K. 2009. *General S. M. Shrinagesh: Soldier, Scholar, Statesman.* New Delhi: Vision Books.

Jaffrelot, Christophe. 1999. *India's Silent Revolution: The Rise of the Lower Castes.* London: Hurst & Co.

Jalal, Ayesha. 1987. "India's Partition and the Defence of Pakistan: An Historical Perspective." *The Journal of Imperial and Commonwealth History* 15, no. 3, 289–310.

————. 1992. *The State of Martial Rule: The Origins of Pakistan's Political Economy of Defence.* New York: Cambridge University Press.

————. 1994. *The Sole Spokesman: Jinnah, the Muslim League and the Demand for Pakistan.* New York: Cambridge University Press.

————. 1995. *Democracy and Authoritarianism in South Asia: A Comparative and Historical Perspective.* New York: Cambridge University Press.

Janowitz, Morris. 1977. *Military Institutions and Coercion in the Developing Countries.* Chicago: University of Chicago Press.

————. 1964. *The Military in the Political Development of New Nations: An Essay in Comparative Analysis.* Chicago: University of Chicago Press.

Jha, Saumitra, and Steven I. Wilkinson. 2012. "Does Combat Experience Foster Organizational Skill: Evidence from Ethnic Cleansing during the Partition of India." *American Political Science Review* 106, no. 4, 883–907.

Jinnah, Muhammad Ali. 1996. "Statement of the Congress Machination to Discredit the Punjab Government, New Delhi, September 8th 1938." In *Speeches, Statements and Messages of the Quaid-e-Azam, Volume 2: 1938–1941,* edited by Khurshid Ahmad Khan Yusufi, 850–851. Lahore: Bazm-e-Iqbal.

————. 1999. *Quaid-i-Azam Mohammad Ali Jinnah Papers—Pakistan at Last: 26 July–14 August 1947.* Islamabad: Government of Pakistan.

Jones, George W. 1948. *Tumult in India.* New York: Dodd, Mead & Co.

Khalidi, Omar. 2002. "Ethnic Group Recruitment in the Indian Army: The Contrasting Cases of Sikhs, Muslims, Gurkhas, and Others." *Pacific Affairs* 74, no. 4, 529–552.

————. 2009. *Khaki and Ethnic Violence in India: Police and Communal Riots in India.* New Delhi: Three Essays Collective.

Kazimi, Muhammad Reza, ed. 2003. *Jinnah-Liaquat Correspondence.* Karachi: Pakistan Study Centre.

Khan, Ayub, 1967. *Friends not Masters.* New York: Oxford University Press.

Khan, Fazal Muqeem. 1963. *The Story of the Pakistan Army.* Lahore: Oxford University Press.

Khanduri, Chandra B. 2000. *Field Marshall K. M. Cariappa: A Biographical Sketch.* New Delhi: Dev Publications.

————. 2006. *Thimayya: An Amazing Life*. New Delhi: Centre for Armed Historical Research, United Service Institution of India.

Khattak, Mohammad Aslam Khan. 2005. *A Pathan Odyssey*. Karachi: Oxford University Press.

Khera, S. S. 1968. *India's Defence Problem*. New Delhi: Orient Longmans.

Kothari, Rajni. 1964. "The Congress 'System' in India." *Asian Survey* 4, no. 12 (December), 1161–1173.

Kumar, Dharma. 2005. "The Fiscal System." In *The Cambridge Economic History of India Volume 2: c.1757–2003*, edited by Dharma Kumar, 905–946. New Delhi: Orient Longman/Cambridge.

Lambert, Richard D. 1959. "Factors in Bengali Regionalism in Pakistan." *Far Eastern Survey* 28, no. 4 (April), 49–58.

Lehl, Lachhman Singh. 1997. *Missed Opportunities: Indo-Pak War 1965*. Dehra Dun: Natraj Publishers.

Leigh, M. S. 1922. *The Punjab and the War*. Lahore: Superintendent, Government Printing, Punjab.

Longer, V. 1980. *Forefront for Ever: The History of the Mahar Regiment*. Saugor: Mahar Regiment Centre.

Luttwak, Edward. 1968. *Coup d'état: A Practical Handbook*. London: Allen Lane.

Mainwaring, Scott, and Timothy R. Scully. 1995. "Introduction: Party Systems in Latin America." In *Building Democratic Institutions: Party Systems in Latin America*, edited by Scott Mainwaring and Timothy R. Scully, 1–34. Stanford, CA: Stanford University Press.

Malhotra, Inder. 1974. "Guns, Ghee and Olive Green." *Times of India*, September 15, 6.

Malik, Iftikhar Haider. 1985. *Sikandar Hayat Khan (1892–1942): A Political Biography*. Islamabad: National Institute of Historical and Cultural Research.

Marston, Daniel P. 2003. *Phoenix from the Ashes: The Indian Army in the Burma Campaign*. Westport, CT: Praeger.

————. 2014. *The Indian Army and the End of the Raj*. Cambridge: Cambridge University Press.

Mason, Philip. 1974. *A Matter of Honour: An Account of the Indian Army, Its Officers and Men*. Harmondsworth: Penguin.

Maxwell, Neville. 1970. *India's China War*. London: Jonathan Cape.

————. 2001. "Henderson-Brooks Report: An Introduction." *Economic and Political Weekly*, August 14–20, 2001.

Mazari, Sherbaz Khan. 2000. *A Journey to Disillusionment*. Karachi: Oxford University Press.

Mazumder, Rajit K. 2003. *The Indian Army and the Making of Punjab*. New Delhi: Permanent Black.

Menezes, S. L. 1999. *Fidelity and Honour: The Indian Army from the Seventeenth to the Twenty-first Century*. New Delhi: Oxford University Press.

Menon, Narayan. 2009. "Downhill from Kargil." *Indian Defence Review* 24, no. 3, 114–118.

Mill, John Stuart. 1861. *Considerations on Representative Government*. London: Parker, Son and Bourn.

Moon, Penderel. 1968. "Review of *Friends not Masters: A Political Autobiography*, by Mohammad Ayub Khan." *English Historical Review* 83, no. 329, 812–814.

Moore, Barrington. 1966. *Social Origins of Dictatorship and Democracy: Lord and Peasant in the Making of the Modern World*. Boston: Beacon Press.

Moore, R. J. 1966. *Sir Charles Wood's Indian Policy, 1853–66*. Manchester: Manchester University Press.

Morris-Jones, W. H. 1967. *The Government and Politics of India*. London: Hutchinson.

Mouat, G. D. 1927. *Madras Classes. Handbooks for the Indian Army*. Government of India Defense Department.

Mukherjee, Anit. 2011. *Failing to Deliver: Post Crisis Defence Reforms in India 1998–2010*. Occasional Paper no. 18. New Delhi: Institute for Defence Studies and Analyses, March. http://www.idsa.in/system/files/OP_defen cereform.pdf.

———. 2014. "Cleaning the Augean Stables." *Seminar*, 658 (June), 41–44.

Munshi, K. M. 1950. *Pilgrimage to Freedom Volume 1 (1902–1950)*. Bombay: Bharatiya Vidya Bhavan.

Naga Regiment. 2009. *A New Sunrise in the East: Story of the Naga Regiment*. Ranikhet: Kumaon Regimental Centre/Colonel of the Naga Regiment.

Nakanishi, Yoshihiro. 2013. "Strong Soldiers, Failed Revolution: The State and Military in Burma 1962–1988." Singapore: Kyoto Center for South East Asian Studies Series on Asian Studies, National University of Singapore Press.

Navlakha, Gautam. 2006. "Collating Information, or 'Communalising' the Army." *Economic and Political Weekly*, February 25.

Nawaz, Shuja. 2008. *Crossed Swords: Pakistan, Its Army and the Wars Within*. Karachi: Oxford University Press.

Nehru, Jawaharlal. 1963. "'Linguistic States,' Speech in the House of the People, New Delhi, July 7 1952." In *Jawaharlal Nehru's Speeches Volume 2 1949–1953*. New Delhi: Publications Division, Ministry of Information and Broadcasting, 33–43.

———. 1982. *The Discovery of India*. New Delhi: Oxford University Press. First published 1946 by Signet Press, Calcutta.

———. 1985. "Letter to Premiers, 16 August 1948." In *Jawaharlal Nehru: Letters to Chief Ministers 1947–1964, Volume 1: 1947–49*, edited by G. Parthasarathi, 175–187. Oxford: Oxford University Press.

Nordlinger, Eric. 1977. *Soldiers in Politics: Military Coups and Governments*. Englewood Cliffs, NJ: Prentice Hall.

Oldenburg, Philip. 2010. *India, Pakistan and Democracy: Solving the Puzzle of Divergent Paths*. New York: Routledge.

Omissi, David. 1994. *The Sepoy and the Raj: The Indian Army, 1860–1940*. London: Macmillan.

Palit, D. K. 1972. *Jammu and Kashmir Arms: History of the J&K Rifles*. Dehra Dun: Palit & Dutt.

———. 1991. *War in High Himalaya: The Indian Army in Crisis, 1962*. London: Hurst and Company.

———. 1997. *Major General A. A. Rudra: His Service in Three Armies and Two World Wars.* New Delhi: Reliance.

Parsons, Timothy H. 1999. "'Wakamba Warriors Are Soldiers of the Queen': The evolution of the Kamba as a martial race, 1890–1970." *Ethnohistory* 46, no. 4, 671–701.

Parthasarathi, G., ed. 1985. *Jawaharlal Nehru: Letters to Chief Ministers 1947–1964 Volume 1 1947–49.* Oxford: Oxford University Press.

Pataudi, Muhammad Sher Ali Khan. 1978. *The Story of Soldiering and Politics in India and Pakistan.* Lahore: Wajidalis.

Patel, H. M. 1963. *The Defence of India: R. R. Kale Memorial Lecture 1963.* Poona: Asia Publishing House/Gokhale Institute of Politics and Economics.

Pettigrew, Joyce. 1987. "In Search of a New Kingdom of Lahore." *Pacific Affairs* 60, no. 1 (Spring), 1–25.

———. 1995. *The Sikhs of the Punjab.* London: Zed Books.

Pirzada, Syed Sharifuddin, ed. 1970. *Foundations of Pakistan: All-India Muslim League Documents 1906–1947.* Karachi: National Publishing House.

———. 1984. *The Collected Works of Quaid-e-Azam Mohammad Ali Jinnah, Volume 1: 1906–1921.* Karachi: East and West Publishing Company.

———. 1986a. *The Collected Works of Quaid-e-Azam Mohammad Ali Jinnah, Volume 2: 1921–1926.* Karachi: East and West Publishing Company.

———. 1986b. *The Collected Works of Quaid-e-Azam Mohammad Ali Jinnah, Volume 3: 1926–31.* Karachi: East and West Publishing Company.

Praval, K. C. 1975. *India's Paratroopers.* London: Leo Cooper.

———. 1976. *Valour Triumphs: A History of the Kumaon Regiment.* Faridabad, Haryana: Thomson Press (India) Limited.

Quinlivan, James T. 1999. "Coup-Proofing: Its Practice and Consequences in the Middle East." *International Security* 24, no. 2, 131–165.

Raghavan, Srinath. 2009. "Civil–Military Relations in India: The China Crisis and After." *Journal of Strategic Studies* 32, no. 1, 149–175.

———. 2010a. *War and Peace in Modern India: A Strategic History of the Nehru Years.* New Delhi: Permanent Black.

———. 2010b. "Soldiers, Statesmen and Strategy." *Seminar* (July), 14–18.

———. 2012. "Soldiers, Statesmen and India's Security Policy." *India Review* 11, no. 2, 116–133.

——— 2013. *1971: A Global History of the Creation of Bangladesh.* Cambridge, MA: Harvard University Press.

Raghavan, V. R. n.d. *By Land and Sea: The Post-Independence History of the Punjab Regiment (1947–86).* Ramgarh Cantt., Bihar: Punjab Regimental Centre, 1986. National Defence College.

Rajagopalan, Rajesh. 2010. "Innovations in Counterinsurgency: The Indian Army's Rashtriya Rifles." *Contemporary South Asia* 13, no. 1, 25–37.

Rao, Kotikalapudi Venkata Krishna. 2001. *In the Service of the Nation: Reminiscences.* New Delhi: Viking.

Rao, P. V. R. 1970. *Defence without Drift.* Bombay: Popular Prakashan.

Regimental Standing Orders, 40th Pathans. 1919. Jhelum: Gouldsbury Press.

Richter, William L. 1978. "Persistent Praetorianism: Pakistan's Third Military Regime." *Pacific Affairs* 51, no. 3 (Autumn 1978), 406–426.

Rizvi, Hasan-Askari. 1974. *The Military and Politics in Pakistan*. Lahore: Progressive Publishers.

———. 1988. *The Military and Politics in Pakistan, 1947–1986*. Delhi: Konark.

———. 2000. *Military, State and Society in Pakistan*. New York: St. Martin's Press.

———. 2008. *The Military and Politics in Pakistan*. New Delhi: Konark.

Rosen, Stephen Peter. 1996. *Societies and Military Power: India and Its Armies*. New Delhi: Oxford University Press.

Ross, J. 1967. *The Jat Regiment: A History of the Regiment Volume 2: 1937–1948*. Bareilly: The Commandant, Jat Regimental Centre.

Roy, Kaushik. 1997. "Recruitment Doctrines of the Colonial Indian Army: 1859–1913." *Indian Economic and Social History Review* 34, 321.

———. 2010. *The Armed Forces of Independent India 1947–2006*. New Delhi: Manohar.

Rudolph, Lloyd, and Susanne H. Rudolph. 1964. "Generals and Politics in India." *Pacific Affairs* 37, no. 1, 9–16.

Sarkar, Sumit. 1983. *Modern India, 1885–1947*. New Delhi: Macmillan.

Scott, Samuel. 1998. *From Yorktown to Valmy: The Transformation of the French Army in an Age of Revolution*. Niwot: University Press of Colorado.

Sethna, A. M., and Valmiki. 1983. *Traditions of a Regiment: The Story of Rajputana Rifles*. New Delhi: Lancers.

Shah, Aqil. 2014. *The Army and Democracy: Military Politics in Pakistan*. Cambridge, MA: Harvard University Press.

Shankar, Prasada, ed. 1971. *Sardar Patel's Correspondence 1945–50, Volume 10*. Ahmedabad: Navajivan.

Sharma, Gautam. 1990. *Valour and Sacrifice: Famous Regiments of the Indian Army*. New Delhi: Allied.

———. 1996. *Nationalization of the Indian Army 1885–1947*. New Delhi: Allied.

———. 2000. *Indian Army: A Reference Manual*. New Delhi: Reliance.

Shrivastava, V. K. 2000. *The Rajputana Rifles*. New Delhi: Lancers.

Siddiqa, Ayesha. 2007. *Military Inc.: Inside Pakistan's Military Economy*. London: Pluto Press.

Siddiqi, A. R. 1986. *The Military in Pakistan: Image and Reality*. Lahore: Vanguard.

Sikh Regimental Officer's Association. 2010. *A Legacy of Valour: An Illustrated History of the Sikh Regiment (1846–2010)*. n.d. Ramgarh Cantonment: The Sikh Regimental Officer's Association.

Singh, Amarjit, ed. 2007. *Jinnah and Punjab: Shamsul Hasan Collection and Other Documents 1944–47*. New Delhi: Kanishka.

Singh, Depinder. 2005. *Field Marshal Sam Manekshaw, MC. Soldiering with Dignity*. Dehra Dun: Natraj.

Singh, Gajendra. 2006. "The Anatomy of Dissent in the Military of Colonial India during the First and Second World Wars." *Edinburgh Papers in South Asian Studies*, no. 20.

Singh, Gurharpal. 2000. *Ethnic Conflict in India: A Case Study of Punjab*. New York: St. Martin's Press.

Singh, Harbaksh. 2000. *In the Line of Duty: A Soldier Remembers*. New Delhi: Lancers.

Singh, Jogindar. 1993. *Behind the Scene: An Analysis of India's Military Operations 1947–1971*. New Delhi: Lancer International.

Singh, J. J. 2012. *A Soldier's General*. New Delhi: HarperCollins Publishers India.

Singh, Khushwant. 1991. *A History of the Sikhs Volume 2: 1839–1988*. New Delhi: Oxford University Press.

Singh, Kirpal. 1972. *The Partition of the Punjab*. Patiala: Punjabi University.

Singh, Serbjeet. 1983. Letter on "Army Chief." *Times of India*, July 30, 8.

Singh, V. K. 2005. *Leadership in the Indian Army: Biographies of Twelve Soldiers*. New Delhi: Sage.

———. 2013. *Courage and Conviction: An Autobiography*. New Delhi: Aleph/Rupa.

Sinha, B. P. N., and Sunil Chanda. 1992. *Valour and Wisdom: Genesis and Growth of the Indian Military Academy*. New Delhi: Oxford/IBH.

Sinha, S. K. 1992. *A Soldier Recalls*. New Delhi: Lancer.

Standing Orders for the 4th Battalion 11th Sikh Regiment. 1939. Landikotal: Sikh Regiment.

Staniland, Paul. 2008. "Explaining Civil-Military Relations in Complex Political Environments: India and Pakistan in Comparative Perspective." *Security Studies* 17, no. 2, 322–362.

———. 2013. "Kashmir since 2003: Counterinsurgency and the Paradox of 'Normalcy.'" *Asian Survey* 53, no. 5, 931–957.

State of Democracy in South Asia Team. 2008. *State of Democracy in South Asia*. New Delhi: Oxford.

Subrahmanyam, K. 1970. "Neville Maxwell's War." *Review of the Institute for Defence Studies and Analysis* 3, no. 2 (October), 268–291.

———. 1997. "Armed Forces 1947–1997: Apolitical Instrument of Security." *Times of India* July 28, 12.

———. 2005. *Shedding Shibboleths: India's Evolving Strategic Outlook*. Delhi: Wordsmiths.

Subramanian, L. N. 2003. "The Rajputana Rifles." *Bharat Rakshak Monitor* 5, no. 1. http://www.bharat-rakshak.com/MONITOR/ISSUE5-1/subra.html.

Talbot, Ian. 1988. *Punjab and the Raj 1849–1947*. New Delhi: Manohar.

Tarbush, Mohammed. 1982. *The Role of the Military in Politics: A Case Study of Iraq to 1941*. London: Kegan Paul.

Thorat, Shankarrao Pandurang Patil S. 1986. *From Reveille to Retreat*. New Delhi: Allied.

Tudor, Maya. 2013. *The Promise of Power: The Origins of Democracy in India and Autocracy in Pakistan*. Cambridge: Cambridge University Press.

Tuker, Francis. 1950. *While Memory Serves*. London: Cassell.

Vakil, C. N., ed. 1950. *The Economic Consequences of Divided India: A Study of the Economy of India and Pakistan*. Bombay: Vora & Co.

Valour Enshrined: A History of the Maratha Light Infantry Volume 2. 1971. Bombay: Orient Longman.

Vas, Eric A. 1995. *Fools and Infantrymen: One View of History (1923–1993)*. Meerut: Kartikeya.

Venkatasubbiah, Hiranyappa. 1958. *Indian Economy since Independence*. Bombay: Asia Publishing House.

Venkateshwaran, A. L. 1967. *Defence Organisation in India*. New Delhi: Government of India.

Verma, Ashali. 2012. *"Victoria Cross: A Love Story*: Interview with Ashali Verma." StratPost, November 21. http://www.youtube.com/watch?v=-yO VZGyPNSw.

Verma, S. D. 1988. *To Serve With Honour: My Memoirs*. Kasauli: S. D. Verma.

Verma, V. S. n.d. "One for All—All for One." India College of Defence Management Casenotes. http://cdm.ap.nic.in/casestudies/casevol319/One %20For%20All%20All%20For%20One.pdf.

Wainwright, A. Martin. 1994. *Inheritance of Empire: Britain, India and the Balance of Power in Asia, 1938–1955*. Westport, CT: Praeger.

Watkins, Shanae J., and James Sherk. 2008. "Who Serves in the U.S. Military? Demographic Characteristics of Enlisted Troops and Officers." CDA08-05, August 21, 2008. Washington, DC: Center for Data Analysis, Heritage Foundation. http://www.heritage.org/research/reports/2008/08/ who-serves-in-the-us-military-the-demographics-of-enlisted-troops -and-officers.

Weiner, Myron. 1989. "Institution-Building in India." In *The Indian Paradox*, New Delhi: Sage, edited by Wynn Weiner, 77–95.

Wilcox, Wayne. 1965. "The Pakistan Coup d'Etat of 1958." *Pacific Affairs* 38, no. 2 (Summer), 142–163.

Wolpert, Stanley. 1993. *Zulfi Bhutto of Pakistan: His Life and Times*. Karachi: Oxford University Press.

Yong, Tan Tai. 2005. *The Garrison State: The Military, Government and Society in Colonial Punjab, 1849–1947*. New Delhi: Sage.

Young, M. Crawford. 1965. *Politics in the Congo: Decolonization and Independence*. Princeton, NJ: Princeton University Press.

———. 1966. "Post-Independence Politics in the Congo." *Transition* no. 26, 34–41.

Zaidi, Z. H. ed. 2001. *Quaid-i-Azam Mohammad Ali Jinnah Papers—Pakistan: Battling Against Odds 1 October–31 December 1947*. Islamabad: Quaid-i-Azam Papers Project, Government of Pakistan.

———. 2002. *Quaid-i-Azam Mohammad Ali Jinnah Papers—Pakistan: Struggling for Survival 1 January–30 September 1948*. Islamabad: Quaid-i-Azam Papers Project, Government of Pakistan.

Zinkin, Taya. 1959. "India and Military Dictatorship." *Pacific Affairs* 32, no. 1 (March), 89–91.

Acknowledgments

In writing on a new topic I have had to rely on the friendship and help of many experts. I especially want to thank Stephen P. Cohen, whose work stands as a model in this field, both for his extensive and generous comments and for making available transcripts of his 1960s interviews with some key figures. Lloyd Rudolph and Susanne Rudolph, whose own work has influenced so many South Asianists, also generously shared their interviews from 1963 and 1964, when they met with a who's who of key figures in civil-military issues. Ornit Shani also very kindly helped me to obtain some archival materials. I also owe thanks to Paul Staniland, Anit Mukherjee, Suamitra Jha, Gareth Nellis, Erica de Bruin, Srinath Raghavan, and an anonymous reviewer for Harvard University Press for additional and very helpful comments along the way, all of which have greatly improved the manuscript, even though time unfortunately prevented me from making all the good changes they recommended. Daniel Marston, Aqil Shah, and Anit Mukherjee were also kind enough to share their own excellent manuscripts with me.

I presented various parts of this book at the India Institute at King's College London, the South Asia Seminar at Cambridge, and the European South Asian Conference meetings in Lisbon, as well as at the Center for the Advanced Study of South Asia at the University of Pennsylvania and the TIGER Conference at the Toulouse School of Economics. Thanks go to Sunil Khilnani, Louise Tillin, and Christophe Jaffrelot at King's; Joya Chatterjee and David Washbrook at Cambridge; Paul Seabright at Toulouse; and Devesh Kapur at Penn for arranging these talks and providing excellent comments and advice, in addition to wonderful hospitality.

Special thanks go to Ram Guha, master historian and wordsmith, for suggesting the book's title while sitting outside in New Delhi. I only wish that the rest of the manuscript could live up to the high standards he sets in his own work.

I have also been very fortunate in terms of research assistance for this book. First and foremost thanks go to Anna Kellar, who has worked very hard and with great intelligence and enterprise throughout. Michael Weaver suggested to me how some of the raw data I had collected could be used to calculate yearly changes in the composition of the forces and turned into charts, then did a lot of that work. David Cline and Carrie Young helped with the regional database and much else besides. And Ashish Mitter used his considerable talents to help with additional research and coding. I am grateful to them all.

Everyone who works on the history of the Indian Army relies on the archivists and librarians at the India Office, the National Archives in New Delhi, and the National Army Museum, and I owe these dedicated and able people my thanks. In addition I owe a special debt to Squadron Leader (Retired) Rana Chhina at the Center for Armed Forces History at the United Services Institution for granting me access to its library, with its superb collection, as well as helping me to locate various difficult-to-find items. I would also like to acknowledge the help I received from staff at the Churchill archive and Centre for South Asian Studies archive in Cambridge, the National Library of Scotland in Edinburgh, and the Nehru Memorial Museum and Library in New Delhi.

At Harvard University Press thanks go to Sharmila Sen and Heather Hughes for putting up with my slow progress at times and knowing when to encourage and when to crack the whip. Rukun Advani at Permanent Black was first to sign on to this as a project and I am very grateful to him as well.

This book is dedicated to Donald L. Horowitz. It was a class with Don in graduate school that first got me interested in the study of political science, and in ethnic conflict. His work on ethnic conflict and the role of the military in politics has been required reading for me and others in the field, and has influenced much of my work. More importantly I have been influenced by his method of working—drawing from many cases and disciplines—and his great encouragement and advice over the years. To him and to Judy go many thanks.

Finally, thanks go to my family, Elizabeth, Alex, and Nick, for making time to let me get this book done, but also for reminding me that there are more important things than books.

Index

Note: An *italicized f* or *t* following a page number indicates a figure or table, respectively.